I0198306

UNDERSTANDING
YOUR
BIBLE

An Old Testament Survey

Michael L. Gowens

SOVEREIGN GRACE PUBLICATIONS

Shallotte, North Carolina

UNDERSTANDING YOUR BIBLE: *An Old Testament Survey*
Published by Sovereign Grace Publications
Post Office Box 1150
Shallotte, North Carolina 28459
Email: sovgracepublications@gmail.com
http://sovgrace.net

Copyright © 2021 by Michael L. Gowens

All rights reserved. No portion of this book may be reproduced or transmitted in any form or by any means, except brief quotations in printed reviews, without written permission from the publisher.

ISBN 978-1-929635-34-4

Scripture quotations are from the *King James Version* of the Bible.

Printed in the United States of America
2021

CONTENTS

PREFACE

Near Columbus, Georgia is an interesting little town called "Westville." Westville unabashedly advertises itself as the town "Where It's Always 1850." It is not uncommon for visitors to the quaint community to sense that they have traveled backward in time to a much simpler, yet arguably more challenging, way of life.

On this corner, a blacksmith heats metal in the fire and shapes it on the iron anvil into a horseshoe; and on that, a craftsman fashions shoes and belts from tanned leather. Across the dirt street, a woman bakes homemade biscuits in a wood stove, and in the building next door, a potter crafts a vessel on his wheel.

Like so many other tourist attractions, Westville is a "counter-culture"—a small world within the larger world. I'm sure the founder(s) was motivated by a desire to preserve a slice of antiquity, lest people who live in the extremely fast-paced world of technology and innovation forget their humble, yet significantly less stressful, beginnings.

The Bible is a book about another "counter-culture"—a community marked by certain cultural characteristics within the larger culture of society. The founder of this "new society" is God, and the community He builds is termed "the kingdom of God."

In the pages that follow, I will attempt to trace the developing plot of the book we call "the Bible" through a survey of Old

Testament history. My objective is to demonstrate that this concept of "the kingdom of God"—i.e. God's purpose to create a new society in which He reigns as King—is the unifying theme of Holy Scripture.

Of course, that statement presupposes a conviction for the unity and harmony of Scripture. I believe that the Bible is a book of one story, not a kind of encyclopedia giving a little information about a variety of subjects which may or may not be connected to each other. Even though the Bible is comprised of two testaments, sixty-six books, and one thousand one hundred eighty-nine chapters; and although it was penned by at least forty human authors on three continents in three languages over a period of about fourteen hundred years; and even though it includes a wide assortment of literary genres and forms, yet the Bible is one book simply because a common theme binds it all together.

The question, then, arises, "What is that common and central theme? What is the primary plot of the Bible? What is the single concept that unifies the book as a whole?" Now, on the surface, the answer to this question may seem to be very simple—a "no brainer", if you please. Many professing Christians, for instance, would answer unhesitatingly, "The central theme of the Bible is obviously Christ Himself". Perhaps most would say, "Of course, the common theme of Scripture is redemption; everyone knows that."

Well, I concede that these answers are not wrong. Both Christ and redemption are integral to the development of the Biblical story. They are both dominant and unifying themes. In fact, I suggest that Divine Revelation reaches its zenith in the themes of Christ's Person and Work and God's plan of redemption. The rising action of the Old Testament climaxes in Christ and His work on the cross. I do not wish to convey even the slightest hint of an attempt to devalue either theme.

But the fact remains that whatever is the central theme of the Bible, it must be broad enough to embrace and allow for an interpretation of every major Biblical idea. Biblical topics such as *creation* (a theme that seems to occupy a place of greater prominence than as a mere backdrop to redemption), *angels, the church, worship, covenant, holiness,* and *final judgment*. While redemption is certainly a major Biblical theme, it does not seem broad enough to encompass the topic of creation, an event that occurred prior to the entrance of sin and any need for redemption.

Is there a theme in the Bible, then, that is comprehensive enough to embrace every other major theme, including redemption and the person and work of Christ? Indeed, there is.

The plot or "big idea" developed in Scripture is *the kingdom of God*. This Biblical concept describes a domain (or environment) in which God governs and is acknowledged as King. We might even say that God's kingdom is best defined as "a theocratic community". Because that terminology will be used frequently in this work, perhaps I need to define the term.

Simply put, a *theocracy* is by definition "a form of government in which God is recognized as the king...and his laws are taken as the statute-book of the kingdom, these laws being usually administered by a priestly order as his ministers and agents."[1] If a democracy is government by the people, and an aristocracy is government by the wealthy, then a theocracy is government by God. The commonwealth of Israel from the exodus to the election of Saul as king was, in the strictest sense of the term, a theocracy.

In these pages, I will build from the premise that God created the universe with precisely this goal—i.e. to establish a theocratic community devoted to His glory and praise—in view. "For [His] pleasure," affirm the four and twenty elders, "they are and were created" (Rev. 4:11). God made the world "for Himself" (Pro. 16:4).

It was not long, however, before sin's entrance marred the scene of Paradise, and Adam and Eve chose to act contrary to the King's word. It appeared that the goal of establishing a theocratic kingdom would remain unrealized.

The Lord God, however, would not be distracted from His plan. Out of the rubble of a rebellious world, God created a nation for Himself: "This people have I formed for myself that they should show forth my praise" (Is. 43:21; cf. vs. 1, 7).

The Old Testament, subsequently, is the story of the formation of this nation and its subsequent struggle to establish a society in which God alone is glorified through unequivocal obedience to His revelation.

---

[1] *The Oxford Universal Dictionary*, 1955; p. 2166.

As this story unfolds throughout the historical narratives and prose of the Old Testament, however, the reader may begin to sense that the plan—I say it reverently—does not seem to be working. This ideal society, governed and sustained by God, seems, in all due respect, less than ideal.

Consider, for instance, Aaron and the Hebrews dancing around the golden calf while Moses is in the mount receiving God's law. Does this scene resemble the theocratic model? Further, ask yourself, "Was Israel functioning as a theocratic people when they rejected God as King and aspired to be like the secular and heathen kingdoms around them?". Was the covenant community faithful to the King's law when it constructed groves and high places for the worship of Baal, Molech, and Chemosh?

Clearly, the nation does not consistently behave like the subjects of a theocratic kingdom. It has not yet attained the ideal of a community totally devoted to the glory of God,. Instead, the covenant community seems to be perpetually and seriously deformed by rebellion and disobedience.

Of course, the fault lay with the people, not God's plan. Like the Law of God which is inherently "holy, and just, and good", yet "weak through the flesh" (Rom. 7:12; 8:3), the plan to establish a society devoted to the glory of God is only weak by virtue of the people's proclivity to wander into sin and disobedience.

Hence, judgment comes, and the people that have been so signally blessed by God are sold into the hands of the enemy. There, in enemy captivity, the nation is sorely chastened.

It is during these dark scenes of the Biblical story, however, that we meet with a surprising development in the unfolding narrative. Now, we learn that God's purposes will not be foiled. He will, in fact, establish His kingdom, but not by means of any purely human monarch. It is during the nation's bondage in Babylon that God's purpose to establish His kingdom through the Messiah surfaces in unmistakable terms.

This eschatological hope of a Messianic kingdom is one of the dominant themes of the prophets. Prophets like Daniel, who ministered while the nation served as captives to the Babylonians, reveal that the anticipated Messianic kingdom would be a spiritual, not political, entity, and His domain, the hearts and lives of men, not a geographical plot of ground. Unlike the "on again—off again" nature of the kingdom heretofore, the Messianic kingdom would continue forever.

So the plot of the Bible might be defined in terms of the fulfillment of God's goal to establish a community devoted to His glory through His own Son, the Messiah. The whole of the Old Testament comprises the "rising action" toward this climactic truth. The many "twists and turns" along the way supply the tension and suspense of the drama.

That is the picture I will attempt to sketch in the following pages, a mere outline, if you please, of the complete portrait that is the Bible. Though this effort to synthesize the various parts of the Old Testament into a unified whole so that a clear plot-line emerges may or may not meet the standards of scholastic breadth of other, similar works, I trust that the information contained in these pages will prove beneficial in the reader's own quest to grow to a fuller and more accurate understanding of the Bible.

Michael L. Gowens
Shallotte, North Carolina
August 2021

Preface

Chapter 1
INTRODUCTION

The use of "special-effects" distinguishes the professional cinematographer from the amateur with a video camera. I'm sure that most everyone would agree that there is something fundamentally different between a network production or motion picture and a home video shot in the backyard.

Recently, I discovered the reason, at least in part, for this visceral "gap" of appeal between the professional and the amateur video production. I was watching a video with my son on the wonders of God's creation. As the narrator spoke of the intricate detail of the world that God made, the camera shot a wide-angle view of planet earth. Little by little, the focus narrowed, first to the United States, then to the State of Florida, then to the city of Tallahassee, then to a particular property in that city, then to an oak tree on that property, then to a single leaf on that oak tree, then to a single cell on that leaf, and then to the various parts of that cell. This visual journey from the macro to the micro took all of about fifteen seconds. But I was literally riveted to the screen.

I've noticed the same technique used in movies. The movie concerns a person who lives in some major city. The initial camera shot, however, pans the skyline of the city. Then, the focus narrows, first to a certain high-rise apartment building, then to a particular apartment in that building, and finally to a certain room in the apartment where the subject is sitting in a

1

chair, and a good bit of background information helpful to the development of the story line is communicated in a matter of mere seconds. This unique tactic "sets the stage" for development of the main plot. It's the kind of "special effect" that makes the cinema significantly more interesting than your neighbor's favorite home videos.

I cite the intriguing use of this telescope-to-microscope technique in the world of cinematography because the Holy Spirit employs the same formula in the first book of the Bible. The Old Testament, consisting of thirty-nine books, is basically a story within a story—a sub-plot developed within a larger context. Think of it in terms of Redemptive History framed against the backdrop of Secular, or World, History.

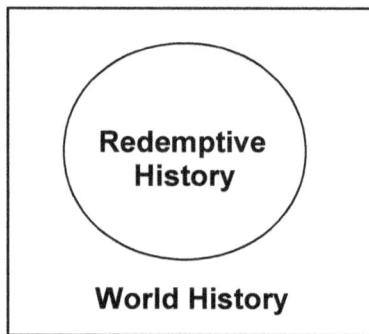

The Theme of the Old Testament

Genesis sets the larger context for the development of the Divine plot in the first eleven chapters. Here we learn that God, as Creator of the universe, exercises sovereign authority in history. The world, in other words, was created as a theocracy, a sphere or domain in which God rules with ultimate and absolute authority. All men and nations, consequently, are under His sovereign sway—accountable to Him as their Creator and Sustainer.

It is within this broad context of world history that Genesis 12 begins to sketch the details of redemptive history. Think of Genesis 1-11, then, in terms of a telescope, and Genesis 12 and following in terms of a microscope. Genesis 1-11 offers us the broad spectrum, wide-angle setting of the Biblical story. Genesis 12, however, narrows the focus and shines the Divine spotlight on the minutia of God's plan for a specific people—the nation of Israel, popularly called the Hebrews or the Jews.

Of course, even after the introduction of the Bible's main story in Genesis 12, the Old Testament continues to expand the focus via periodic references to other nations—Gentile nations, if you will—even beyond the primary focus.[1] Two reasons account for this: (1) God is still the Creator of all men and continues His involvement among the nations. He insists on man's compliance with His moral law and holds man accountable for his actions; (2) Since He has a covenant people even beyond the nation of Israel—in fact, a people Christ will redeem "out of every nation"—God intends to expand the horizons of special revelation to embrace the Gentiles as well as the Jews.

The story of the Old Testament, then, is the account of God's special plan for the Jews set within the broader context of His

---

[1] Notice for instance the prophecies of Jonah and Nahum to Assyria, the numerous messages sent to various nations in Isaiah 13-21, and Obadiah's prophecy to Edom.

more general plan for the world. It is the story of the theocratic Ruler of the universe entering into a covenant relationship with a particular people in that universe, in order to establish His theocratic kingdom.

The Structure of the OT

This theme is developed in the Old Testament by a four-tiered division. The respective books may be categorized as follows:

```
I.   History
II.  Poetry
III. Wisdom
IV.  Prophecy
```

The historical section of the Old Testament is comprised of Genesis through Esther. Psalms, the Song of Songs, and Lamentations fall into the category of the poetical books. The philosophical section, or the Old Testament's "wisdom literature" consists of the books of Job, Proverbs, and Ecclesiastes. Finally, the prophetic section is comprised of the four major prophecies of Isaiah through Daniel and the twelve minor prophecies of Hosea through Malachi.

The dominant emphasis of the Old Testament, however, is historical. The three remaining categories (poetic, philosophic or wisdom, and prophetic) are intertwined within the historical development of the Biblical plot. For example, the Psalms were composed by David and other important figures at various junctures in Jewish history. Proverbs and Ecclesiastes were composed by Solomon, the king of Israel. Each of the prophets, furthermore, ministered God's word at a specific point on the timeline of history.

In a word, the Old Testament is not necessarily laid out in a sequential or chronological format. Like so many pieces to a jigsaw puzzle, the various parts must be arranged properly if the big picture will be intelligible. The following study, consequently, is an attempt to systematically arrange the details, and sketch the main historical developments and the way the various parts (e.g. "Which prophets prophesied before the Babylonian captivity? Which…during? Which…after?") go together to form that big picture.

The Three Periods of OT History

Understanding the three historical periods in the Old Testament story is essential to the ability to synthesize its message. Together, these three periods comprise the first 3600 years of Biblical history. They are as follows:

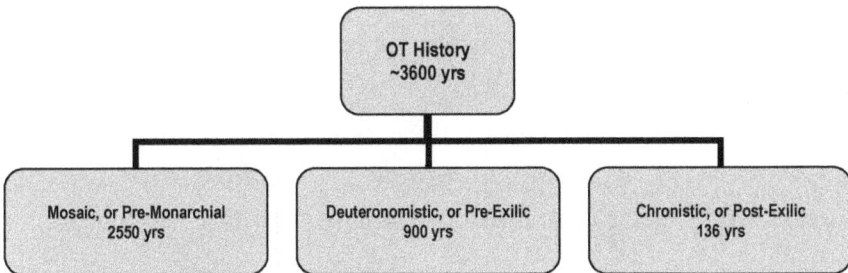

```
                    ┌─────────────────┐
                    │   OT History    │
                    │    ~3600 yrs    │
                    └─────────────────┘
        ┌───────────────────┼───────────────────┐
┌───────────────────┐ ┌───────────────────────┐ ┌───────────────────────┐
│ Mosaic, or Pre-   │ │ Deuteronomistic, or   │ │ Chronistic, or Post-  │
│ Monarchial        │ │ Pre-Exilic            │ │ Exilic                │
│ 2550 yrs          │ │ 900 yrs               │ │ 136 yrs               │
└───────────────────┘ └───────────────────────┘ └───────────────────────┘
```

(1) **The Mosaic, or Pre-Monarchial, Period** (4004 – 1452 B.C.). This period lasted for approximately 2550 years, from creation to the death of Moses. The books of Genesis through Deuteronomy

record the historical events comprising the Mosaic, or Pre-Monarchial period. Notice how Genesis begins the history; Exodus builds on the events of Genesis; Numbers extends the history further; and Deuteronomy develops it further still. The Mosaic Period of Old Testament history describes *the establishment of Israel as a theocracy*.

(2) **The Monarchial (Deuteronomistic), or Pre-Exilic, Period** (1452 – 536 B.C.). The second major division of Old Testament history covers approximately 900 years and concerns the period from the conquest of Canaan to the release from Babylonian captivity. It is often called the Monarchial period, for it was the period of the Kings. The books of Joshua through 2 Kings describe the details of this era.

As stated, the single theme or motif that unites the Old Testament is the ideal of Israel as a theocracy—a nation ruled by God. Whereas the previous literary division, i.e. the Mosaic Period, showed the establishment of the theocracy, the Deuteronomistic, or Pre-Exilic, period describes *the theocracy's continuation and decline*. Within the 900 or so years covered by these books, Israel will rise to the pinnacle of national peace and prosperity, then sink to the depths of Divine judgment for their disobedience. In rebellion, they will reject Jehovah as the theocratic ruler of the nation, opting instead for a monarch (i.e. king) like the other nations around them.

(3) **The Post-Exilic, or Chronistic, Period** (536 – 400 B.C.). The final historical section is the Chronistic, or Post-Exilic period, a 136 year span of time consisting of the release from Babylonian

captivity, the migration of the exiles back to Jerusalem, the rebuilding of the city of God, and the subsequent life of the people. The books 1 Chronicles through Esther were composed during this period, with Ezra, Nehemiah, and Esther detailing the historical events. The dominant theme is *Israel's restoration as a theocracy*. The Chronicler wrote his history to give guidance and direction for restoring the nation during the post-exilic period.

Interestingly, the Song of Moses recorded in Deuteronomy 32 outlines these three periods in the history of the nation of Israel. In verses 9-14, Moses discusses the nation's humble beginnings —the Mosaic Period, if you please: *"[Jehovah] found [Jacob] in a desert land...He led him about, He instructed him, He kept him as the apple of His eye...He made him ride on the high places of the earth...".* Then, in verses 15-35, the focus shifts to the nation's rebellion and the judgment meted out upon them by God—the Deuteronomistic Period, if you will: *"But Jeshurun waxed fat, and kicked...then he forsook God which made him, and lightly esteemed the Rock of his salvation...And He said, I will hide my face from them, I will see what their end shall be...They have moved me to jealousy with that which is not God; they have provoked me to anger with their vanities: and I will move them to jealousy with those which are not a people; I will provoke them to anger with a foolish nation...".* Finally, in verses 36-43, Moses speaks of the restoration and spiritual renewal of the nation—the theme of the Chronistic Period: *"For the Lord shall judge [lit. do justice for] His people, and repent Himself for His servants, when He seeth that their power is gone, and there is none shut up, or left…Rejoice, O ye nations, with His people: for He will avenge the blood of His servants, and will render vengeance to His adversaries, and will be merciful unto His land, and to His people."*

These three sections, then, comprise the story of the Old Testament—the nation established, the nation sold into bondage, and the nation revived and restored. Let's begin our survey, then, by setting the stage for this compelling drama. Genesis 1 through 11 will provide the historical background for the gripping story about to unfold.

Part 1

The

Mosaic Period

(or Pre-Monarchial Era)

The Patriarchs

Chapter 2
THE PATRIARCHS
Genesis

The Mosaic History describes that period of time in which the nation of Israel was established as a people governed, delivered, guided, protected, and provided for by Jehovah, the Creator God, who had entered into covenant with them. If we think of it in terms of human development, this period might be classified as Israel's "childhood" (see Hos. 11:1 and Deut. 32:9-14). The narratives of Genesis through Deuteronomy record the events of this era—a period embracing approximately 2550 years of human history.

The majority of that time-span (all except ~175 years) is covered by the book of Genesis, a history of selected events from creation to the death of Joseph. Further, the majority of that 2375 year span of human history recorded in Genesis—namely, the first 1500 years—is covered in the first eleven chapters.

To put the point in perspective, the entire Pentateuch (Genesis through Deuteronomy) covers 64% of the entirety of Old Testament history; Genesis itself covers 59% of that entire period; and Genesis 1-11 covers 38% of the first 4000 years of human history.

In a word, the integrity of Genesis is crucial to the message of the whole Bible. Perhaps that is the reason that skeptics have launched such a relentless assault on the reliability and historical accuracy of Genesis, particularly the first eleven chapters. The devil knows that if he can undermine confidence in the Creation narrative, the historicity of Adam and Eve, and the account of the global flood in Noah's day, he has dealt a formidable blow to the trustworthiness of the entire Bible.

Genesis 1-11 – World History

Genesis 1-11 is the wide-angle context in which the Holy Spirit proceeds to develop his dominant story of Israel, the covenant people of God. It is, if I may mix metaphors, the general "stage" on which the more specific "set" that begins in chapter twelve is built.

Or, again, one might think of Genesis 1-11 as the broad canvas on which the artist proceeds to depict a single, detailed scene. The dominant plot of the Bible, i.e. Sacred History, begins with the inspired record of World History.

These important chapters teach us that God reveals Himself as Creator before revealing Himself as Redeemer. They remind us that every man is accountable to Him by virtue of the fact that He is the Giver of life. Further, they set the stage for the global scope of God's eternal purposes.

Because they are written in the literary style of historical narrative, these chapters should be interpreted literally, not as allegorical symbols. The creation narrative in Genesis 1-2, the deluge of Genesis 6-9, and the confusion of languages (and subsequent dispersion of people-groups into their respective societies and nationalities) of Genesis 11 are actual, historical events. The biographical style in which Part 2 of the book is written, i.e. chapters 12 through 50, also argues for a literal interpretation of Genesis chapters one through eleven.

Virtually every major Bible doctrine is revealed Genesis 1-11. First, *the doctrine of God* (theology proper) is here. Notice the sovereignty of God in creation, the justice of God in the Fall, the wrath of God in the deluge, the mercy of God in promising a remedy for man's sin, and the covenant-faithfulness of God exhibited in both the covenant with Adam and with Noah (Gen. 2:16-17; Gen. 8:22).

Second, *the doctrine of man* (anthropology) is here. Genesis 1:26-27 teaches that man is made in God's image. Genesis 3 teaches that because of sin, the image of God in man is marred. Genesis 4 demonstrates the extent to which that image was marred in the narrative of the first act of malicious murder.

Third, *the doctrine of sin* (hamartiology) is here. Genesis 1-11 teaches that sin is essentially an act of treacherous disobedience to God that brings death, disease, and destruction. It had its beginning with one man who was the representative head of the entire human family.

Next, *the doctrine of Christ* (Christology) is also here. Genesis 3:15, a passage known as the *proto-euangelion* ('first gospel') is the first Messianic promise and prophecy of the Bible.

Finally, *the doctrine of salvation* (soteriology) is here. The coats of animal skin with which God clothed the guilty pair in Genesis 3, an act that necessarily required the shedding of innocent blood, is a striking type, forecasting the atonement, substitutionary nature of the cross, and the imputation of an alien righteousness to sinners.

These chapters, then, are both historically and doctrinally crucial to an understanding of the Biblical message. They provide the 'big picture' grid for interpreting all that follows.

Genesis 12-50 – Patriarchal History

Beginning in Genesis 12, the Holy Spirit through Moses narrows the focus and shines the spotlight of revelation on the Bible's main theme—God's covenant with one nation. Four primary figures—men known as the Patriarchs—stand out in these chapters: Abraham (chs. 12-25), Isaac (ch. 26), Jacob (chs. 27-36), and Joseph (chs. 37-50).

The events recorded in these chapters form the foundation for the plot that will be developed in the remainder of Scripture. This history explains both the significance of every subsequent event in the Old Testament narrative, as well as the future, Messianic hope realized in the New Testament.

That God deals with men on the basis of *covenants* is the main point to be deduced or derived from Genesis 12-50. These chapters teach that God takes the intiative to enter into a covenant relationship with the people of His choosing in order to accomplish His purposes.

When God called Abram from idolatrous paganism (Gen. 12:3), He literally "created" a new nation (cf. Is. 43:1, 7; 44:2). Just as surely as He created the universe for His own glory (Rev. 4:11)—a world that soon fell into condemnation—so, the Lord created a particular nation for His own glory (Is. 43:21). To the created world, God had given a general revelation of Himself in nature (Ps. 19:1-6; Rom. 1:20), but to this newly created nation, He would give a special revelation of Himself via both the Law and the Prophets (cf. Rom. 3:1-2).

The entrance of sin onto the stage of history perverted the very purpose of man's existence (Gen. 6:5-6). God had made man for His own glory, but now "it repented the Lord that He had made man." Now, however, through His covenant relationship with Abraham and his descendents, God would indeed receive the glory that is His due. This nation would be a new theocracy—a people, on the one hand, obedient to His sovereign authority and committed to His glory and praise, and, on the other, a people to whom He would pledge Himself in covenant commitment to be their provider, protector, and defender. The historical record of the Abrahamic Covenant is found in Genesis 15.

The remainder of Genesis displays God fulfilling His self-imposed, covenant obligations—multiplying Abraham's descendents and providing for Israel physically, morally, and materially in the face of gross wickedness, physical violence, enemy threats, personal sin, human exploitation, and an extensive regional famine. The book closes with the Patriarchal multitude in Egypt, sustained by Divine providence, awaiting the day when they would possess the inheritance that God had promised.

Now, let's consider Genesis 12-50 in more specific terms. The purpose of this passage is to document how God established the nation of Israel as His covenant people, and fulfilled His covenant promise to give them possession of the land of Canaan. The dominant themes of Genesis 12-50 are the numerical expansion of the nation, possession of the promised land, and the relationships they had with surrounding nations. These themes are developed as follows.

The Call of Abraham (Gen. 12)

The narrative begins with God's call to Abram to leave his native land for "a land that I will show thee" (v. 1). A promise that he would be a Divinely appointed channel for international blessing served as the impetus for obedience: "*And I will make of thee a great nation, and I will bless thee, and make thy name great; and thou shalt be a blessing: and I will bless them that bless thee, and curse him that curseth thee: and in thee shall all families of the earth be blessed*" (vs. 2-3).

By faith (i.e. acting on God's testimony), Abram obeyed the call of God (v. 4; Heb. 11:8). He was seventy-five years of age when he left his homeland (v. 4b). As he came into the land of Canaan, the Lord, just as He had promised, appeared to him, saying, "*Unto thy seed will I give this land*" (v. 7). God confirmed the promise again after Abram's separation from Lot (13:14-18).

But still, Abram's actual possession of the land was a future prospect, as was the realization of God's promise of a "son" (Acts 7:5).

The Abrahamic Covenant (Gen. 15-17)

God's promise to Abram was formally ratified in a solemn covenant (Gen. 15)—the "covenant of circumcision" (Acts 7:8). The symbolism involved in this ceremony is revealing. After Abram divided the animals and arranged them so that a sort of alley lay between the divided pieces, God manifested himself in theophany and passed between the pieces of the slain animals (v. 17).

What was the significance of this Divine act? It was a powerful testimony to the fact that the fulfillment of the promises to Abraham rested on God alone, being guaranteed by His very nature. God, in other words, pledged Himself and His own being as the guarantor of His promise (Heb. 6:13). Its fulfillment rested entirely on God's faithfulness, not Abraham's.

In the course of this ceremony, however, God revealed that the chosen seed would be temporary residents in a strange land (i.e. Egypt). After four hundred years of bondage, they would be delivered in a mighty way (v. 12-14; cf. Acts 7:6-7).

When Abram was 86 years of age, Hagar bore Ishmael to him (16:16). Thirteen years later, at age 99, God appeared to him again, confirming His promise and changing his name to Abraham—"father of a multitude" (17:1-8). He gave him the rite of circumcision as the sign of the covenant, requiring every male offspring and servant to be circumcised (vs. 10-14). Then the Lord repeated His promise to give Abraham a son—the promised "seed"—through Sarah (vs. 15-16). Through Isaac, not Ishmael, God's covenant would be established with Abraham's seed (vs. 19-21).[1]

Birth of Isaac, the Covenant Son (Gen. 21-23)

The next year, when Abraham was 100 and Sarah 90 years of age, Isaac was born (21:1-5). Twenty-five years had passed since the initial promise of a "son", but God had kept His "word of promise" (Rom. 9:9) in a miraculous way (cf. Rom. 4:18-21). The "covenant son"—the one in whom Abraham's "seed would be called" (Rom. 9:7b) was alive.

But not many years hence, God tested Abraham's faith, calling him to sacrifice "his only begotten son" (Heb. 11:17-18) at Mount.Moriah (Gen. 22), an event that foreshadowed the One who would be the ultimate fulfillment of the Abrahamic Covenant. Here, on Mount Moriah, Abraham began to understand the far-reaching implications and significance of God's covenant promises (Jno. 8:56; Heb. 11:19). It would be in the Christ, the Father's "only begotten Son" and Abraham's "seed" (Gal. 3:16; Heb. 2:16), that the covenant promises would be realized. In Him, the promise of international blessing (Gen. 12:3) and of a land possessed by God's covenant people as an

---

[1] The ongoing conflict between the Arab (Ishmael) and Jewish (Isaac) peoples has its origin here.

everlasting inheritance would be ultimately realized (Heb. 11:13-16).

Twenty-seven years after Isaac's birth (and probably twelve years after Mount Moriah), Sarah died. She was buried in the land of Canaan at the cave of Machpelah (Gen. 23). But Abraham's heritage in the land was still marginal. Besides the birth of Isaac and the possession of a burial cave at Machpelah, the covenant promises—i.e. of an innumerable offspring and a permanent inheritance in and occupation of the land—had not, as yet, been realized.

Jacob's Blessing (Gen. 24-29)

Fifty-plus years had passed since God said "*I will make of thee a great nation.*" Still, there was only one son—Isaac. But Isaac's marriage to Rebekah was soon blessed with the birth of twin boys (Gen. 25:19ff)—Esau, the elder, and Jacob, the younger.

The fulfillment of God's covenant promises would continue, however, through Jacob, the younger, not Esau—a surprising development, testifying to God's sovereignty in grace. Isaac's blessing upon Jacob that "the blessing of Abraham" might be upon him and that he might "inherit the land...which God gave unto Abraham" (28:3-4) is reminiscent of the original covenant promises.

No sooner had Jacob left home than God appeared to him at Bethel, confirming the covenant: "*I am the Lord God of Abraham thy father, and the God of Isaac: the land whereon thou liest, to thee will I give it, and to thy seed; and thy seed shall be as the dust of the earth...and in thee and in thy seed shall all the families of the earth be blessed"* (28:13-14).

The Twelve Sons of Jacob (Gen. 30)

The birth of eleven of Jacob's twelve sons is recorded in Genesis 30 (Benjamin, the youngest, was born later – 35:18). These twelve sons became the patriarchal heads of the twelve tribes of Israel. Through them, God would fulfill his promise to give Abraham a family as innumerable as the stars of the heaven and the sands on the seashore. Abraham begat Isaac; Isaac begat Jacob; Jacob begat twelve sons; those twelve begat seventy sons, and those seventy would begat a great multitude.

The Migration of the Chosen Seed to Egypt (Gen. 37-50)

The growing family of Israel, however, was soon to face a grave threat to its survival—a famine of far-reaching proportions. But the God who had pledged Himself in covenant-faithfulness to fulfill His promise to Abraham would not abandon them. Through a series of remarkable providences, Jehovah sent Joseph ahead to preserve life.

Though he was in fact the next to the youngest of the twelve sons, Joseph was elevated by God to the position of family patriarch—the one who would provide bread for the entire family. Just as the Lord had said when He made the covenant with Abraham, the children of Israel sojourned in the "strange land" of Egypt for the next 400 years. There they flourished and became a great multitude.

As he was dying, Joseph reminded them, "*God will surely visit you, and bring you out of this land unto the land which He sware to Abraham, to Isaac, and to Jacob*" (50:24). He made them swear by an oath that when the day of departure arrives, they would carry his remains with them. The patriarchal history concludes with the words, "*So Joseph died, being a hundred and ten years old: and they embalmed him, and he was put in a coffin in Egypt*" (50:26).

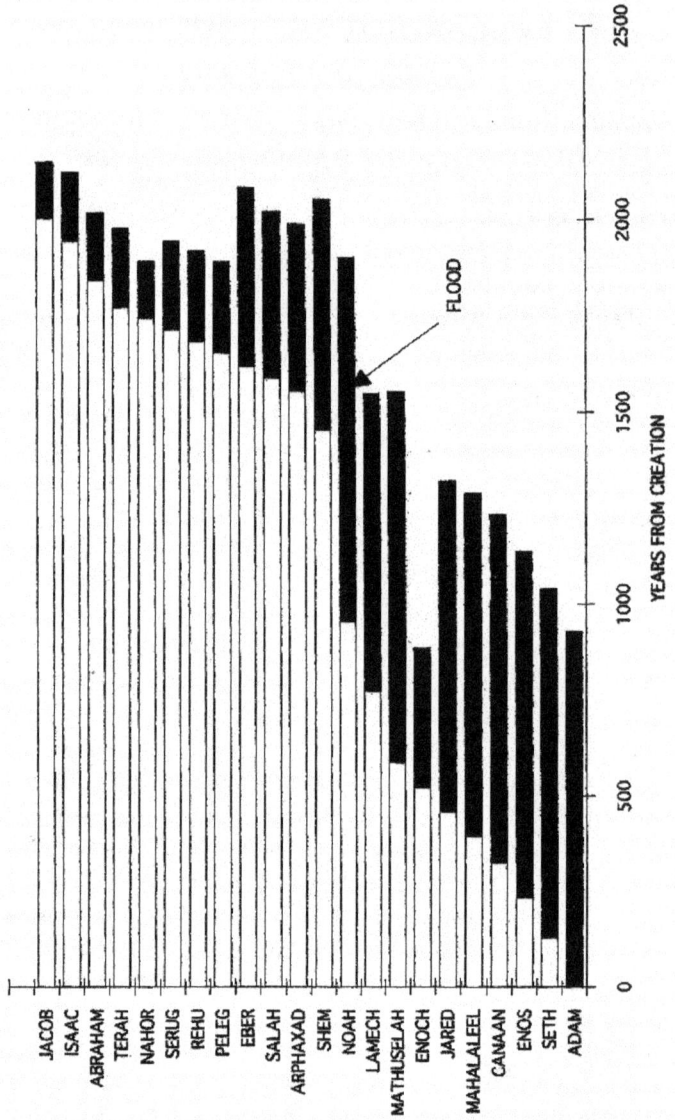

LIVES OF THE PATRIARCHS
by Alan Hisel, Lexington, Kentucky

FLOOD

YEARS FROM CREATION

JACOB
ISAAC
ABRAHAM
TERAH
NAHOR
SERUG
REHU
PELEG
EBER
SALAH
ARPHAXAD
SHEM
NOAH
LAMECH
MATHUSELAH
ENOCH
JARED
MAHALALEEL
CANAAN
ENOS
SETH
ADAM

Chapter 3
ESTABLISHING THE THEOCRACY
Exodus and Leviticus

The Pentateuch, i.e. first five books of the Old Testament, is a composition of individual books, each with a distinctive purpose, in a unity of progressive revelation. From book to book, the narrative of God's covenant relationship with Israel gradually unfolds in a seamless and unified way.

For example, the narrative of Genesis ends with the death of Joseph and the covenant people in Egypt. Exodus resumes the narrative of sacred history after some time has passed, probably about three hundred fifty years. The theme of Exodus is the establishment of Israel as a theocracy. It shows how the nation that Jehovah created as a people for whom He would care was further established as a people under His theocratic rule.

Exodus develops this theme in two sections: (1) Israel's *redemption* by the power of God and blood of the Paschal lamb (chs. 1-15); (2) Israel's *consecration* as God's servants by ordinances, laws, and judgments (chs. 16-40). First, in other words, the book shows God dealing with Israel as His "son", then as His "servant".[1]

---

[1] Note the sequence of "sonship" then "service" (or "salvation" then "worship", or "relationship" [union] followed by "fellowship" [communion]) inherent in the way God deals with Israel. This sequence is consistent throughout the Scripture. Sonship is always antecedent to worship and service.

Israel's Redemption from Egypt (Ex. 1-15)

The trusted 19th century scholar Alfred Edersheim explains the historical setting of the Exodus narrative:

> "On the boundary of the Holy Land the Lord had encouraged Israel: 'Fear not to go down into Egypt; for I will there make of thee a great nation' (Gen. 46:3). And the book of Exodus opens with the record that this promise had been fulfilled, for 'the children of Israel were fruitful, and increased abundantly, and multiplied, and waxed exceeding mighty; and the land was filled with them' (Ex. 1:7)."[2]

To prevent a possible mutinous revolt, Pharoah officially classified the Jews as slaves and instituted a program of hard bondage (1:11). When that did not retard the growth of the burgeoning nation, he increased the work load (1:13-14). He also commanded the midwives to kill every male baby among the Hebrews as soon as it was born, but the midwives did not obey, for they "feared God" (1:17). Pharoah issued an official edict, consequently, that every newborn son be drowned in the Nile River (1:22).

Against this dark background of unprecedented persecution, God raised up a deliverer for His covenant people. By a series of extraordinary providences, the child Moses was spared from the king's infanticide program, nursed by his own mother, and reared by Pharoah's own daughter as her adopted son (2:1-10; cf. Heb. 11:23; Acts 7:20-22). At the age of forty, Moses determined to visit his brethren, the Hebrews (Acts 7:23). But when he saw an Egyptian master abusing a Hebrew servant, Moses killed the

---

[2] Edersheim, *The Bible History* (Vol. 2), p. 24.

Egyptian, hiding his body in the sand. When the news reached Pharoah, he set out to kill Moses, who, in turn, fled for his life into the land of Midian. There, in the wilderness of Sinai, he spent the next forty years of his life—a stranger in a strange land (2:11-22).

But Jehovah, the covenant-keeper, did not forget His promise to Israel (2:23-25). When Moses was eighty years old, the Lord called him (just as He had called Abram some five hundred years earlier) from the midst of the burning bush: *"I am the God of thy father, the God of Abraham, the God of Isaac, and the God of Jacob...I have surely seen the affliction of my people which are in Egypt...And I am come down to deliver them out of the hand of the Egyptians, and to bring them up out of that land unto a good land... Come now therefore, and I will send thee unto Pharoah, that thou mayest bring forth my people the children of Israel out of Egypt"* (3:7-10). God was about to deliver His people with a mighty deliverance and Moses, His servant, was especially commissioned and equipped as the mediator, or instrument, of redemption (3:11 – 4:17).

But deliverance did not come at once. When Moses made his initial demand for release to the king, Pharoah increased the pressure yet again, requiring the slaves to satisfy the same daily quota of brick while denying them straw, a key ingredient for their manufacture (5:5-19). The people, then, complained to Moses, who, in turn, complained to the Lord (5:20-23). But the Lord replied with yet another confirmation of His covenant-promise: *"I have remembered my covenant...I will bring you out from under the burdens of the Egyptians...and I will redeem you with a stretched out arm and great judgments: and I will take you to me for a people, and I will be your God..."* (6:1-7).

There followed ten great plagues upon the Egyptians—the smiting of the Nile, the plague of frogs, lice, flies, murrain, boils, hail, locusts, darkness, and the death of the firstborn. Many of these miraculous plagues took the form of a direct strike at the pagan deities worshiped by the Egyptians.[3]

At each turn, Pharoah's heart was hardened and he refused to comply with God's command; nevertheless, the plan of God was not thwarted. According to His overruling providence, the Lord intended *"to show [His] power in [Pharoah] that [His] name might be declared throughout the whole earth"* (Rom. 9:17).

In every one of the ten plagues, for example, the children of Israel were protected by God, for their sovereign God "put a difference between the Egyptians and Israel" (11:7), graciously discriminating between His chosen, covenant people and the land's native inhabitants. Though the houses of the Egyptians were full of swarms of flies, the land of Goshen was severed so that no flies were there (8:22). Though all the cattle of Egypt died, not one head was lost among the children of Israel (9:6).

---

[3] The Nile was considered to be the bloodstream of the deity named *Osiris*. *Heqt*, the god of resurrection, possessed the form of a frog. The plague of murrain on cattle was a strike at *Apis*, the bull god and symbol of fertility. The plague of boils demonstrated the impotence of *Imhotep*, the god of medicine. Hail and locusts decimated the crops, exposing the inability of the deity *Seth*, protector of crops, to do his job. Darkness humiliated the sun gods *Re*, *Aturn*, and *Horus*. And the death of the firstborn was a fatal blow to Pharoah's deity, *Osiris*, the giver of life.

Though the hail smote both man and beast in all the land of Egypt, the land of Goshen was spared (9:25-26). And though thick darkness covered the land of Egypt so that they saw not one another for three days, yet "all the children of Israel had light in their dwellings" (10: 23).

What made the difference between the Egyptians and God's covenant people in the final plague—i.e. the death of the firstborn? The only protection from the plague of death was the blood of the Passover Lamb (11-12). *"When I see the blood,"* said the Lord, *"I will pass over you, and the plague shall not be upon you to destroy you, when I smite the land of Egypt"* (12:13).

Pharoah's plot to exterminate the Jews had miserably failed. In fact, the Hebrews multiplied exceedingly, surviving the rigor of hard taskmasters, the catastrophe of the plagues, and the sweeping deaths of the tenth plague. It was the Egyptians, on the contrary, who suffered such tremendous casualties. God was fighting for His people to redeem them by a great deliverance. At the conclusion of a vivid, poetic summary of these incredible events, the Psalmist says, *"Egypt was glad when [Israel] departed"* (Ps. 105:23-38; cf. also Ps. 78:43-54).

Through the blood of the Passover Lamb, Jehovah wrought out redemption for his own people. The battle was the Lord's— no man could have accomplished this fantastic deliverance. He brought them forth from the bondage of the iron furnace with "a high hand"[4] (Ex. 14:8; cf. Deut. 4:20).

---

[4] A covenant expression, alluding to the image of lifting the right hand when swearing an oath.(cf. Ps. 89:13; Gen. 14:22)

When they found themselves trapped by Migdol on the right, Pi-hiharoth on the left, the Red Sea in front, and Pharoah's six hundred pursuing chariots from behind, God again delivered them, opening the waters of the Red Sea so that they crossed on dry ground, safely to the other side (Ex. 14:22). The final blow of the Divine rout of Egypt came as Pharoah and his army attempted to follow them. Jehovah fought for His own by loosing the wheels of the chariots. The crashing waters drowned the entire enemy army in the depths and brought the ancient empire of Egypt to ruins.

The account of Israel's redemption from Egyptian bondage concludes with a song of victory, celebrating Jehovah's glorious triumph on behalf of His chosen people (Ex. 15). Under the leadership of God's servant, Moses, the people set out to possess their God-given inheritance in the land of promise, where they will live under His sovereign sway as a people devoted to His name.

◆——————————◆

As the first part of Exodus concludes, Israel has become a nation in a two-fold sense. God has both "created" it for Himself, and "redeemed" it to Himself. As Jehovah's covenant people, they have been beneficiaries of His faithful providence, having received blessing on top of blessing. Now, it only remains for this new nation to be consecrated to Him in a covenant of worship and service.

This new covenant, the Sinaitic or Mosaic covenant (often called "the Law"), is not intended to replace the covenant with Abraham, but to supplement it (cf. Gal. 3:17-29). It is, in fact, a subset of the relationship between God and the nation of Israel. The unilateral covenant God made with Abraham established them *as a nation*. The bilateral covenant God made with Israel through Moses would establish them *as a theocracy*—i.e. a people ruled and governed by God.

In other words, the focus of the umbrella covenant concerned those things that God would do for them. The thrust of this further covenant concerned their obligations and responsibility to serve Him (see Deut. 5:15). Or, to state the point yet further, the Abrahamic covenant gave them *identity*; the covenant at Sinai gave them *instruction* for worship and service. God had set them apart from every other nation by His blessings upon them (Amos 3:2a; Deut. 7:6-8; 10:15); now, He would consecrate them to Himself by laws and ordinances (Ps. 147:19-20; Deut. 10:12-22).

The Consecration of the Nation at Sinai (Ex. 16-40)

From the banks of the Red Sea, the children of Israel turned toward the wilderness of Shur ('the wall'), or the Sinai Peninsula —a tract of mountainous desert that lies between the Gulf of Suez and the Persian Gulf. Thus the Hebrews, numbering about two million people[5], set out on pilgrimage to "the land that God

---

[5] Edersheim writes: "Their 'army' consisted in round numbers of '600,000 on foot—men, beside children' (Ex. 12:37), or, as we may compute it, with women

had promised." From this point forward, every blessing or provision made for them is coupled with a law or an ordinance imposed upon them.

Three days journey brought the fatigued and weary nomads to a pool of water called Marah (meaning "bitter"). The water was unfit for consumption, and the people began to murmur (Ex. 15:22-24). How quickly does faith fail, said A. W. Pink, when provisions wear thin! But God showed Moses a tree that, when cast into the water, would heal the poisoned waters. *"There he made for them a statute...and there he proved them"* (v. 25). Alfred Edersheim writes,

> "The lesson was twofold...The 'statute' or principal...was this, that in all seasons of need and seeming impossibility the Lord would send deliverance straight from above, and that Israel might expect this during their wilderness-journey...But He also ever 'proves' us by this, that the enjoyment of our right and privilege [i.e. of God's providence] is made to depend upon a constant exercise of faith."[6]

From Marah, they proceeded to Elim, a very fertile spot, where they encamped for about a month (15:27; cf. 16:1). From Elim, they journeyed south-westward into the Wilderness of Sin (modern *El Markha*). Here their provisions ran out and the people again murmured against Moses and against the Lord for hunger (16:2-3, 7). And again, Jehovah provided for them by "raining bread from heaven" (v. 4), a small round wafer that the

---

and children, about two millions." (cf. Num. 1:46)
[6] *Bible History*, Edersheim, p. 93.

people called "manna" (v. 15). But with the provision came an "ordinance" or "statute" that they were not to gather it on the Sabbath. Every morning for six days, they were to gather that day's supply, and God would give them a two day supply on the sixth day, for no manna would be given on the Sabbath (vs. 19-36).

This recurring motif—namely, that God intended Israel to live not only under His providence but also under His authority —anticipates the giving of the Law at Sinai (Ex. 19-31). The Sinai covenant is a revelation of God's will regarding both the ethical behavior of His people (20:1 – 23:13) and their religious observances (23:14 – 31:18). In a word, God instituted in the Law both *a social* (i.e. moral laws) and *a sacrificial* (i.e. ceremonial laws) code of conduct.

The ethical obligations imposed upon them are embellishments of the "Second Table" of the Ten Commandments (20:12-17). These involved instructions on how to treat servants (21:1-11), prohibitions against violence (21:12-36), directives concerning the sanctity of personal property, sexual purity, another's reputation, the principle of truth, and the principle of Sabbath-rest (22:1 – 23:13).

The ceremonial obligations are enlargements of the "First Table" of the Law (20:1-11). These concerned the observance of Holy days (23:14-19), the specifications and uses of the various items of furniture in the Tabernacle worship, and the vesture and function of the Aaronic priesthood (25:1 – 30:38).

31

No sooner had God given Moses these civil and ceremonial ordinances, however, than He informed him of the people's quick apostasy: *"Now therefore let me alone, that my wrath may wax hot against them, and that I may consume them: and I will make of thee a great nation"* (32:10).

Note that God indicates that the sin of His people would incur His severe judgments, but He would not break His covenant promise to Abraham, even though it meant starting again with Moses.

But Moses, in a striking display of foreshadowing the mediatorial ministry of Christ, made intercession: *"Remember Abraham, Isaac, and Israel, thy servants, to whom thou swarest by thine own self...'I will multiply your seed as the stars of heaven, and all this land that I have spoken of will I give unto your seed, and they shall inherit it forever"* (32:13). Just as Moses made intercession on behalf of God's covenant promise to Abraham, in like manner, the Lord Jesus Christ, our Moses, pleads the blood of the everlasting covenant when He makes intercession for the saints.

When Moses returned to the camp, he found them engaged in gross idolatry and immorality. In anger, he cast the two tables of stone, on which God had written His Laws with His own finger, to the ground and broke them at the foot of the mountain (32:19). That day, about three thousand Israelites were slain for their sin. Moses returned to the Lord and begged forgiveness, pledging his own life in vicarious sacrifice as an atonement for their sin (32:30-32), another very striking type of Christ.

In His mercy, God gave the revelation to Moses a second time, and Moses inscribed the covenant on new tables of stone (Ex. 33-34). It was on this occasion that Moses requested a complete manifestation of the Divine character: "*I beseech thee, show me thy glory*" (33:18). Though the Lord refused to grant Moses a visual revelation of His glory ("...for there shall no man see me, and live" – v. 20), He did give him a verbal revelation ("...I will proclaim the name of the Lord before thee..." – v. 19). The verbal portrait of Jehovah in Exodus 34:6-7 discloses the fact that He is both good ("...merciful and gracious, longsuffering... forgiving iniquity...") and holy ("...and that will by no means clear the guilty; visiting the iniquity of the fathers upon the children..."). His covenant of redemption, in other words, did not mean that He would negotiate His holiness. Justice must be served. His righteous law must be upheld.

To say it another way, the people of Israel must be cautious about the attitude that presumptuously receives the Lord's covenant mercies. They must never presume upon His grace. Instead, they must demonstrate their gratitude for His grace by bowing submissively to His government. As long as they did this, they would eat the good of the land, but if they rebelled against Him, they would be devoured with the sword (Is. 1:18-19). Those that Jehovah had redeemed were to sanctify and devote themselves to His service.

Exodus 35-40 describes the actual construction of the tabernacle and the various pieces of furniture for Divine worship. God intended these items and the ceremonial laws accompanying their religious use to be central to the life and worship of the nation from this point forward. Where ever they might go, the tabernacle was to travel with them.

When the work was completed, the glory of the Lord filled the house. The people, subsequently, left Mount Sinai (after an extended stay of almost one year) for the promised land, the Lord guiding them via cloud by day and fire by night (40:34-38).

The Consecration of the Nation in the Wilderness (Leviticus)

Leviticus is a book about worship. It has been said that in Genesis, man is ruined. In Exodus, he is redeemed. And in Leviticus, he worships.

The Jewish rabbis called the Book of Leviticus the "Law of the Priests" or the "Book of the Law of Offerings". It was the Levite's official manual for conducting religious worship and regulating the spiritual life of Israel. Like the ethical and religious code outlined in Exodus 16-40, the sacrificial system described in Leviticus was given to Moses at Sinai as part of the Law (Lev. 27:34).

Leviticus is a sequel, then, to Exodus. The late Bible teacher J. Vernon McGee writes,

"In Exodus, we have God's approach to man; in Leviticus, it is man's approach to God. In Exodus, Christ is the Savior; in Leviticus, He is the Sanctifier. In Exodus, man's guilt is prominent; in Leviticus, man's defilement is prominent. In

Exodus, God speaks out of the mount; in Leviticus, He speaks out of the tabernacle."[7]

The subject of both the last half of Exodus and the entire book of Leviticus is the consecration (or "setting apart") of the people to God as His possession—a "holy nation" devoted exclusively to Him and not to idols. This contrast between the holy and the unholy—between the sacred and the profane—is basic to an understanding of Leviticus.

Like Exodus, again, the book may be divided into two sections. Part 1 of the book (chapters 1-16) describes the way of approach to God in *religious worship*. It outlines Jehovah's prescribed "sacrificial system". The first part of the book closes with a description of the Day of Atonement (Lev. 16). Part 2 (chapters 17-27) describes the necessity of *holiness of life*. It specifies a code by which the priests might determine fitness for worship. The second part of Leviticus concludes with the instructions for observing the Year of Jubilee (Lev. 25).

THE "SACRIFICE" MOTIF (Lev. 1-16): The book opens with a very elaborate system of laws concerning sacrifices (chs. 1-7), indicating that the only way of access to God is through sacrifice (Lev. 17:11; Heb. 9:22). The word "atonement" (meaning "covering") is used forty-five times in Leviticus.

A "sacrifice" symbolized the worshipper's consecration to God. When an Israelite ceremoniously gave up some item of his

---

[7] *Thru the Bible Commentary*, Vol. 6, p. xii

possession, he was, by that act, dedicating himself anew to God. Each of the five sacrifices prescribed by God—the Burnt Offering (ch. 1), the Grain Offering (ch. 2), the Peace Offering (ch. 3), the Sin Offering (ch. 4 – 5:13), and the Trespass Offering (5:14 – 6:7) —was made on the brazen altar. In Leviticus 1:1 – 6:7, the worshipper is instructed regarding which particular sacrifice is necessary on each specific occasion. In Leviticus 6:8 – 7:38, the priesthood is instructed concerning the ceremonial rituals of each sacrifice.

These various offerings may be subdivided into two categories: (1) The first three (the Burnt, the Meal, and the Peace) are sweet-savor offerings—voluntary sacrifices made with incense, thereby producing a sweet aroma; (2) The final two (the Sin, and the Trespass) are non-sweet-savor offerings—required sacrifices made without incense. The sweet-savor offerings are primarily *acts of worship*—offerings made to seek God's blessing or to give thanks for blessings received. The non-sweet-savor offerings are primarily *acts of atonement* by which a sinner is ceremonially purified from either unintentional or willful sin.[8]

The sacrificial system outlined in Leviticus is foundational to an understanding of the sacrifice of Christ on the cross. Hebrews employs the Levitical concepts of sin, sacrifice, and atonement as the grid for interpreting the meaning of the cross (cf. Heb. 9). Of course, the blood of bulls and goats never expiated one sin, but every animal sacrifice of Leviticus foreshadowed the

---

[8] Consider Heb. 13:12-16 for a NT application of this distinction.

substitutionary nature of the sacrifice that Jesus Christ, the Lamb of God, would make in the stead of His covenant people.

THE "HOLINESS" MOTIF (Lev. 17-27): The noun "holy" and its corresponding verb "to sanctify"[9] (words occurring 87 times in Leviticus) mean *separate*. The term conveys the thought of something that is different and set apart from that which is common so that it may be dedicated or consecrated to the Lord. When God took the initiative to enter into covenant with Israel, He separated them from the nations (Deut. 7:6-8); consequently, He calls them to consecrate themselves to God by living holy lives.

Consider the language of Leviticus 11:44-45: *"For I am the Lord your God: ye shall therefore sanctify yourselves and ye shall be holy; for I am holy; neither shall ye defile yourselves with any manner of creeping thing that creepeth upon the earth. For I am the Lord that bringeth you up out of the land of Egypt, to be your God: ye shall therefore be holy, for I am holy."* God had "put a difference" between Israel and the nations (Ex. 11:7); now they were to *"make a difference between the unclean and the clean..."* (Lev. 11:47a). Consider also Leviticus 20:23-26 where the same thought is developed.

God, then, not man, determines and defines what is "holy". Contemporary author and theologian R. C. Sproul writes:

---

[9] Both terms derive from the same family in the Hebrew (*qadash*), and in the Greek (*hagios*).

"Only God can put the touch on something that changes it from the commonplace to something special, different, and apart... When we call things holy that are not holy we commit the sin of idolatry."[10]

The account of Nadab and Abihu in Leviticus 10 is meant, no doubt, to impress both the priests and people with the holiness of Divine worship. It spoke poignantly to their concept of and attitudes and actions toward God. He wanted them to learn that He means business: *"I will be sanctified* [i.e. regarded as holy] *in them that come night me, and before all the people I will be glorified"* (Lev. 10:3).

In Leviticus, God calls His redeemed people to consecrate themselves to Him by obeying His laws and ordinances. Such consecrated service would necessarily involve complete compliance with His will at every level, even at the most basic levels of their daily diet and sanitation. Leviticus discloses God's standards of sanctification by drawing very clear distinctions between that which God calls clean and that which He calls unclean—between the sacred and the profane.

Beginning in Leviticus 17, God specifies the numerous ways that the people of Israel might defile and disqualify themselves from Divine worship. The guilt of shedding the blood of an animal without sacrificing it to the Lord (ch. 17), sexual impurity (ch. 18), and exploitation of other people (chs. 19-20) defile the worshipper. Leviticus 21-22 talks about the necessity of holy conduct within the priesthood, lest they disqualify themselves

---

[10] *The Holiness of God*, pp. 56,58.

from service. Chapter 23 and 24 describe the necessity of observing holy days, and chapter 25, the hallowing of the land every seven years.

All in all, Leviticus teaches that holiness is the order of the House of the Lord. It is not an option. It is a necessity. *"Be ye holy, for I am holy,"* saith the Lord.

Summary

The developing Biblical plot, therefore, is the story of a single nation—formed, protected, guided, multiplied, delivered, instructed, and sustained by God. They, in turn, are called to consecrate themselves exclusively to His glory. The consequent life of community is to function as a theocracy, submissive to Jehovah's absolute authority and governed, ruled, and defended by Him. Among all the nations and empires of the world, Israel is to be the Lord's domain—a theocratic community devoted to His praise and honor alone.

Would the dream of a society ruled by God and devoted to God be realized? The book of Numbers reveals that living as a theocracy was not a simple or easy thing for the people of God. Though they were still His covenant people, yet with many of them, God was not well pleased. And that will be the subject of our focus in the next chapter.

Establishing the Theocracy

Chapter 4
ISRAEL'S WILDERNESS WANDERINGS
Numbers

Numbers resumes the narrative style of Genesis and Exodus. The book takes its name from the census figures that dominate the first four chapters as well as chapter 26, but Numbers is more than a simple statistical tally of the people of Israel. It is a detailed, historical account of their forty years in the wilderness, living as a theocratic society.

A brief review of the developing plot may be helpful at this point. Israel's ancestors, like those of the nations, had worshiped idols (Jos. 24:2). But God had chosen them from among the nations to be his covenant people. He pledged Himself to multiply the nation and give them the land of Canaan for an everlasting inheritance.

To this end, He raised up Joseph as patriarch to sustain the nation in famine, and Moses as deliverer to redeem the people from Egyptian bondage. Through Moses, God gave the people His revelation and set them apart from the nations in a covenant of worship and service. Through this revelation, Israel would function as a theocratic kingdom—a nation governed by Jehovah as the sovereign King—a distinct counterculture in the midst of the various religious cultures of the nations. The laws, statutes, and ordinances of Exodus 16-40 and the book of Leviticus define in detail the form that God's kingdom, as expressed through the nation of Israel, would take.

God had promised to lead, protect, defend, and prosper the nation. All He required from them was obedience to His commands and dependence on His promise. Yet Israel found it difficult to be faithful to God's revelation. The book of Numbers is essentially a development of this theme of Israel's struggle with unbelief.

By way of practical application, this record of Israel's experience in the wilderness teaches that God's people must walk by faith. Hebrews 3-4 offers the New Testament commentary on this period of Israel's history. Both Numbers and Hebrews affirm that when God's people succumbed to unbelief, they wandered aimlessly into tragedy. But when they trusted in God's promises and depended on His strength, they made steady, forward progress. The Old Testament Professor Gleason Archer writes,

> "The purpose of the census prior to the failure at Kadesh (Num. 1-4) and of the census of the later generation at the plains of Moab (Num. 26) was to show that they were not kept out of Canaan by their insufficient numbers. It was not the size of their army that mattered, but only the size of their faith."[1]

Like a Mighty Army (Num. 1-8)

The book of Numbers records stage three of Israel's history. Stage one—Genesis 11 through Exodus 15—depicts Israel as Jehovah's "sons". Through Abraham, God established a covenant relationship with the nation. Stage two—Exodus 16

---

[1] *A Survey of Old Testament Introduction*, p. 265.

through Leviticus—focuses on Israel as Jehovah's "servants". Through Moses, the servant of God, the Lord was shaping His covenant people into a theocratic counter-community. Stage three—Numbers through Deuteronomy—pictures Israel as Jehovah's "soldiers". Under Moses' leadership, the nation was formed into the holy army of God.

Numbers begins by describing the constitution of the army and the regulations it must observe as the people marched toward conquest of the land of promise (chs. 1 - 10:10). Part two of the book describes the mighty army's actual march from Sinai to the plains of Moab with their attendant failures and successes (chs. 10:11 – 25:18). Part three describes the organization of a new army and their preparations for entering Canaan's land (chs. 26 – 36). The basic outline of Numbers, then, looks like this:

I.	**Formation of the Army (1:1 – 10:10)**
II.	**Failures of the Army in the March (10:11 – 25:18)**
III.	**Formation of a New Army (26:1 – 36:13)**

As the new army prepared to leave Mount Sinai for the promised land, God commanded Moses to "take the sum of all the children of Israel" (1:2). The number of males, twenty years old and upward—those who "were able to go forth to war"— was 603,550 (1:46). God has indeed made Abraham the "father of a multitude."

Chapter three and following concern Israel's marching orders. First, before the people could move forward, instructions must be given regarding the transportation of the tabernacle and its furniture, for the worship of Jehovah was central to the community. The sons of Levi, being from the priestly tribe, were given charge of various portions of the dismantling, transportation, and reconstruction of the tabernacle as the nation journeyed in the wilderness.

Each of the families of Levi's three sons was commissioned as "burden bearers." The Gershonites were commissioned to care for and transport the tent and curtains. The Merarites were charged with the care of the external framing (pillars, boards, etc.) of the sacred tent. To the Kohathites was committed the care of the contents, vessels, and furniture of the sanctuary (Num. 3:18-38).

The Army Mobilized (Num. 9 -10)

After further civil and ceremonial instructions concerning their march through the wilderness, the Lord gave the command for the people to observe the second celebration of the Passover (9:1). One year had elapsed since Israel left Egypt and on the anniversary of their Exodus, the entire company commemorated the most significant deliverance in their history.

Numbers 9:15 begins the actual account of their departure from Sinai and journey toward the land God had promised. God manifested His ongoing presence with them by means of a theophany[2]: "*And on the day that the tabernacle was reared up the cloud covered the tabernacle...and at even there was upon the*

---

[2] A theophany is a visible manifestation of God's presence.

tabernacle as it were the appearance of fire, until the morning. So it was always: the cloud covered it by day, and the appearance of fire by night" (Num. 9:15-16). No doubt, the sight of these perpetual, supernatural phenomena, the same elements seen by Abraham when God covenanted with him (Gen. 15) and by the children of Israel at the Red Sea, must have exercised a profound effect upon the people.

How did they know when to journey and by what course they were to move forward? The "cloud" would guide them: *"And when the cloud was taken up from the tabernacle, then after that the children of Israel journeyed: and in the place where the cloud abode, there the children of Israel pitched their tents. At the commandment of the Lord the children of Israel journeyed, and at the commandment of the Lord they pitched: as long as the cloud abode upon the tabernacle they rested in their tents"* (Num. 9:17-18). With Jehovah as their Commander-in-Chief, the whole impressive entourage— encompassing approximately three square miles—marched forward "like a mighty army".

The actual signal to march was to be given by the sons of Aaron on two silver trumpets (Num. 10:1-10). Instructions were given regarding the different occasions for the sounding of the trumpets, whether for the purpose of gathering the tribal heads (v. 4), or for the general gathering of the entire congregation (vs. 7-8), or for war (vs. 9), or for festive occasions (v. 10). Edersheim writes,

"Israel was a host [i.e. army], and as such [was] summoned by blast of trumpet. But Israel was a host of which Jehovah was Leader and King, and the trumpets that summoned this host were silver trumpets of the sanctuary, blown by the priests of Jehovah. Hence these their blasts brought Israel as the Lord's host in remembrance before their God and King".[3]

About one month after the second Passover observance, the cloud lifted from above the tabernacle and Israel marched forward (10:11). The rest of the chapter describes the juxtaposition of each tribal "army" (10:28) to the tabernacle (which was always in the center) as the nation journeyed. The language of Numbers 10:35 (repeated in Psalm 68:1) captures the essence of the militant spirit with which they moved forward: *"Rise up, Lord, and let thine enemies be scattered: let them also that hate thee flee before thee."*

This repetition of military imagery is revealing. The imagery suggests that Israel—this group of Bedouins in the Sinai peninsula—would be Jehovah's army. He had redeemed them from bondage by His own mighty power and would now use them to fight for His glory against the idolatry and paganism that prevailed in His world. The practical lesson is clear: *The Kingdom of God exists in time in a fundamental conflict with the kingdoms of this world.* Whether we are speaking of Israel, in the Old Testament, or the Church, in the New, both are called to a counter-cultural existence in this present world—a calling that necessarily involves spiritual conflict.

---

[3] *Bible History*, p. 152. (Cf. v. 9b).

Israel's Unbelief (Num. 10:11 – 21:20)

Part 2 of the book of Numbers begins with chapter 10 and continues to the end of the book. This section develops the theme of Israel's unbelief and various failures in the course of marching to Canaan's land by describing seven major episodes of Israel's unbelief and rebellion. The Lord indicts the nation for murmuring, mutiny, rebellion, insubordination, more murmuring, ingratitude, and tempting God.

1) MURMURING. On the twentieth day of the second month after the Exodus, the cloud lifted from the tabernacle, and the nation began its march across the wilderness (10:11). But it wasn't long before the people began to murmur. Journeying with the people on the outskirts of the procession was a "mixed multitude" (11:4)—foreigners who had come out of Egypt with Israel (Ex. 12:38). Since they were not part of the covenant family and had no relationship with Jehovah, they soon tired of the manna and began to grumble: "*We remember the fish, which we did eat in Egypt freely; the cucumbers, and the melons, and the leeks, and the onions, and the garlic*" (11:5).

The complaints angered the Lord and he sent judgment by fire that consumed a number of people "in the uttermost parts of the camp" (11:1). But the murmuring spirit of the mixed multitude had already infected the children of Israel and they began to cry out for "flesh", i.e. meat, to eat (11:10ff). They wanted flesh and the Lord gave them flesh—so much that it came out at their nostrils (11:19-20). Yes, He gave them meat, but He also gave them "leanness of soul" (Ps. 106;15). The people gathered for the quail stacked three-feet deep around the camp, but before they began to chew the meat, "the Lord smote the people with a very great plague" and multitudes died (11:31-34; cf. 1 Co. 10:10). God will not bear long with those who murmur against Him (Num. 14:27).

Is murmuring such a great sin? Yes, it is a very heinous sin, for it expresses a quarrel with His goodness and ingratitude for His providential care. Thomas Watson writes,

> "The murmurer says...that God hath not dealt well with him, and that he deserves better from Him. The murmurer charges God with folly...[saying] 'God might have been a wiser and a better God'."

God's displeasure with the people was due to their discontent with what He had provided and distrust of His promise to sustain them.

2) MUTINY. Not long after, a mutiny erupted in the troops. Miriam and Aaron voiced a complaint about Moses' exalted position as mediator between God and the people (12:1-2). Though Moses, in self-effacing meekness (12:3), did not defend himself, God spoke to validate Moses' authority (12:6-8). Because Miriam initiated the insurrection and was "not afraid to speak against" God's servant (v. 8b), the Lord smote her with

leprosy and she was quarantined from the camp for seven days (12:10-15).

3) REBELLION. Following shortly on the heels of this episode, the people revealed just how obstinate and rebellious they were. The ten spies returned from their reconnaissance mission to Canaan with a huge cluster of grapes, pomegranates, figs, and the following report: *"Surely [the land] floweth with milk and honey; nevertheless the people be strong that dwell in the land, and the cities are walled, and very great: and moreover we saw the children of Anak there...We be not able to go up against the people; for they are stronger than we"* (13:27-33). Only Caleb and Joshua believed God (13:30).

The report of unbelief discouraged the people and they began to murmur again: *"Would God we had died in the land of Egypt..."* The rebellion grew to a fevered pitch, with someone suggesting that they choose a new captain and return to Egypt (14:1-4). When Joshua and Caleb reminded the people that the Lord was with His people and would deliver their enemies into Israel's hand, the congregation wanted to stone them to death (14:6-10). Suddenly the Lord appeared and spoke to Moses, saying, *"How long will this people provoke me? And how long will it be ere they believe me, for all the signs which I have showed among them?"* (14:11).

Moses intercession on behalf of the people stayed the complete annihilation of the nation (14:12-19), but God, because of their unbelief and disobedience, judged them sorely. All who were twenty years of age and above when they came out of Egypt, i.e. the entire original army, the Lord revealed, would die in the wilderness (14:29). Only their children would be blessed to inhabit the land (14:31). Furthermore, the nation would "wander in the wilderness forty years" according to the number of days that they spied out the land (14:33-34).

The ten unbelieving spies died immediately by a plague (14:36-37). The next morning, the congregation gathered with a change of mind: *"Lo, we be here, and will go up unto the place which the Lord hath promised"* (14:40). But it was "too little, too late" though Moses counseled them to forbear "for the Lord is not among you", a number of them "presumed to go up" anyway, and the army was routed by the Amalekites and Canaanites (14:42-45).

4) INSUBORDINATION. Some time later, there was yet another incident of rebellion and unbelief. The sons of Korah from the tribe of Levi raised support among some of the leaders to challenge Moses and Aaron (16:1-3). They were not content with the role of service God had entrusted to them, but wanted to usurp the Aaronic priesthood as well (16:9-11). When Moses called Dathan and Abiram, the two sons of Eliab[4], they obstinately refused to comply with his subpoena to "come up" for negotiation (16:12-14). When the day of reckoning arrived,

---

[4] Eliab was the official representative of the tribe of Zebulun (Num. 1:4-5,9,16); hence, his sons were among the "men of renown" gathered with the sons of Korah (Num. 16:2).

the sons of Korah, their two accomplices Dathan and Abiram, and Aaron stood before the Lord with their respective censers in hand (16:16,24). Korah had managed to marshal the support of practically the entire congregation, who assembled to see the contest (16:19). It was a showdown of the first order.

Moses said, *"Hereby ye shall know that the Lord hath sent me to do all these works; for I have not done them of mine own mind"* (16:28). Suddenly, the ground opened beneath the sons of Korah and the earth swallowed them up (16:31-32).

5) MURMURING AGAIN. As if this were not sufficient to impress the people with the danger of rebellion, the very next day *"all the congregation murmured against Moses, saying, Ye have killed the people of the Lord"* (16:41). At once, the Lord sent a plague that consumed 14,700 more of the mutineers before it was stayed (16:42-50).

6) INGRATITUDE. At Kadesh, the thirsty army formed a mob and again "chided with Moses", saying, *"Would God we had died when our brethren died before the Lord! And why have ye brought up the congregation of the Lord into this wilderness...and wherefore have ye made us to come up out of Egypt, to bring us in unto this evil place? It is no place of seed, or of figs, or of vines, or of pomegranates; neither is there any water to drink"* (20:1-5). Note the ungrateful spirit of their words. Was the land to which they were headed an "evil place" or the land of promise?

Moses, in frustration, says, *"Hear now, ye rebels, must we fetch you water out of this rock?"* Instead of "speaking" to the rock as God had commanded, Moses smote it with his rod. The water gushed forth in abundance, but God disciplined Moses and Aaron severely: *"Because ye believed me not, to sanctify me in the eyes of the children of Israel, therefore ye shall not bring this congregation into the land which I have given them"* (20:10-13). Here, at Kadesh, both Miriam and Aaron died.

7) TEMPTING THE LORD. The seventh episode of rebellion occurred as the people journeyed around the land of Edom (for the king of Edom refused them passage through his land – 20:14-21). On the journey, the morale of the army fell. *"And the people spake against God, and against Moses, Wherefore have ye brought us up out of Egypt to die in the wilderness? For there is no bread, neither is there any water; and our soul loatheth this light bread"* (21:4-5). God judged the murmuring Israelites by fiery serpents that bit the people (21:6; cf. 1 Cor. 10:9).

When Moses made intercession for the people, God commanded him to construct a brazen serpent and erect it for the healing of those who had been bitten (21:8-9). According to John 3:14, this event foreshadows the cross of Christ and the healing benefits of looking by faith on Him.

Triumphs in Battle (Num. 21:21 – 25:18)

The focus changes in Numbers 21 from the ominous scenes of disobedience and judgment to the thrilling accounts of military triumph and conquest. First, at Hormah, Israel responded to king Arad's attack by turning to the Lord in humility and faith. He honored their faith by giving them the victory (21:1-3).

Then, when they arrived in the land of Moab, Israel triumphed over Sihon, king of the Amorites, and Og, king of Bashan (21:21-35). News of these victories reached Balak, the king of Moab. Realizing that his military was not capable of defeating the armies of Israel, and that they had occupied his territory, Balak resorted to the use of sorcery to defeat Israel (22:1-4). He sent repeated appeals to Balaam, a well-known prophet who lived near the Euphrates in an attempt to hire him to pronounce a curse that would insure Israel's defeat. Finally, Balaam consented, but on the way, encountered the angel of the Lord with his sword drawn, who registered God's displeasure that the prophet had agreed to cooperate with Moab. Balaam proceeded on his mission, but committed himself to saying only those things that the Lord told him to speak, whether or not it pleased Balak (22:21-35).

Balak took the prophet to three different hills from which he might see the army of Israel. But each time, much to Balak's chagrin, Balaam spoke words of promise and blessing upon Israel (23:7-11; 23:18-25; 24:2-9). Balak refused to pay the prophet, ordering him to go home. In a final parting shot, Balaam uttered yet a fourth prophecy in which he predicted Israel's conquest of Edom and Amalek, Israel's future captivity by the Assyrians, and the Kittim's (i.e. Greeks and Romans) conquest of the Babylonians and rule over the Hebrews (24:15-24).

It is a remarkable prophecy of Israel's future, sprinkled with rich predictions of the coming Messiah. On a strictly historical note, this episode demonstrates how God fought for His people, turning the proposed curse into a blessing.

Though Balaam did not pronounce a curse upon Israel, he did, as chapter 25 indicates, teach Balak how to gain an advantage over them (cf. Num. 31:16; Rev. 2:14). He advised Balak to use Moabite women to seduce the Israelites into idolatry. He knew that Jehovah would judge His people for syncretism. Sure enough, when Israel joined himself to Baal, the judgment of God fell in the form of a plague and 24,000 Israelites died (25:1-9). Only the swift action of Phinehas, Aaron's grandson, stayed the plague. When he saw the audacious immorality of an Israelite man and a Midianite woman, Phinehas followed the couple into the tent and thrust them through with his javelin (25:6-15). And this courageous act "was counted unto him for righteousness" (Ps. 106:30-31).

Preparing to Enter the Promised Land (Num. 26 – 36)

There are repeated references in the last ten chapters to Jericho, indicating that the book of Numbers was probably composed by Moses while the army camped trans-Jordan, near the end of Moses' life (26:3, 63; 31:12; 33:48, 50; 34:15; 35:1; 36:13). Almost 40 years have elapsed, and the army has traveled from Sinai to the border of Canaan's land.

Almost all of the first generation army has perished in the course of their journey. Now, it is here, "in the plains of Moab by Jordan near Jericho" (26:3), that God mercifully reconstitutes the second generation into His holy army.

In Numbers 27, the Lord names Joshua as Moses' successor. In chapter 31, He commissions Moses for one final military campaign against the Midianites. Numbers 32 records the decision by two and one-half tribes (Gad, Reuben, and half of Manasseh) to settle trans-Jordan, and the questions raised by that decision about their loyalty to Jehovah and willingness to participate in Israel's military campaigns. Numbers 33 recaps the itinerary of their forty years of wilderness wandering. Numbers 34-36 contains instructions about the division of the land of Canaan.

All in all, the book of Numbers demonstrates the fact that God had fulfilled His promise to Abraham concerning an innumerable offspring. The covenant people were now not only a great multitude, but they were also within a hairs-breadth of seeing the fulfillment of the second part of the promise—the occupation of the land of Canaan for an everlasting inheritance.

Israel's Wilderness Wanderings

Chapter 5
THE MOSAIC COVENANT RENEWED
Deuteronomy

Deuteronomy, a book consisting of Moses' farewell addresses to Israel as they prepare to enter the land God had promised to them, closes the Mosaic period of Old Testament history. In it we see Moses exercising his prophetic office (Deut. 34:10) as Jehovah's spokesman to the covenant people.

The nation has been established as a theocratic society—a people founded, preserved, delivered, directed, sustained, protected, and governed by Jehovah (Deut. 32:9-14). He is their "Judge, Lawgiver, and King" (Is. 33:22)[1], and they, His subjects and army. He is their God; they are His people. Now, standing on the threshold of their God-given inheritance, it is appropriate that Moses review their journey thus far, remind them of their obligations to God's Law, and urge them to a renewed commitment to the covenant. These three emphases make up the content of Moses' three orations in Deuteronomy.

Deuteronomy means "second law". It is Moses' farewell address, given in the plains of Moab, to the second generation army as they prepare to enter Canaan. Reading Deuteronomy is like listening to a general giving his last-minute instructions to

---

[1] Note that Jehovah satisfies all three "branches" of government—the judicial ("Judge"), legislative ("Lawgiver"), and executive ("King"). There could be no clearer definition of a *theocracy* than this verse from Isaiah.

the troops before they enter battle. After he interprets the Law to the new generation, Moses will relinquish his leadership in death.

The book of Deuteronomy is a compendium of the specific form the new theocracy would take in the land of promise. It is written in the format of an ancient covenant treaty, the parts of which are as follows:

I.   The *historical prologue*, reviewing the past relationship between the parties of the covenant is recorded in chapters 1-4.

II. The *stipulations of the covenant*, outlining the expectations of covenant life, are listed in chapters 5-26.

III. Chapters 27-30 concern the *ratification of the covenant*, spelling out how God will respond to their adherence to or violation of the treaty in specific "blessings" and "curses".

IV. The fourth section, chapter 31, records the *witnesses of the treaty*.

V.   Finally, Chapters 32-34 concern the *ongoing administration of the covenant* through Joshua after Moses' death.

The key word of the book is "remember" (5:15; 7:18; 8:2; 9:7; 16:3,12; 32:7). The imperative verb (i.e. 'thou shalt remember') appears, together with its negative corollary (i.e. 'do not forget' – 4:9; 6:12; 8:11,14; 9:7; 32:18) over twenty-five times in Deuteronomy. As the nation prepared to possess the land of promise, it faced a number of challenges. Moses writes Deuteronomy to remind them of who their God is, how He had delivered them and led them through the wilderness, and what He required from them.

A simple outline of the book in terms of Moses' three orations may be helpful to the synthesizing of its message:

I. First Address – "Review of History" (1-4)
II. Second Address – "Repetition of Law" (5-26)
III. Third Address – "Renewal of Covenant"(27-31)
IV. "Requiem of Moses" (32-34)

The fact that Deuteronomy is couched in homily (i.e. the style of a sermon) indicates that it is not simply an explanation, but an application of the Law. Moses wants each individual Israelite to take seriously Jehovah's call to holiness.

At least three major themes dominate Moses' message in Deuteronomy. As the nation prepares to invade Canaan, they must remember these various principles.

The Exclusivity of God

Deuteronomy emphasizes the true character of Jehovah and the danger of idolatry. God's unique nature—His spirituality (4:12,15-24) and unity (4:35, 39; 6:4; 7:9; 10:17)—is the basis of the repeated warnings against idolatry (6:14-15; 7:4; 8:19-20; 11:16-20; 13:2-12; 30:17-18).

Israel was entering a culture steeped in polytheism (the worship of many gods). Idol worship and its accompanying culture of immorality was pervasive in the land of Canaan. The Canaanites worshipped Baal, the sun god, and Ashtoreth (or

Astarte), the Queen of Heaven—the chief god and goddess of an entire pantheon. The possibility that Israel might be influenced by polytheism was very real. The threat of syncretism, i.e. blending Divine revelation with man-made religion, was the greatest danger the nation faced.

The Principle of Love

Another theme developed in the various discourses of Deuteronomy is the primary role of love between God and His people. The word "love" occurs twenty-two times in the book—both in terms of God's love for the nation and of love as the basis of their service to Him.

Deuteronomy reveals that the covenant relationship between God and Israel is based on His love, not man's merit (4:37; 7:7-8, 13; 10:15; 33:3; cf. Ps. 47:4; Hos. 11:1). All of the wonderful things He has done for them are due to His love. Sovereign love is the motive behind all of Jehovah's dealings with the nation.

The book also develops the reciprocal truth that love for God is the basic requirement of the law (6:5; 10:12; 11:1, 13, 22; 13:3; 19:9; 30:6, 16, 20). Everything they do in service to God is to be motivated by love for Him, not self-serving interests. This note of love responding to love is one of the most refreshing features of Deuteronomy, for it anticipates the New Testament message that love is the fulfillment of the law.

The Priority of Obedience

The third dominant theme of Moses' messages is the importance of resolute obedience to God's word. The startling language of chapters 28-30, with their powerful pronouncements of "blessing" and "cursing", teaches that there are blessings to be had in obedience to God that simply may not be enjoyed in disobedience. Every act of obedience will be met with blessing, and every violation will receive a just recompense of reward.

All in all, Deuteronomy is Moses' final challenge to the people of Israel as they prepare to conquer the land God has promised to them. The forty year journey through the wilderness is complete. God has marvelously sustained His people. Now they are just a month or two away from possessing their possessions. Let's consider the content of the book, now, in more specific terms.

Historical Reflections (Deut. 1-4)

The first address reviews God's gracious guidance on their journey from Horeb (i.e. Sinai) to Moab. The key events rehearsed by Moses include the call to march (1:6-8), the appointment of tribal judges (1:9-18), the unbelief of the twelve spies and rebellion of the people (1:21-46), and the thirty-eight years of wandering in the wilderness "until all the generation of the men of war were wasted out from among the host" (2:1-14).

On the course of this journey, Moses reminds them, God prohibited them from engaging the Edomites (2:5), the Moabites (2:9), and the Ammonites (2:19) in battle, for He had given these lands to Esau and the children of Lot as an inheritance. But God did deliver the trans-Jordanian kingdoms—ruled by Sihon, the Amorite, and Og, the king of Bashan, into their hands (2:24 – 3:11).

It is evident that Moses is driven by a pastoral motive. He reflects on their history for the sake of encouraging them to trust the Lord. Hence he reminds them repeatedly in this section of the great truth of God's sovereignty (2:7, 25, 30) and admonishes them to "fear not nor be discouraged" (1:21; 3:22).

Finally, Moses concludes this first address by reviewing Joshua's commission as the new leader (3:23-29) and urging the people of Israel to cherish God's Law (4:1-49), a theme he will develop in greater detail in the next address.

The Law Reiterated (Deut. 5-26)

Moses' second oration begins in 5:1. It is from this section that the book derives its name, for this is "a second giving", or reiteration, of the Law. The Law given at Sinai is now repeated in the plains of Moab for the sake of instructing the new generation of Israelites of their several responsibilities to God. Though the circumstances of their existence would soon change from the environment in which their fathers had initially received this word, God's standards had not changed. This second law is meant to remind them of that fact.

Chapter five repeats the Ten Commandments and charges the people to obedience. Chapter six urges the people to "fear the Lord [their] God" (6:2, 13, 24)—i.e. to regard Him and Him alone as holy—and to love Him exclusively (6:5). This command is based on the well-known passage known as the *Shema*, the most important text in the Old Testament to the Jew: "Hear, O Israel: The Lord our God is one Lord..." (6:4). Because Jehovah is the only true and living God, idolatry is strictly forbidden and will be judged severely (6:13-15). Fearing God and loving Him with one's total being involves making Him the center of one's whole life (6:6-9), recognizing Him as the source of every blessing (6:10-12), faithfully keeping His statutes (6:16-19), and diligently teaching the meaning of His word to one's children (6:7, 20-25). Fearing, loving, serving and obeying Jehovah is enjoined upon them as essential to the nation's future well-being and blessedness (6:3, 18, 24; cf. 10:12-13).

Chapters seven through eleven is a call to separation, or holiness. In these chapters, Moses warns the people of the dangers of corrupting themselves with the pagan practices of Canaan's inhabitants. God had made them "a holy people unto Himself" (7:6); therefore, they were to destroy every idol that rivaled His glory (7:25-26) and remain completely devoted to Him (10:20-21; 11:1).

Chapters twelve through twenty-six repeat the laws of religious worship and personal conduct. It is interesting to note the several warnings in this passage concerning participation in the occultic practices of the Canaanites (12:30-31; 14:1-2 [cf. Lev. 19:28; 21:5]; 18:9-14).

It is in this section also that two important prophecies appear. The first anticipates the nation's desire for a human king like the nations around it (17:14-20). Though God indicates that He would permit the request to be granted, He makes it plain by the stipulations imposed that He would still retain ultimate authority. This is the first hint that Jehovah's theocratic rule would be challenged by a monarchy—a paradigm shift that will be developed as the dominant theme of the Deuteronomistic Period of Israel's history.

The second prophecy anticipates Moses' greater successor— the "Prophet like unto Moses" (18:15-19). This "Prophet" is not Joshua, but the Messiah. Hence, in the middle of this historical context, the Holy Spirit broadens our perspective and reminds the reader of the fact that the immediate plot of Israel's history is really a sub-plot of the larger redemptive theme of Messiah's advent.

The Covenant Renewed (Deut. 27-31)

The third discourse begins in 27:1. This passage records the ratification, or endorsement, of the covenant by the people. It corresponds to the "application" phase of a sermon—the homiletic tactic in which the truths that have been stated and explained are personally applied and the hearers are called upon to respond. Moses, here, brings to bear upon the people the previous two messages and calls them to rededicate themselves anew to God in covenant commitment: *"I call heaven and earth to record this day against you, that I have set before you life and death, blessing and cursing: therefore choose life, that both thou and thy seed may live"* (30:19).

In chapter 31, Joshua is formally and publicly commissioned as the new leader, thus insuring the continuation of the covenant's administration after Moses' death. John Wesley put it correctly: "God buries His workmen, but carries on His work."

Moses' Requiem (Deut. 32-34)

The Pentateuch concludes with a section appended to Deuteronomy (probably written by Joshua, Moses' successor) after Moses' death. It includes the "Song of Moses" (ch. 32), the record of His final benediction on the nation (ch. 33), and the account of his death (ch. 34).

The "Song of Moses" recorded in Deuteronomy 32 is a remarkable poetic composition. Similar to the prophecies of Balaam (see especially Num. 24:16-24), this song encompasses the entirety of Israel's existence—past, present, and future. The Mosaic history (Abraham to Moses) is poetically outlined in verses 9-14. The Deuteronomistic history (Joshua to Babylonian Captivity) is described in verses 15-21. The Chronistic history (Restoration of Exiles and Rebuilding of Jerusalem) is the subject of verses 35-43.

This song refers to God as "the Rock", an image suggesting the thought of stability and faithfulness (32:4). Revelation 19 echoes the eschatological hope of Moses' song, with its prediction that God will avenge the blood of His servants (vs. 41-43).

Moses' final benediction, recorded in Deuteronomy 33, is reminiscent of Jacob's dying blessing upon his twelve sons. Like the song of chapter 32, it is poetic in genre. It concludes with a celebration of Israel's God and the victory He would accomplish for them: *"There is none like unto the God of Jeshurun, who rideth upon the heaven in thy help...The eternal God is thy refuge, and underneath are the everlasting arms...Happy art thou, O Israel: who is like unto thee, O people saved by the Lord, the shield of thy help, and who is the sword of thy excellency! and thine enemies shall be found liars unto thee; and thou shalt tread upon their high places"* (33:26-27, 29).

The book of Deuteronomy itself concludes with the account of Moses' death. From Pisgah's lofty heights in Mount Nebo, Moses surveyed the promised inheritance: *"And the Lord said unto him, This is the land which I sware unto Abraham, unto Isaac, and unto Jacob, saying, I will give it unto thy seed: I have caused thee to see it with thine eyes, but thou shalt no go over thither. So Moses the servant of the Lord died there in the land of Moab, according to the word of the Lord"* (34:4-5). And so concludes the Mosaic period of the nation's history.

Part 2

The

Monarchial Period

(or Deuteronomistic Era)

Introduction to Part 2

The books of Joshua through Kings describe the events that transpired during the next 850 years. This second major period of Israel's history, sometimes termed the Deuteronomistic, or Monarchial era, begins with Israel's incursion into and conquest of Canaan, continues with the theocracy's decline, and concludes with the account of the nation's exile in Babylon. During the Deuteronomistic period, Israel will rise to the peak of prosperity, then sink to the depths of adversity for rejecting Jehovah as the theocratic ruler of the nation.

The Deuteronomistic history embraces events between 1452 and 536 B.C. It is within this time frame that most of the prophets ministered the word of God to the people. In fact, this second major division in Old Testament history is actually called in the Hebrew Canon "the prophets" (*nby' ym*). Understanding how the prophecies of Isaiah, Jeremiah, Hosea, Amos, and the rest synchronize with the events related to this era is a significant key to the interpretation of the Old Testament. Likewise, a grasp of the major events during this period in the nation's history will prove to be a great help in the interpretation of the prophets.[1]

---

[1] For example, Hosea addresses his message to "Ephraim" and "Samaria." He says things like "Ephraim is joined to idols' and "Ephraim is a silly dove without heart." On the surface, these statements appear to be unintelligible, but when they are viewed through the grid of the Deuteronomistic period of history with its emphasis on the Divided Monarchy, it becomes apparent that Hosea's message is directed to the Northern kingdom of Israel—Ephraim being its principal tribe and Samaria its capital city—in contrast to the Southern kingdom of Judah. The need to set Hosea's prophecy within this historical context is, then, an important hermeneutical key.

The narrative section (Joshua through Kings) develops the historical theme of judgment. During this period in Israel's history, the nation struggles to live as a theocracy, finally opting for a king (monarch) like the other nations around it. God allows them to have their desire, but still retains plenipotentiary, or ultimate, authority, rejecting the king the people chose for themselves (i.e. Saul), and establishing his own king (i.e. David) over them. Their rejection of Jehovah as King and concern to accommodate the spirit of the age, however, leads to the nation's decline and ultimate fall under Divine judgment.

But beyond the dominant and most apparent motif of God's judgment on the backslidden people, the prophetic section (Isaiah through Zechariah) interjects a further dimension. In addition to the historical theme of judgment, the prophets develop an eschatological theme—the messianic hope of a Davidic King who would reign over God's people forever—in the clearest terms yet. It is here, in the Deuteronomistic period of Israel's history, that the grand plot of special revelation, i.e. the Messianic hope, emerges and begins to assume prominence.

In single words, the Deuteronomistic period of Israel's history can be summarized in terms of Victory (Joshua), Anarchy (Judges), Monarchy (Samuel & Kings), and Captivity (the prophets). A more specific outline of this era might look like this:

I.   **Conquest of Canaan (Joshua)** II. **Decline & Deliverance (Judges)** III. **The United Monarchy (Samuel)** IV. **The Divided Monarchy (Kings)** V. **The Assyrian Conquest of Israel** VI. **The Babylonian Captivity of Judah**

Chapter 6
THEOCRACY OR ANARCHY?
Joshua, Judges & Ruth

Part 2 of Israel's history begins with the account of the conquest of Canaan and occupation of the Promised Land under Joshua. This defining moment in Israel's history marked the fulfillment of God's original promise to Abraham. No longer would the nation live as a nomadic people, wandering in the desert and living in tents. The long-anticipated day has arrived. The arduous journey through the wilderness is over. The people of Jehovah are home at last.

Joshua: An Abundant Entrance

The book of Joshua, named for its primary character, resumes the narrative of Numbers and Deuteronomy, with the commissioning of Joshua as Moses' successor (1:1-9). It strikes a triumphant note, marking the transition of Israel from a nomadic existence in Egypt and the wilderness to its possession of the inheritance God had promised as the nation's permanent dwelling-place. The book of Joshua is, then, both the triumphant conclusion of Israel's redemption and the bridge to the next chapter in the ongoing saga of Biblical history. It is composed of three parts:

> I.   Entering the Land (Jos. 1-12)
> II. Settling the Land (Jos. 13-22)
> III. Living in the Land (Jos. 23-24)

The theme of the book might be expressed by the call to "possess your possessions." The popular Bible teacher J. Vernon McGee writes,

> "The book of Joshua corresponds to the Epistle to the Ephesians in the New Testament where we see that the believer is blessed with all spiritual blessings. The practical possession and experience of them depends upon conflict and conquest. These are never attained through the energy of the flesh, but through the power of the Holy Spirit in the yielded life of the believer. The Book of Joshua is the pattern, and it illustrates the method by which the believer can possess what God has given to him."[1]

Joshua was forty years old at the Exodus. Among the twelve men sent to spy out the land of Canaan at Kadesh-barnea, only Joshua and Caleb believed God. Now, at the age of eighty, God commissions him to lead the people into their rest.

Rest, however, would not come without conflict. Joshua would need "strength and courage" to lead the people in holy war (1:6,7,9,18). Battles against the strongholds of Jericho (ch. 6) and Ai (chs. 7-8), together with battles against the five kings at Gibeon (ch. 10) and throughout southern and northern Canaan (chs. 11-12) awaited them. The book of Joshua teaches the

---

[1] McGee, *Thru the Bible Commentary Series*, Vol. 10, p. X.

important principle that "rest is attained through labor" (cf. Heb. 4:11).

The book also teaches that rest is the product of faith in God. The "abundant entrance" they enjoyed was due to the army's dependence on the Lord. It was God who parted the waters of the Jordan when the sole of the priest's foot touched it, so that the people crossed on dry ground (chs. 3-4). It was God that outlined the battle tactic at Jericho. Strange as it may have seemed to them, the Lord honored their obedience to His word, and the walls of Jericho fell down flat to the ground (ch. 6; cf. Heb. 11:30).

The book of Joshua teaches that God honors faith with His blessing, whether in the sense of protection from danger (as in the case of Rahab – ch. 2) or military success in battle (e. g. the victory at Jericho). Moreover, the book illustrates the principle that when God's people rely on their own strength and ingenuity, they meet with defeat and failure. The initial defeat of Israel by the little city of Ai is a case in point (ch. 7).

Chapters 13–22 outline the tribal apportionment of the land and chapters 23-24, Joshua's final charge to Israel before his death, including his famous confession of faith, *"As for me and my house, we will serve the Lord"* (Jos. 24:15). The primary purpose of the book is to teach Israel how to live according to the covenant in the land that God had given them. As long as they heed the word of Jehovah, their theocratic King, they will prosper (cf. 1:7-8). But if they rebel against Him, they will be sorely judged (cf. 1:18; 24:20).

Would the nation be able to sustain its covenant to obey the word of God? Would they be successful in the quest to live as a theocracy? The book of Judges supplies the tragic answer to that question.

Judges: An Attempt at Autonomy

The history of Israel in the land of Canaan really begins with the book of Judges. This book covers a time-span of approximately 350 years, from 1385 to 1055 B.C., though the period of the judges itself continued another one hundred years to include the tenure of Eli and Samuel (Acts 13:20).

During this interval between the conquest of Canaan and the beginning of the monarchy, God raised up "judges" to deliver the people from enemy oppression (Jud. 2:18). The book reveals no new developments in Israel's history, but describes a repetitive cycle of decline and deliverance reminiscent of Psalms 78 and 106. Over and again, Judges tells the same story: Israel's apostasy and compromise, God's judgment in the form of enemy oppression, Israel's repentance, God's faithfulness to raise up a deliverer, Israel's subsequent peace and prosperity, and Israel's precarious slide back into apostasy and compromise, beginning the cycle again. The message of Judges is summarized in Judges 2:11-23.

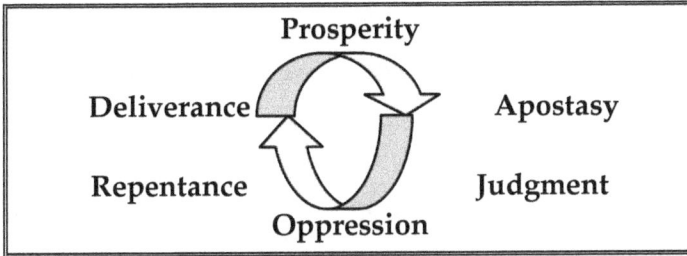

What was the reason for Israel's repeated lapses into apostasy? Since Peor, when Israel intermarried with the daughters of Moab and joined themselves to Baal (Num. 25:3), they had not been completely free of idolatry. The nation was tainted with syncretism. Judges 3:1-6 explains the fact that after the death of Joshua, many of the native inhabitants of Canaan remained unconquered. The effect of living among these idolatrous nations would prove disastrous for Israel (cf. 1:21, 27-33; 2:1-3).

Gleason Archer, a reputable voice on the Old Testament, writes about the book of Judges:

> "The basic theme of the book is Israel's failure as a theocracy to keep true to the covenant even under the leadership of men chosen of God to deliver them from oppression by the pagan world. The frequent and repeated failures of the twelve tribes to remain true to God and His holy law prepared the way for the institution of a central monarchy."[2]

Israel's struggle during this initial period of tribal leadership in Canaan—a period without any centralized form of

---

[2] *A Survey of Old Testament Introduction*, p. 299.

government—was comparable to the challenge facing the thirteen original colonies in America prior to the Revolutionary War. Like the New World colonists, the various Israelite tribes lived virtually independent of one another. They were not united under a common government. Instead, "every man did that which was right in his own eyes" (Jud. 21:25). The nation established to function as a theocracy had slid precariously into anarchy.

The historical purpose of the book of Judges is to explain the reason Israel became a monarchy. The spiritual purpose of the book is to magnify God's covenant faithfulness to deliver His people even though they repeatedly displayed their infidelity to Him. After the introduction to the book (chs. 1-2), Judges contains two primary sections: (1) History of the Judges (chs. 3-16); (2) Snapshots of the Spiritual Condition of Israel (chs. 17-21).

History of the Judges (3 – 16)

Six times, the author introduces his story by the formula, *"And the children of Israel did evil in the sight of the Lord"* (cf. 3:7, 12; 4:1; 6:1; 10:6; 13:1). Each time Israel compromised with the pagan nations around them, God sold them into bondage. And each time Israel repented and sought the Lord, a deliverer was exalted from among the people to lead them back to peace and prosperity. Many of these sections close with the refrain, "And the land had rest [a certain period of time]" (cf. 3:11, 30; 5:31; 8:28).

The Judges				
Opponent	**Deliverer**	**Tribe**	**Yrs**	**Scripture Reference**
Mesopotamia	Othniel	Judah	40	3:7-11
Moab	Ehud	Benjamin	80	3:12-30
Philistines	Shamgar	--	--	3:31
Canaanites	Deborah	Ephraim	40	4:1-24
Midianites	Gideon	Manasseh	40	6:1 – 8:35
Ammonites	Jephthah	Gilead	6	11:1-33
Philistines	Samson	Dan	20	13 – 16

The book of Judges spotlights thirteen of these "judges," of which seven are the most prominent: Othniel (3:7-11), Ehud (3:12-20), Shamgar (3:31), Deborah (4:1-24), Gideon (6:1 – 8:35), Jephthah (11:1-33), and Samson (13 – 16). Of these, Gideon, Barak, Samson, and Jephthah are mentioned among the "heroes of faith" in Hebrews 11:32.

Many of these "judges" were ordinary people living very simple and ordinary lives. But when "the Spirit of God" came upon these ordinary people (3:10), He transformed them into people who made a significant impact for God and His glory. Judges teaches us that we should never underestimate God's ability to use weak and unspectacular instruments to accomplish mighty feats (cf. 1 Cor. 1:26ff).

God used a left-handed Benjamite named Ehud to deliver Israel from eighteen years of Moabite domination. He blessed Shamgar to slay six hundred Philistines with an ox goad (3:31).

He even used a mother in Israel (5:6-7), named Deborah—an Old Testament "Molly Pitcher"—to motivate Barak, the leader of Israel's army, to courageous action against the Canaanites (4:6). When God gave them a great deliverance, Deborah composed a song of praise to Jehovah (ch. 5) and judged Israel for the next forty years. The celebration of the Gentile heroine Jael instead of Barak in Deborah's song (v. 24) demonstrates that when Israel lacked the wise leadership of godly men, Jehovah was able to deliver his people by wives and mothers.

Gideon was one of these apparently "unlikely heroes." He was timid and cowardly—reluctant to assert himself. The Midianites had oppressed Israel for seven years. The invasion of the Midianites had brought the nation to the brink of economic ruin (6:6). But when the people cried to the Lord, He answered by calling Gideon to deliver them.

Gideon's call to service, described in Judges 6:11-24, is an example of Divine patience and kindness. The Lord meets every one of Gideon's objections with assurances of His providential care and assistance. When Gideon finally engaged the enemy— an army of 135,000 trained soldiers—he had with him 300 men and a battle strategy that included the use of lamps, pitchers, and ram's horns. By the hand of the 300 Israelites, God gave Gideon a categorical victory (8:10).

Each of these judges, however, demonstrated flaws and weaknesses. Gideon's fear, Jephthah's rash vow in which his only daughter was resigned to a life of perpetual virginity (11:29-40), and Samson's lust and anger (chs. 13-16). Though Samson was mightily used by God to deliver Israel from the Philistines, he appears throughout his story as someone who thinks life is a game—a fun-loving fellow with an explosive temper. Samson's is a tragic tale of a life ruined by the passions of the flesh. His story teaches the principle that spiritual strength is a by-product of one's commitment and devotion to God. Flirting with the world, as if life is a game, jeopardizes the very thing that makes a person great in God's service.

Snapshots of Israel's Spiritual Condition (17-21)

The book of Judges concludes with a series of "snapshots" that serve to reveal the moral and religious confusion that reigned in Israel during this period. The first "snapshot" is of an Ephraimite named Micah. He was a maverick. He had stolen money from his mother. When he restored it, she made a graven image with the silver and he set it up in his own house of worship. Then he hired a traveler to be his resident priest. When some visitors from the tribe of Dan came to inquire, the hired "priest" told them precisely what they wanted to hear. The Danites subsequently robbed Micah of his idols, kidnapped his "priest", and violently seized the city of Laish as their own (17-18).

The second "snapshot" describes a Levite whose concubine ran home to her father. He pursued her and convinced her to return with him. On the journey home, his concubine was brutalized and abused by some ungodly Benjamites. So severe were her injuries that she died. At home, the Levite divided her into twelve pieces and mailed a piece of her to every tribe. The deed was shocking enough to rally the tribes of Israel to take up arms against the tribe of Benjamin in a bloody, civil war. Over 25,000 men of Benjamin were killed. Lest the tribe of Benjamin cease to exist, however, the remaining tribes determined to secure wives for the men that remained (19-21).

All in all, this was a period of corruption, compromise, and confusion. The ruthlessness and violence that prevailed during the time of the judges is, indeed, shocking.

Practical Lessons

The book of Judges highlights the difficulty of living by faith. After each deliverance, the nation quickly tended to forget God, the Unseen King who had given them His revelation, and assimilate themselves into the culture around them.

When a nation loses a sense of God's reality, its people tend to think of themselves in autonomous (or independent) terms. When Israel failed to recognize the Lord as their God, every man became his own god and did that which was right in his own eyes. The resulting chaos described in Judges 17-21 demonstrates the disastrous results of living as one's own authority. Judges teaches that political, economic, and social decline always has its roots in the disintegration of a culture's moral and spiritual foundations.

Ruth: An Exception to the Chaos

The book of Ruth is a snapshot of a very ordinary and average family living in Israel during the turbulent period of the Judges. Like a fresh breeze in the stifling heat of summer, this book is a welcome reprieve to the violent and vicious tone of Judges.

Against the dark background of moral chaos and civil war, the Holy Spirit paints this portrait of personal godliness, Divine providence, and fidelity to Jehovah. This historical glimpse into the house of Elimelech adds a melody to the cacophony of the Judges. It demonstrates God's ongoing providence in the lives of ordinary people, even in a time of great apostasy and confusion.

The genealogy that concludes this "love story" indicates that the book of Ruth is not merely a romance novel or work of historical fiction. Rather, the purpose of the book is to establish the legitimacy of King David's right to the throne. This personal portrait of a single family that lived during the period of the Judges, therefore, is more than a mere sideline to the developing plot of the Bible. *Ruth* demonstrates that God was already at work to prepare the way for His chosen king at least four generations before David was born.

Ruth is an apologetic for David's kingship in spite of the introduction of non-Israelite blood into his family lineage. Though a Moabitess was, in fact, in David's line, she was, through God's providence and the legal practice of levirate marriage, a genuine convert to Israel's God (Ruth 1:16). From the paganism and idolatry of the land of Moab, Ruth was brought to "trust under the shadow of Jehovah's wings" (2:12). This little foreign girl found refuge in the Lord God of Israel. She would even be included in the royal lineage of the Messiah (Mt. 1:5). Ruth's story, set in the land of Bethlehem-judah, sets the stage for the birth of Jesus in Bethlehem-judah many years later.

We might view the book from a two-fold perspective. (1) First, in terms of its very obvious and apparent lessons. The narrative of *Ruth* is a classic example of the providence of God. (2) Secondly, in terms of its less obvious yet equally valid lessons. Underneath the historical surface, *Ruth* foreshadows two great truths: the important role of the *goel*, or "kinsman-redeemer", and the expansive scope of the Abrahamic Covenant to include even Gentiles in its number.

Divine Providence

The book of Ruth is the Old Testament version of the parable of the prodigal son (Lk. 15). It is the story of a frightened Jewish family turning to the world in compromise rather than leaning on Jehovah in confidence.

The famine that troubled the land of Canaan was especially severe. Under these adverse circumstances, Elimelech made a decision that almost proved fatal to his family. He left "the house of bread" and took his family transjordan to the land of Moab. His sons compromised even further and married two Moabite girls, Orpah and Ruth. Before any offspring were born, however, Elimelech and his two sons died. His widow, Naomi, was not only deprived of her husband but her two sons. When she returned to her home in Bethlehem-judah, Naomi interpreted the calamity in terms of Divine chastening: *"Call me not Naomi, but call me Mara, for the Almighty hath dealt very bitterly with me. I went out full, and the Lord hath brought me home again empty"* (1:20-21).

At her behest, Orpah, Naomi's daughter-in-law, returned to her people to restart her life. Ruth, however, would not leave Naomi. Her uncommon devotion is a refreshing change to the self-absorbed spirit of compromise that marked that day. Ruth 1:16-17 is undoubtedly the loveliest expression of commitment in the entire Bible. When she said, *"Thy people shall be my people and thy God my God"*, Ruth made a conscious decision to turn from idolatry and consecrate herself to the God of Israel. Here is genuine conversion.

Chapter two is a showcase of Divine providence. Though it appeared that Ruth just "happened" upon the field of Boaz, the unfolding drama reveals that God was directing her steps (2:3). Boaz' inclination to protect, speak kindly to, and instruct his workers to leave her some "handfuls of purpose" all indicate that the Lord had a hand in these events.

When Naomi discovered how the day's events had turned out, she recognized at once the Lord's providence. She instructed Ruth to apply to Boaz, who had demonstrated such "kindness" (Heb. *hesed* = covenant loyalty) already, to "do the kinsman's part" as the *goel*, or the near kinsman, to redeem his brother's name in Israel (ch. 3).

The noble Boaz, humbled by the request of this "virtuous woman", made provision to satisfy all the legal requirements to redeem Ruth as his bride and preserve the name of Elimelech from extinction (chs. 3-4). From start to finish, the book of Ruth is an illustration of the marvels of Divine providence.

The Kinsman-Redeemer

Less conspicuous in the book (albeit of paramount significance) is the principle of the kinsman-redeemer, or *goel*. This brief narrative offers an important and helpful look at the function of this office in Jewish society.

Why is the official role of the kinsman-redeemer so important? It is important because the concept of redemption was built into the very fabric of the nation of Israel. They had experienced God's redemption from Egypt. All of their interpersonal relationships were to be built, consequently, on that great fact. The function of a *goel* reminded the Jewish people that they were called to perpetually remember His redemptive work by living together redemptively in community. In New Testament terms, "freely they had received"; now they were called to "freely give". God intended for them to demonstrate the same grace toward others that He had extended to them.

The criteria for levirate marriage (laid out in Deuteronomy 25:5-10 and illustrated here) were three: (1) The redeemer must be a near kinsman, or blood relative; (2) The redeemer must be *able* to purchase the forfeited inheritance; (3) The redeemer must be *willing* to buy back the forfeited inheritance. Boaz fulfilled all three qualifications.

Of course, this episode foreshadows Boaz' greatest descendant, the Lord Jesus Christ. Our "Boaz" is a worthy redeemer. He is a near kinsman to His people, for Jesus assumed human nature and was "made like unto his brethren" (Heb. 2:14-17). He is able to redeem, for He alone is sinless and in possession of the redemption price (Heb. 9:12, 22). Finally, He is willing to redeem. Without obligation or coercion, the Lord Jesus voluntarily assumed the sin debt of His people and suffered as their substitute (Heb. 13:12).

The Inclusion of Gentiles

The book of Ruth also foreshadows God's purpose to expand the scope of gospel blessings to include even the Gentiles. The inclusion of the Gentile woman Ruth in the developing saga of Israel's story anticipates God's plan to bring "the blessing of Abraham on the Gentiles through Jesus Christ" (Gal. 3:14). This note will be struck with increasing frequency as the pages of the Old Testament continue to unfold.

Theocracy or Anarchy?

Chapter 7
THE UNITED MONARCHY
1ˢᵗ & 2ⁿᵈ Samuel

The period of the Judges revealed just how challenging it was to live as a theocratic community. It meant that they were different from every other nation around them. They had no visible king like everyone else. Instead they were required to live by faith—to trust their unseen King to protect and provide for them and to pattern their lives according to the revelation, i.e. word or law, that He had given them. Eventually, the difficulty of living by faith coupled with the relentless pressure to conform to popular standards took its toll.

The books of 1ˢᵗ and 2ⁿᵈ Samuel mark the most strategic point yet in the unfolding drama. Here, the nation registers its preference for a human, as opposed to a Divine, king. Although God intended to establish His King over the people in His time, the people's demand for a king was premature, and tantamount to a collective rejection of Jehovah as King. By taking this step, they were saying, "We prefer to be governed as a monarchy instead of a theocracy."

Samuel: Last of the Judges, First of the Prophets

Samuel appears as a transitional figure in the unfolding drama of the sacred story. As the last of the judges (Acts 13:20) and the first of the prophets (Acts 3:24), he bridges the gap between the period of the judges (pre-monarchial era) and that of the kings (monarchial era).

This sense of *time* is critical to a synthesis of the developing plotline of the Old Testament. Israel's history can be divided into four epochs:

```
1. pre-monarchial
2. monarchial
3. exilic
4. post-exilic
```

The general theme of the Old Testament, of course, is "the Theocratic Kingdom", i.e. Jehovah's sovereign government over His covenant people (cf. Is. 33:22). But the question still begs an answer, "Just how would God exercise His theocratic rule over the nation? What particular form, in practical terms, would Divine government take?"

First and Second Samuel provides the answer to this question. Here we learn that Jehovah intended to govern His people by means of various theocratic officials—the priesthood, the prophets, and the kings. These three Divinely-ordained institutions would function as officers of the theocracy, or intermediaries between God and the nation. Jehovah would maintain ultimate (or *plenipotentiary*) authority, but would interact with the people through these mediators (cf. Gal. 3:19).

At the beginning of 1st Samuel, the priesthood is already in place and functioning as guardians of Divine worship in the theocratic community. The fact that the Lord established the office of the priesthood before the offices of both prophet and king illustrates the centrality of worship in the Divine economy and ties the identity of the nation to their service to God, for Israel was established to be a worshipping community, devoted to the glory of God. Only as the nation maintained fellowship with God would they prosper politically, monetarily, and socially. The vertical focus, in other words, would be critical to horizontal success.

First Samuel records the beginning of the remaining office bearers in the theocracy—the prophets and the kings. But unlike the priesthood which represented the people to God, these two institutions were intended to represent God to the nation. As the last of the judges in the pre-monarchial period and the first of the prophets—through whom the Lord would install a king to rule His people—Samuel appears as one of the most strategic figures of the Old Testament.

The Character of Samuel

Samuel was not only a "prophet" (1 Sam. 3:19-21) and a "judge" (1 Sam. 7:15), but a "priest" (1 Sam. 7:9). He was qualified to serve as a priest for Samuel was a descendent of Levi (1 Chr. 6:27-28; cf. 1 Sam. 8:2).[1] He interceded for the nation (1 Sam. 12:19, 23), judged the twelve tribes as he rode a regular circuit from Ramah, to Bethel, to Gilgal, to Mizpeh, and back to

---

[1] The fact that Samuel's family lived in one of the cities in Ephraim, according to 1 Sam. 1:1, does not contradict his Levitical descent, for the Levites had no inheritance except in the forty-eight Levitical cities disseminated throughout the other tribal territories.

Ramah again (1 Sam. 7:16-17), and acted as God's spokesman to the king (1 Sam. 15:16ff) and the people (12:1-25). All in all, Samuel was a faithful servant of God like Moses (Ps. 99:6; Jer. 15:1), a "guardian of the unfolding theocracy."[2]

The Career of Samuel

First and Second Samuel describe the origin of the monarchy. It may be outlined in terms of the leading figures of the narrative:

I. Samuel's Career (1 – 7)
II. Saul's Career (8 – 15)
III. David's Career (16 – 2 Sam)

Part I depicts Samuel as "the kingmaker";[3] Part II pictures Saul as the unfaithful king who rebelled against Jehovah's theocratic rule; Part III describes David as the "truly theocratic king" from whose dynasty the Messiah would come.[4]

Samuel's story begins with the account of his birth (1 – 2). His mother, Hannah, was a very devout woman, but she was barren. In her extremity, she cried out to God for a son and promised to consecrate the child to God's service. When Samuel ("God hears") was weaned, Hannah took him to Shiloh and presented

---

[2] Geerhardus Vos, *Biblical Theology: Old and New Testament*, p. 204.
[3] Archer, *A Survey of Old Testament Introduction*, p. 311
[4] Ibid.

him to Eli as a perpetual Nazarite, one dedicated exclusively to God.[5]

His call and apprenticeship in the Tabernacle under Eli's tutelage is recorded in chapter 3. His first God-given assignment set the pace for his entire career of courageous ministry. God required him to confront Eli with a message of doom upon his house, *"for his sons made themselves vile and he restrained them not"* (3:13-14). This act of announcing impending judgment establishes a precedent for the role of the prophets as covenant prosecutors—a task to which almost every successive prophet would be called to fulfill.

The promised judgment on Eli's house fell some time later. As Samuel functioned in his prophetic office, the army of Israel engaged its perennial nemesis, the Philistines, in battle. When the Philistines killed approximately four thousand soldiers, the elders of Israel concluded the defeat was due to the absence of the ark of the covenant: *"Let us fetch the ark of the covenant of the Lord out of Shiloh unto us, that when it cometh among us, it may save us out of the hand of our enemies"* (4:3).

Somewhere along the way, the people began to think of the ark as a kind of lucky charm, instead of a symbol of the Lord's presence. Though the Philistines were initially intimidated by the presence of the ark, they rallied and fought even harder.

---

[5] Amos 2:11-12 mentions both "prophets and Nazarites" as gifts that Jehovah had given to His people. As a prophet, Samuel *instructed* the people in God's law. As a Nazarite, He modeled the kind of separation God required of them by *example*.

Israel lost 30,000 soldiers, including the two sons of Eli, and the ark of the covenant was captured by the enemy.

When tidings came to Eli of the death of his sons and the capture of the ark, he fell from his chair and broke his neck. At that instant, his daughter-in-law travailed in birth and bore a son whom she called "Ichabod", meaning "the glory has departed" (4:21). Immediately after naming the child, she died. In one day, Eli, his two sons, and his daughter-in-law died. This tragedy marked the beginning of Samuel's public career as Israel's priest/prophet. Talk about 'the fast track to success'!

But the hand of God was heavy on the Philistines while they possessed the sacred ark (5). After numerous deaths and widespread suffering, they returned it to the city of Kirjath-jearim, where it stayed for twenty years. During these two decades while this most sacred article of tabernacle furniture was missing from its place in Shiloh, "all the house of Israel lamented after the Lord" (7:2).

But Samuel called the people to repentance: "*If you do return to the Lord with all your hearts and put away the strange gods...from among you...He will deliver you out of the hand of the Philistines*" (7:3). He then gathered the tribes at Mizpeh and interceded for them before the Lord by prayer and sacrifice. When the Philistines heard that the nation was gathered at Mizpeh, they deployed an army to attack. But while Samuel was offering the sacrifice, "the Lord thundered with a great thunder upon the Philistines and discomfited them; and they were smitten before Israel" (7:10).

At Mizpeh, Samuel built an altar of remembrance and called it *"Ebenezer, saying, Hitherto hath the Lord helped us"* (7:12). It was a day of revival and deliverance, continuing for many years hence until Samuel was old (7:13 – 8:1).

Samuel renewed the theocratic ideals of the nation during his early tenure as Israel's judge. His later years, however, were marked by another decline in national godliness.

He had delegated a number of his duties to his two sons—Joel and Abiah—but they did not share their father's integrity (1 Sam. 8:1-2). First Samuel 8:3 reads, *"And his sons walked not in his ways, but turned aside after lucre, and took bribes, and perverted judgment."*

Disillusioned by the failure of their leaders, Israel rejected the judicial authority of Samuel and his sons. The tribal "elders" proposed a change in the form of government: *"Make us a king to judge us like all the nations"* (1 Sam. 8:5b). Samuel felt personally abandoned and unwanted, but God interpreted their request in the context of graver concerns: *"They have not rejected thee, but they have rejected me, that I should not reign over them"* (1 Sam. 8:7b).

Though they were called to "be different" from other nations and completely dedicated to Jehovah, Israel had failed as a theocratic community. Peer pressure had taken its toll. They found it difficult to sustain the vertical gaze of faith in a horizontal environment with so many distractions. Perhaps they were a bit embarrassed that they were different—that they were so unlike "all the nations" (vs. 5, 20). After all, they alone had no ruler—at least, none that they could see.

No doubt, if Israel had originally obeyed the Lord's command to expunge the land of its native inhabitants, they would not now be so interested in accommodating the culture. But past concessions inevitably lead to further compromises. It seems so much simpler to live by sight, like all the other nations, than to walk by faith. Rare is the individual, church, or nation that can sustain the focus necessary to live in the world and yet resist the subtle magnetic pull to become like the world; yet, God calls His people to precisely such a holy walk.

Israel already had a King (cf. Is. 33:22; Jud. 8:22-23). The demand for another king, therefore, was tantamount to a rejection of Jehovah's sovereign rule. It was nothing short of a revolutionary move to attempt to "change the form of government from a pure theocracy to a hereditary monarchy".[6]

At the same time, the Old Testament indicates that God had anticipated and even planned to establish a king over Israel.[7] How may these two apparently contradictory facts, i.e. that in the request for a king, Israel rejected Jehovah as their true King, and that God did, in fact, intend to establish an official king over Israel from the very beginning, be reconciled? Why would He

---

[6] Alfred Edersheim, *Bible History: Old Testament*, Vol. IV, p. 32.

[7] Consider Deut. 17:14-20, a passage in which God reveals His laws for the kings that would reign over His people. Even the original covenant with Abraham mentioned the fact that his descendants would include kings (Gen. 17:6; 35:11).

condemn their desire for a monarch when He planned to give them one anyway?

The answer is rooted in the motives behind the request, not the request itself. Instead of accepting blame to themselves for the social and military problems they faced, the nation was, in effect, ascribing the blame for their failures to the present system of government. It was a sin of unbelief—an act of vile ingratitude to the God who had made, multiplied, and maintained the nation these many years. In a word, it was a renunciation of the very bedrock principle that gave them identity as a nation.

The Lord told Samuel to grant their petition, but to "solemnly protest" and inform them of the kind of kingdom they could expect from a king of their own choosing. First Samuel 8:10-18 records Samuel's protest.

But they were unmoved by his objection. Their purposes would not be thwarted (vs. 19-20). Did they want a king? Very well, then; they would have their desire. Little did they know, however, that they were jumping out of the proverbial frying pan and into the fire. Israel was "courting a despotism whose intolerable yoke it would not be possible for them to shake off in the future."[8]

Over the next 120 years, Israel would function as a "united monarchy". Three kings—Saul, David, and Solomon—each reigning for forty years, would sit on the throne of Israel. This new centralized authority would have the effect of replacing social anarchy with civil order, unifying the tribes under a

_____
[8] Edersheim, p. 34.

common head, and promoting the interests of Israel as a single nation rather than a loose confederation marked by tribal loyalty.

Saul was "the people's choice" as king. He was subsequently appointed by Samuel and held in admiration by the people. Saul reigned from approximately 1050 to 1010 B.C. His successes included the military conquest of the Ammonites. Saul disobeyed God's instructions concerning the Amalekites, however, and was deposed by God from the throne.

David was the Lord's choice—"a man after God's own heart". He reigned from 1010 to 971 B.C. Though he was not as physically impressive as Saul, God judged David fit to reign, not because of the strength of his body, but because of the integrity of his heart. He, too, was appointed by Samuel, but the people hesitated to recognize him as their king because he was not in Saul's line of descent. Just as, centuries later, various people would challenge the apostolic credentials of Paul (for he came into the apostleship from the outside, being not one of the original apostles), so David's right to the throne in this "hereditary monarchy" was constantly questioned.[9] Eventually, however, all Israel would acknowledge David as the rightful king.

David's successes included the capture of Jerusalem for Israel (a city which was then under Jebusite occupation), the conquest of the Philistines, the recovery of the lost ark and transfer of tabernacle worship from Shiloh to Jerusalem, and the

---

[9] See the study on the book of Ruth in Chapter 6.

unprecedented territorial expansion of the empire from 6000 to over 60,000 square miles. Through the line of David, God would establish His own Son as the everlasting King over His kingdom. The Lord Jesus Christ is the ultimate Davidic King, a theme that assumes increasing prominence as the Biblical story unfolds.

Solomon, David's son, assumed the throne upon the death of his father. He was appointed by David, and confirmed as the king by Zadok the priest and Nathan the prophet. His 40 year reign upon the throne (971 to 931 B.C.) was characterized by military peace and the building of the Temple for Divine worship. Upon Solomon's death, the kingdom divided into the Northern Kingdom of Israel and the Southern Kingdom of Judah.

A Potential Peril

The message of 1st Samuel is that though the nation of Israel substantially compromised its commitment to Jehovah as its King, yet He did not abandon the nation. Though the people's focus was earthbound and man-centered, God still maintained theocratic rule.

Regardless of the identity of the particular man who might sit on the throne of Israel, the Lord made it clear that He would still be the ultimate authority. The people might select rulers that suit their preference (like Saul), but God would appoint rulers who recognized that they, too, were under His sovereign authority (like David). Through these God-fearing monarchs, Jehovah would continue to govern Israel as a theocracy.

The introduction of a human king between God and the nation, however, raised a new potential for peril. What if the king assumes too much authority to himself? What if he begins to improvise and innovate according to his own personal whims? If, as the saying goes, "power corrupts and absolute power corrupts absolutely," what if the king begins to think that he has absolute authority and is corrupted by his position of power?

As an antidote to the temptation to rule by personal preference instead of God's law, the Lord reminded these various kings that they must never begin to think of themselves as sovereign. Instead, each king must "be just, ruling in the fear of God" (2 Sam. 23:3; cf. Ps. 72), recognizing their own accountability to God. In this way, they would be fit to lead the nation. If the monarch once begins to play the maverick, however, God will judge him as a despot.

And that is precisely what would happen to King Saul, the quintessential maverick. Let's take a closer look at his tenure as Israel's king.

The Rise and Fall of King Saul

A man of the tribe of Benjamin named Saul was Israel's first king. The sacred narrative of King Saul stands as an object lesson of a life coming unraveled at the seams. His story is a classic "tragedy"—a woeful account of spiritual and moral declension —a sad tale of "good gone wrong."

Saul's Coronation (1 Sam. 9-10)

At the outset of his reign, Saul's character was impressive. He was a courageous, humble, and immensely talented young man. Well endowed with both physical beauty and personal charisma, Saul was the people's choice. He came from a wealthy family. He was also eloquent before crowds. He stood "head and shoulders above the rest" (1 Sam. 9:2). Saul looked like a king.

The first glimpse the Holy Spirit offers of his heart suggests that Saul was humble (1 Sam. 9:21), and "little in his own eyes" (1 Sam. 15:17). At the public inauguration ceremony at Mizpeh, Saul hid himself among the stuff [lit. baggage] (1 Sam. 10:22), a bit of information that suggests the presence of an unassuming spirit.

After his anointing by Samuel, God gave him "another heart." He had holy thoughts, grand resolve, and resolute determination. He even prophesied so that the people wondered, "Is Saul also among the prophets?" Without a doubt, Saul was very unique. He stood out in the crowd—"there was none like him among all the people" (10:24).

Military Conquests (1 Sam. 11-12)

In his first battle as commander-in-chief, God gave Saul victory over the Ammonites at Jabesh-gilead (1 Sam. 11). There he distinguished himself for bravery and loyalty to the people under his care. He also refused to accept credit for the victory, attributing the army's success to Jehovah alone (11:12-13). This military conquest silenced the last of the critics, and prompted Samuel to lay aside his office as Judge—a post that was evidently, no longer necessary—once and for all (1 Sam. 12).

The Beginning of the End (1 Sam. 13-14)

For two years, Saul reigned with integrity. First Samuel 13, however, records the beginning of the end of his royal career. In this chapter, we are given the first hint of Saul's decaying spirituality.

A new crisis against Israel's archenemy, the Philistines, arose when Jonathan attacked the Philistine garrison at Gilgal. As he waited for Samuel to arrive, Saul became impatient. Sensing that he was losing control of the people and that morale was faltering, Saul usurped the role of the priest and offered the burnt offering to the Lord. It was a tragic compromise.

Immediately, Samuel arrived and confronted him with the question, "What hast thou done?" Instead of acknowledging his presumptuous sin in contrition and repentance, Saul rationalized his behavior. The situation demanded the course of action he took, Saul argued. By this reckless act under the guise of piety, Saul demonstrated that he was willing to obey God only so long as God's commandments did not cross his self-will. The first step in the downward spiral of personal disintegration was compromise. As far as Saul was concerned, "the end justified the means".

He also displayed on this occasion an inappropriate concern for his own reputation: *"The people were scattered from me."* Saul, in other words, was serving Saul, not Jehovah.

Samuel replied, *"Thou hast done foolishly...now thy kingdom shall not continue: the Lord hath sought him a man after his own heart, and the Lord hath commanded him to be captain over his people, because thou hast not kept that which the Lord commanded thee"* (1 Sam. 13:13-14). Jehovah would tolerate a king only as long as the king recognized the Lord as the theocratic ruler of the nation — the One to whom even the king must bow. Saul's maverick and innovative tendencies effectively challenged Divine authority, substituting personal preference in its place. The Lord could not countenance such rebellion.

Again, Saul displayed his own lack of judgment and spirit of self-interest by forbidding food to his army until the enemy was conquered (1 Sam. 14). Had it not been for the people, whose opinion was so important to Saul, Jonathan, who had not heard his father's oath, would have died for tasting a little honey (14:44-45).

Saul soon disobeyed again in reference to the command to "utterly slay" the Amalekites (1 Sam. 15). He spared Agag, the Amalekite king, and the best of the sheep and the oxen. Samuel replied that partial obedience is essentially the same as disobedience: *"Behold, to obey is better than sacrifice...for rebellion is as the sin of witchcraft, and stubbornness is as iniquity and idolatry"* (1 Sam. 15:22b-23a).

In the confrontation that followed, Saul discloses his real motivation: *"I feared the people."* Even after Samuel repeated the dreaded refrain—*"God hath rejected thee from being king"*—Saul was more concerned that his reputation in the eyes of the people be preserved than he was in repentance before God: *"Turn again with me...honor me now, I pray thee, before the elders of my people, and before Israel..."* (1 Sam. 15:25, 30). He was more interested in the honor of men than the honor that comes from God (Jno. 5:44; 12:43). After that day, Samuel "sought no more after Saul."

An Evil Spirit (1 Sam. 16ff)

Remarkably, Saul sat on the throne another 35 or 36 years, but those years were marked by a dark brow, a haunting spiritual emptiness and vacuum, and an embittered heart. First Samuel 16:14 says, *"But the Spirit of the Lord departed from Saul and an evil spirit from the Lord troubled* [lit. terrified] *him"*. Even the king's servants witnessed the dramatic alteration in his mood (v. 15).

Devoid of a close walk with God, Saul shrank before Goliath's challenge (1 Sam. 17). When the women of Israel lauded David's achievements above his own, Saul was gripped by an insane jealousy and paranoia. Twice he attempted to kill David with his javelin (1 Sam. 18:11). When that was unsuccessful, Saul transferred David from palace duty to active service in the military, but "the Lord was with David" and his popularity increased on a daily basis (18:12-16).

The king tried to entrap him again and again (cf. 18:17-30), but David behaved himself with greater wisdom. Saul's obsession with "his enemy" David then grew to more public proportions. He attempted to convince his own son and David's loyal friend Jonathan to kill him (19:1). Finally, Saul himself launched an all-out military campaign to hunt him down. He chased David for approximately ten years, but God delivered his humble servant out of Saul's hand.

Application

How could a life of such promise run so far amok? How could it reach such a low point? The ruin of King Saul began in his own heart. Slowly and imperceptibly, Saul forgot his Divine commission. Motivated not by a sense of his calling but by his own proud ambition and self-concern, King Saul disintegrated from the inside-out. God had departed from Saul, for Saul had departed from the Lord.

On a practical note, Saul's life stands as a warning against spiritual and ethical declension. On a theological note, his story reveals the principle that even the king occupied a subservient role in Jehovah's theocratic kingdom. King Saul forgot that important principle. His successor, however, would be the antithesis of this tragic story. David would function as a true officer of the Divine theocracy.

The United Monarchy

Chapter 8
DAVID'S DYNASTY
1 Samuel 16 – 1 Kings 11

The book of Samuel[1] is designed to show that the house of David, despite all of its internal shortcomings, was the legitimate dynasty in which Israel should hope. Saul's kingdom was rejected by God because of his rebellion and unfaithfulness to the covenant. David's kingdom, however, was established by God as the permanent dynasty from which the Messianic King would arise. Samuel is a book of hope, pointing the nation to the Davidic line as the instrument by which God would bring restoration to the kingdom.

David's Rise to Power (1 Sam. 16 – 31)

The narrative indicates that David's ascent to the throne was orchestrated by Providence. He did not come to power by his own ambition or contrivance. At every turn, the Lord paved the way for David's path to the kingdom.

First, his selection was providentially directed. When Samuel went to the house of Jesse to anoint one of his sons as Saul's successor, God instructed him, *"Look not on his countenance, or on the height of his stature: because I have refused him: for the Lord seeith not as man seeth; for man looketh on the outward appearance, but the Lord looketh on the heart"* (16:7). Each of Jesse's sons was successively introduced to Samuel, then dismissed. Finally,

---

[1] 1st & 2nd Samuel comprised one book in the Hebrew canon.

David, the youngest, was brought, and the Lord said, "*Arise, anoint him: for this is he*" (16:12). When Samuel anointed him, "*the Spirit of the Lord came upon him from that day forward*" (16:13), qualifying him by might and power as "God's anointed."

Secondly, God's providence in David's rise to power can be seen in the circumstances of David's selection as Saul's musician (16:14ff), his victory over Goliath (17), and his friendship with Saul's own son, Jonathan (18). Just as "great doors turn on very small hinges", so each apparently insignificant development in the narrative positions the Lord's anointed ever closer to the throne. No doubt, God used the time spent in Saul's court as his resident harpist and protégé to familiarize David with political and military affairs—a sort of "on the job" training program, though evidently neither David nor Saul was aware of the far-reaching implications of these events.

When a spirit of envy and jealousy seized Saul, God again protected David in the wilderness. Saul's dementia assumed murderous proportions and for a period of at least ten years, David lived the life of a fugitive and vagabond. But God providentially intervened to foil Saul's infernal plot and to protect His anointed king. On two occasions, God delivered Saul into David's hand, but David refused to lift his hand against him.

Saul ultimately digressed to such a low point that he resorted to the same pagan sorceries for which God had judged the Canaanite nations so severely. In the face of a potential battle with the Philistines, Saul sought the Lord, but the Lord answered him not (28:4-6). He then consulted the witch at Endor and called up Samuel, who informed the apostate king that tomorrow would bring both Israel's defeat and his demise (28:19). First Samuel concludes with the account of Saul's death and the tragic end of his career.

All in all, the book of Samuel indicates that Saul's displacement as Israel's king was Divinely orchestrated. God put down one—a man who forfeited his privileged position by personal ambition and compromise—and raised up another—a man after His own heart.

The Davidic Covenant (2 Sam. 1-10)

Second Samuel chapters 1 through 10 records David's coronation as Israel's king and the "glory years" of his reign. It was a time of prosperity (2 Sam. 5:12). He took Jerusalem from the Jebusites and established it as the new capital city (5:7-10). He defeated the Philistines (5:17-25), recovered the lost ark displaced for the past fifty years (cf. 1 Sam. 4), and brought it to his newly established capital (2 Sam. 6). During his tenure as king, David expanded Israel's borders to the limits originally promised to Abraham in Genesis 15:18.

In 2 Samuel 7, David proposed construction of a permanent house for the Lord, but God refused his offer. The Lord, however, made a covenant with David, promising to build him "a house" [or dynasty] and to "establish the throne of his kingdom forever" (vs. 11, 13). This "everlasting covenant" (2 Sam. 23:5) with David, like the original covenant with Abraham, is a unilateral covenant, the promises and blessings of which depend on God alone for their fulfillment.

Indeed, if David or his children disobeyed God, they would incur chastisement and the loss of various temporal privileges, but the covenant itself would never be disannulled (cf. Ps. 89:30-35). David would have a "son" to sit on the throne of God's Kingdom forever. This promise of an enduring Davidic kingdom has been called "the summit of the entire Old Testament".[2]

It is at this point in the sacred narrative that the hope of a Messianic kingdom—the primary plot of the Old Testament—surfaces. Prior to this point, the history of the nation of Israel appeared to be the dominant plot, with hints here and there of a coming Messiah as a subplot. Now, however, the narrative has developed to a point that challenges our initial assumptions. Now, it appears that the history of Israel is not the main plot at all, but a subplot to the larger theme of God's purpose to establish an everlasting Kingdom—a pure theocracy—governed by His own Son as the King.

As evidence to support this case, notice that the covenant promises of 2 Samuel 7 say too much to apply to Solomon alone. The passage, in fact, possesses a distinctively eschatological and messianic tone. I suggest that 2 Samuel 7 finds its ultimate fulfillment in David's "greater son", the Messiah, who would come from his loins (Acts 2:29-30; Ps. 132:11; Rom. 1:3; 2 Tim. 2:8; Lk. 1:32-33).

---

[2] Footnote on 2 Samuel 7:4-17 in the *New Geneva Study Bible*.

Psalm 89:27, the poetic version of 2 Samuel 7, reveals that David's "son" would also be God's "Son", a fact that can only be understood in terms of the two natures of the Lord Jesus Christ. And it would be in Him, this One who would be called the "Root and the Offspring of David" (Rev. 22:16), that Jehovah would reign over His people forever (Is. 9:6-7).

This Messianic hope based on the "sure mercies" of the Davidic covenant (Is. 55:3) would sustain Israel's faith for many years to come, even in the face of the coming exile in Babylon (Jer. 23:5-6; Jer. 30:9; 33:15-22; Eze. 34:23-24; 37:24ff). Though David's "house" was in a state of chaos and disarray[3], yet the "house" or "dynasty" that God purposed to build through the coming Messiah was "ordered in all things and sure". Truth concerning God's covenant loyalty gave David consolation in his dying hour, and provided the people of Israel a reason to hope and a firm foundation for the future of the theocracy (2 Sam. 23:1-5).

Solomon's Career

Old Testament history develops the motif of the superiority of the kingdom of God to every secular kingdom. This Divine plan to establish His kingdom as a world empire, however, would not be predicated on military power, intellectual supremacy, or economic prosperity. "The exaltation of Zion above the hills, and

---

[3] The reference to David's "house" in 2 Sam. 23:5 may speak of: (1) His family troubles (see 2 Samuel 11-19 for a record of the turmoil in David's family in the aftermath of his sin); (2) His dynasty, which seemed, because of David's own sin, so far removed from the everlasting kingdom promised to him. I lean toward the latter explanation.

the flowing of all nations unto it, was to be brought about by the going forth of the Law out of Zion, and of the Word of Jehovah from Jerusalem (Is. 2:2,3)".[4] At its zenith, Solomon's reign embodied this ideal of international influence as the premier empire of the world. Even years later, the prophets pointed to the Solomonic era as the epitome of Kingdom blessings (Mic. 4:4 [cf. 1 Kings 4:25]; Zech. 3:10).

Solomon assumed power in 971 B.C. as the last of the kings in the united monarchy. His forty-year reign was characterized by unparalleled peace and prosperity, but ethical compromises in his later years marked the beginning of the end of national solidarity.

The writer of Kings begins his explanation of the cause and remedy of the exile with Solomon's story. The career of Solomon illustrates the principle that fidelity to God issues in glory, but rebellion brings judgment and ruin.

The book of Kings[5] presents the history of Israel, not from a secular, but, from the prophetic viewpoint of 2 Samuel 7:12-16. It traces the cause of the Babylonian captivity to the kind of syncretism[6] that began with Solomon's reign and continued in the various dynasties of the divided monarchy. The purpose of Kings is to establish the point that the nation's welfare is intricately connected to the leader's personal fidelity to God's covenant. Personal failure and compromise at the leadership

---

[4] Edersheim, *Bible History: Old Testament*, Vol. V, p. iv.

[5] 1st and 2nd Kings comprises one book in the Hebrew canon.

[6] *syncretism*: an attempt to combine opposite or different systems of thought or religion.

level tends to the moral and spiritual disintegration of the whole society.

Solomon's Glory (chs. 1-10)

God, in an exercise of His sovereign authority, selected Solomon from all of David's other sons to be his successor to the throne (1 Chr. 28:2-10). 1 Kings 1-2 concerns the events by which "the kingdom was established in the hand of Solomon" (2:46). The successive chapters describe a time of unprecedented peace and prosperity in the history of Israel.

Why did God so signally favor and bless the nation under Solomon's reign? Because King Solomon publicly acknowledged Jehovah as the God of Israel. First Kings 3 records his sense of personal inadequacy in the face of the tremendous responsibility of governing such a vast multitude of people. That night as he dreamed, God appeared to him, saying, *"Ask what I shall give thee"* (3:5). Instead of the expected selfish requests for wealth, military victory, and personal comfort, Solomon asked for wisdom (3:9). So pleased was God that He promised to give him not only wisdom, but riches, honor, and length of days (3:12-13).

It was not long before Solomon began to give evidence of God's answer to his request. In a case too difficult for ordinary judges, the king pronounced a sentence designed to reveal the identity of the true mother and expose the imposter: *"Divide the living child in two, and give half to the one, and half to the other"* (3:25). When the dispute was resolved and the real mother identified, the fame of Solomon spread throughout the land (3:28).

Solomon's God-given wisdom is also displayed in the book of Proverbs. Here is a philosophy for interpreting human behavior and approaching daily circumstances that is incomparably insightful.

First Kings 4:20-34 describes the glory of Solomon's kingdom. The people were happy (v. 20), confident and personally fulfilled (v. 25). His subjects loved him (v. 21) and his enemies were at peace with him (v. 24). God blessed him with abundance, both in material (vs. 26-28) and spiritual terms (vs. 29-30). He promoted education and the study of literature, not only of his own philosophical and poetic material but of the different branches of the natural sciences (vs. 32-33). His international reputation as a man of honor and wisdom grew and increased so that people from every conceivable society, ethnicity, and nationality sought to hear the wisdom of Solomon (4:31, 34).

But the building of a "house unto the name of the Lord [his] God" (5:5) was the most magnificent achievement of his reign. Chapters 5-6 describe the initial preparations and actual construction of the new and permanent house for Jehovah's worship known as "Solomon's Temple". From start to finish, construction of the Temple took seven years (6:38) and thus, was the original dream of King David realized. The Temple replaced the Tabernacle and underscored the fact that the transient, nomadic existence of the nation was over. The year following, at the Feast of Tabernacles, the Temple was dedicated. The timing of the dedication, a service reminiscent of the days when Israel dwelt in tents in the wilderness, reminded the nation of the pilgrim nature of their lives.

Solomon, acting as the servant of Jehovah, led the proceedings at the dedication service. When the ark of the covenant was placed in the most holy place, the glory of the Lord filled the house in a solemn and very affecting theophany (8:10-11). Solomon then reminded the people that "the Lord said that he would dwell in the thick darkness" and he blessed the vast congregation in the name of the Lord (8:12-21).

Next, Solomon offered the dedication prayer, praising and thanking God for his covenant faithfulness, petitioning Him to receive their worship and prayers and to forgive the sins they confess to Him, and to continue to provide for the needs of His people that His name might be glorified (8:22-53). Following this very moving prayer, he admonished the people to be faithful to the Lord and to walk in His statutes (8:54-61). The service concluded with a sacrifice of peace offerings that consisted of 22,000 oxen and 120,000 sheep (8:62-64) and a seven day feast. When the people departed on the eighth day, they returned to *"their tents joyful and glad of heart for all the goodness that the Lord had done for David his servant, and for Israel his people"* (8:65-66). God appeared to Solomon following the dedication service, confirming the Davidic covenant, yet reminding him of the fact that the promise of an everlasting dynasty did not preclude sore and severe chastisement on the people in the event of their disobedience (9:1-9).

So prosperous was Solomon's kingdom and so wise was Israel's King that his fame spread far and wide. Many foreign dignitaries were attracted to Jerusalem by Solomon's fame (10:24), among the most distinguished of which was the queen of Sheba. She came from a great distance in southern Arabia[7] with a royal entourage to *"prove [him] with hard questions"* (10:1-2). She wanted to test for herself whether the things she had heard were true.

But the queen was actuated by more than sheer curiosity. By comparing the phrase *"concerning the name of Jehovah"* in 1 Kings 10:1 with the words of Jesus in Matthew 12:42, it is likely that she came to learn about Solomon's God. Thus was name of Jehovah increasingly glorified and known in the earth.

Solomon's Apostasy (ch. 11)

First Kings 11 begins with the dreadful word "But...". Though Solomon exceeded all the kings of the earth in both wealth and wisdom, his heart was not perfect with the Lord as was the heart of David his father. *"But king Solomon loved many strange women, besides the daughter of Pharoah...and his wives turned away his heart after other gods"* (11:1-4). To appease his seven hundred wives, princesses, and three hundred concubines, Solomon constructed groves for the worship of Chemosh and Molech, the deities of the Moabites and Ammonites, respectively (11:7-8), and Ashtoreth, the goddess of the Zidonians (11:33).

---

[7] Not "Seba" in Ethiopia, as some suppose, but a kingdom in Arabia.

In His righteous anger, God pronounced judgment on Solomon and stirred up two adversaries against him in the form of Hadad the Edomite and Rezon the ruler of Syria (11:9-25). Further, Jeroboam, a mighty man of valor in Solomon's own kingdom, also revolted against the king. The prophet Ahijah prophesied that indeed Jeroboam would be successful in seizing control of the kingdom (though God did not endorse this ambitious and unscrupulous man), but that David's line would not be left without a "light in Jerusalem" (v. 36).

Edersheim editorializes on the dark and foreboding scenes that characterized Solomon's last days:

> "The introduction of heathen worship commenced with the decline of Solomon's spiritual life. After his death, the apostasy from God attained fearful proportions, partially and temporarily in Judah, but permanently in Israel. In the latter, from the commencement of its separate national existence under Jeroboam, the God-chosen Sanctuary at Jerusalem, and the God-appointed priesthood were discarded; the worship of Jehovah transformed; and by its side spurious rites and heathen idolatry introduced, till, under the reign of Ahab, the religion of Baal became that of the State. This marks the high point of apostasy in Israel."[8]

Indeed, with the death of Solomon, the glory days of the monarchy passed away and the long slide down the slippery slope toward ruin and judgment had begun.

---

[8] Edersheim, *Bible History*, Vol. V, pp. iv – v.

David's Dynasty

Chapter 9
THE DIVIDED MONARCHY
1 Kings 12 – 2 Kings 8

Solomon's demise under God's judgment left the nation vulnerable to tribal jealousies, especially between Ephraim in the north and Judah in the south. Ephraim had long desired preeminence, but Solomon had made Jerusalem both the religious and political center of the nation. Further, the tribe of Ephraim, together with other northern tribes, was required to shoulder the various and sundry burdens imposed by the monarchy, even though the throne was situated many miles to the south.

Just as Samuel had predicted in 1 Samuel 8:10-18, the Israelites paid a heavy price for their king. Their men were required to labor in Solomon's seemingly endless architectural enterprises. Further, the support of the king and his court required a significant financial commitment from the entire nation. Alfred Edersheim writes,

> "To have to pay enormous taxes, and for many long years to be deprived during so many months of the heads and bread-winners of the family, that they might do what seemed slaves' labor for the glorification of a king, whose rule was every year becoming weaker, would have excited dissatisfaction even among a more enduring people than those tribes who had so

long enjoyed the freedom and the privileges of a federated Republic."[1]

Under Solomon's reign, national morale sunk to a very low ebb.

The climate was ripe for revolution. The year was approximately 931 B.C. The leader of the revolt was a man from the tribe of Ephraim named Jeroboam. Once a servant of King Solomon, Jeroboam wrested control of ten of the twelve tribes, i.e. every tribe except Benjamin and Judah, from the house of David (1 Kings 11:30-35). These ten tribes became "the Northern Kingdom", known as *Israel*. But true to His promise that David would never lack for a royal descendant, God preserved the tribe of Judah (and Benjamin) for the house of David (1 Kings 11:36). Solomon's son Rehoboam assumed the throne after his death (11:43). He ruled over the two tribes that comprised "the Southern Kingdom" of *Judah*.

First Kings 12 describes the revolt of the ten Northern tribes and the power struggle for dominance between Jeroboam and Rehoboam. Though civil war was averted (12:21-24), the division between Israel and Judah would continue and the subsequent history of the people of God would be told as separate stories.

The history of the divided kingdom extended over the next three centuries. During that time, approximately twenty kings each would reign over Israel and Judah. Ephraim would be the

---

[1] Edersheim, *Bible History: Old Testament*, Vol V., p. 116.

principle tribe in the Northern Kingdom of Israel [2] with Samaria as its principle city[3]. Judah would be the dominant tribe in the Southern Kingdom with Jerusalem as its capital. Israel would continue until 722 B.C. until it was conquered by the Assyrians. Judah would continue another 136 years beyond Israel's demise until the Babylonian exile in 586 B.C.

Why did the Southern Kingdom of Judah outdistance the Northern Kingdom of Israel? Because Israel's apostasy was unchecked by godly leadership. Of the twenty kings that would subsequently reign over Israel, none were true servants of Jehovah. The sad epithet over the lives of every king of Israel is, *"He walked in the ways of Jeroboam, the son of Nebat"* (1 Kings 15:26, 34; 16:19, 26; *et al.*). The worst of these Northern monarchs was Ahab and his two sons, Ahaziah and Joram. Ahab went beyond the syncretism of Jeroboam, making Baal worship the official religion of the State.

Unlike the Northern Kingdom, Judah had several kings who were·devoted to the worship of Jehovah. Six kings of Judah— Asa, Jehoshaphat, Uzziah, Jotham, Hezekiah, and Josiah—were remarkable because they *"did that which was right in the sight of the Lord, walking in the way of David their father"*. At least two more kings—Joash and Amaziah—spent the bulk of their respective reigns in godliness and piety.

---

[2] Hence, when the prophet Hosea speaks of "Ephraim" such as "Ephraim has joined himself to idols; let him alone" (Hos. 4:17), he is speaking to the entire Northern Kingdom of Israel.

[3] Hosea 7:1; 8:5

Principle Kings of Israel and Judah (and length of reign)	
Israel	**Judah**
Jeroboam (22 yrs)	Rehoboam (17 yrs)
Nadab (2 yrs)	Abijam (3 yrs)
Baasha (24 yrs)	Asa (41 yrs)
Elah (2 yrs)	Jehoshaphat (25 yrs)
Omri (12 yrs)	Jehoram (6 yrs)
Ahab (22 yrs)	Ahaziah (1 yr)
Ahaziah (2 yrs)	Athaliah (6 yrs)
Jehoram (12 yrs)	Joash (40 yrs)
Jehu (28 yrs)	Amaziah (29 yrs)
Jehoahaz (17 yrs)	Uzziah (52 yrs)
Joash (16 yrs)	Jotham (16 yrs)
Jeroboam II (41 yrs)	Ahaz (16 yrs)
Menahem (10 yrs)	Hezekiah (29 yrs)
Pekahiah (2 yrs)	Manasseh (55 yrs)
Pekah (20 yrs)	Amon (2 yrs)
Hoshea (9 yrs)	Josiah (31 yrs)
Jehoiakim (11 yrs)	
Zedekiah (11 yrs)	

The Prophets

Concurrent with the division of the monarchy, God raised up a new class of men—the prophets—who would function as servants of Jehovah during the days of apostasy. The proliferation of prophetic activity beginning with Ahijah in 1 Kings 11:29 and "the man of God" from Judah in 1 Kings 13:1, and continuing to Elijah (1 Kings 17ff), Micaiah (1 Kings 22), Elisha (2 Kings 1ff), and embracing both the pre- and post-exilic prophets (Isaiah to Malachi), is a significant development in the unfolding drama of the nation's history. For the next 900 years plus, the role of the prophets would be dominant in Jewish society.

Prophets and their Respective Eras

Pre-exilic (922-605)	**Exilic** (605-536)	**Post-exilic** (536)
Amos	Ezekiel	Haggai
Hosea	Daniel	Zechariah
Joel		Malachi
Isaiah		
Jonah		
Nahum		
Micah		
Habakkuk		
Jeremiah		
Zephaniah		

These prophets came in different shapes and sizes. Some were court prophets, i.e. Divinely appointed advisers and critics of the king. Nathan and Gad are examples of court prophets (2 Sam. 7; 2 Sam. 24). As long as the kings were submissive to God's word, virtually every prophet was a court prophet. In the aftermath of the divided kingdom, however, God commissioned the classical (literary) prophets. Among the classical prophets, some delivered their oracles verbally (like Elijah), and others both by speaking and writing (like Isaiah and Jeremiah). Still further, the prophets prophesied during different eras—some before, others during, and yet others after the exile in Babylon.

The Prophetic Role

The prophets served Jehovah in a threefold way: (1) as guardians of the theocracy; (2) as covenant prosecutors; and (3) as heralds of a future hope.

Guardians of the Theocracy

If Israel was a theocracy, then how did Jehovah exercise His theocratic rule over His people? He dealt with them through "mediators" or intermediaries—the priesthood, the monarchy (kings), and the prophets (Gal. 3:19). Through the medium of these official representatives of the theocracy, God executed His sovereign authority over the nation.

Like the priests and the kings, the prophets comprised a special class of theocratic officers through whom the Lord gave guidance to His covenant people (Amos 2:11). Their official role as spokesmen[4] for God began with Moses (Deut. 18:15ff) and continued through Samuel (Acts 3:24), both of whom taught the covenant community God's word and communicated the revelation of His will in specific situations.

To what, then, do we attribute the sudden increase of prophetic activity after the division between Israel and Judah? The failure of the monarchy to develop and maintain a nation united in obedience to Jehovah created a crisis of accountability. Hence, God dispatched one prophet after another as "guardians of the theocracy"—to call both king and people to repentance before God. Through their ministry, God protected His truth,

---

[4] The Hebrew word translated "prophet" (*nab i*) means "a spokesman for God".

lest it become obscure and obsolete in these days of apostasy, and guarded His covenant against abuse.

Isaiah's vision of Jehovah "the King" in the year that King Uzziah died illustrates the God-centered focus of the prophetic mission (Is. 6:1ff). Though earthly monarchs fail, the Kingdom of God would remain intact, for the Lord is on the throne.

Covenant Prosecutors

The prophets were also instruments in the hand of God by which the nation was called to account for her sins. Dispatched during times of crisis in the history of Israel and Judah, they brought a covenant lawsuit against God's disobedient people, accusing them of sin and pronouncing the threat of Divine judgment.

Elijah was God's first covenant prosecutor. He brought an accusation of infidelity against not only King Ahab, but all Israel. He charged them with rejecting God's covenant, desecrating His altars, and killing His prophets (1 Kings 18:21). From the very place God had originally given His Law to Moses, i.e. Mt Sinai, Elijah not only warned and threatened, but accused the nation of breaking the covenant. Subsequent prophets continued Elijah's prophetic tradition of prosecuting and confronting the nation for real sins.

Prophets and Their Contemporary Kings

Year	Prophet(s)	King of Israel	King of Judah
~875 BC	Elijah	Ahab	
~860 BC	Micaiah	Ahab	Jehoshaphat
~850 BC	Elisha	Jehu	
~775 BC	Amos/Hosea	Jeroboam II	
~750 BC	Isaiah/Micah		Uzziah-Hezekiah
~630 BC	Zephaniah		Josiah
~625-586	Jeremiah		Jehoiakim-Zedekiah
~600 BC	Habakkuk		Jehoiakim

Because their ministry was essentially confrontational, the true prophets of God were generally unpopular figures (Neh. 9:26; Jer. 7:25-26). Their word was frequently resisted and they were imprisoned, persecuted, and even slain (Mt. 23:37). Theirs was a life filled with tension, for though they loved God's people, faithfulness to the Lord called upon them to bring messages that were unpalatable to the audience.

The unpopularity of the prophet's message was often compounded by his own prophetic colleagues. False prophets proclaimed a socially-acceptable message, tickling the ears of the king and people alike, and increasing the public's animosity toward the true spokesman for God. Jeremiah and Ezekiel lamented the "professional" prophets of their respective times. Ezekiel compared them to "whitewash" (Eze. 13:10-15; 22:28). Jeremiah impugned the self-serving motives that actuated their message of false peace (Jer. 8:10ff; cf. Jer. 23).

In contrast to these false prophets, the true prophet of God was distinguished by an openness to Divine instruction (Is. 50:4), obedience to his Divine commission (v. 5), the willingness to suffer persecution (v. 6), personal dependence on the Lord for strength (vs. 7-9), and a God-centered message to his hearers (v. 10).

Heralds of Hope

Yes, the prophets functioned in the tradition established by Moses at Mount Sinai. They called God's people to an account in the light of the Law and the Mosaic Covenant. When king and people were disobedient, the prophets brought a message of confrontation. But their message was not only related to the Mosaic, but also to the Davidic covenant—to Zion as well as Sinai.   That means that the prophets proclaimed a message of hope as well as of judgment. They spoke of the coming of God in redemption, the promise of restoration, the renewal of the theocracy, and the new age that would be inaugurated by the coming Messiah.

This double "motif" (i.e. judgment and restoration) pervades the prophetic literature of the Old Testament. Both the themes of judgment and restoration are present in Isaiah (chs. 1-39 = judgment; chs. 40-66 = hope), Jeremiah (chs. 1-28 = judgment; chs. 29-50 = hope), Ezekiel, and most of the minor prophets (cf. Hos. 13:9ff; Amos 9:11ff; Micah 7:14ff; Hab. 2:14, 20; Zeph. 3; Zech. 4:6; 9:9; 10:6; etc.). This note of "hope" finds its ultimate fulfillment in the Messiah, David's greater son, who would ultimately reign over the Kingdom of God and fulfill God's covenant purpose.

Elijah, Elisha & King Ahab

The writer of Kings focuses first on the history of the northern kingdom, i.e. Israel. Over the next two centuries of Israel's separate existence as a nation, there would be nine dynasties (royal family lines) of northern kings:

Dynasty of:	Descendants serving as King:
1. Jeroboam I	Nadab
2. Baasha	Elah
3. Zimri	(none)
4. Omri	Ahab, Ahaziah, Joram
5. Jehu	Jehoahaz, Jehoash, Jeroboam II, Zechariah
6. Shallum	(none)
7. Menahem	Pekahiah
8. Pekah	(none)
9. Hoshea	(none)

As the foregoing chart reveals, the dynasties of Omri and Jehu were the most extensive. Omri's house ruled Israel from 885 to 841 B.C. (44 years), and the house of Jehu, from 841 to 753 B.C. (88 years). The prophetic careers of Elijah and Elisha were contemporaneous with the dynasties of Omri and Jehu; consequently, their respective ministries are central to the book of Kings.

It was during this 130-year span that Israel sunk to the lowest ebb yet of moral and spiritual decadence.

"The northern kings opposed the worship of Yahweh in Jerusalem, treated any expression of allegiance to the dynasty of David as treachery, and rejected the word of God's servants."[5]

The crisis was great and God raised up two prophets as messengers from the heavenly tribunal to proclaim a sobering note of impending judgment. They were "men of God" (1 Kings 17:24),[6] totally devoted to His cause and faithful to proclaim the message He communicated to them.

Ahab's Character: The "spirit" of the Age

Elijah, Israel's greatest prophet, was God's man for desperate times. Omri, a very ambitious king who did "worse than all that were before him" (1 Kings 16:25b) had established Samaria as the capital of the northern kingdom. His son, Ahab, married a Phoenician princess named Jezebel[7] and began a career that would mark him as Israel's most notorious monarch.

Ahab, influenced by his marriage to the daughter of Ethbaal, made the worship of Baal the official religion of Israel (1 Kings 16:30-33). He daringly built multiple groves and high places for Baalite worship, and persecuted the priests and prophets of Jehovah even unto death.

Baal, the "sun god", was the chief deity of the Phoenicians and Assyrians. He was served by 850 state-sponsored priests/prophets (1 Kings 18:19). Baal worship was the native

---

[5] Willem VanGemeren, *Interpreting the Prophetic Word*, p. 49.
[6] A label applied to such outstanding characters as Moses (Deut. 33:1), David (1 Sam. 13:14), John the Baptist (Jno. 1:6), and Timothy (1 Tim. 6:11).
[7] According to the Jewish historian Josephus, Jezebel's father, Ethbaal, was originally the high-priest of the temple of Astarte (the moon goddess) in Tyre.

religion of Jezebel, Ahab's unscrupulous wife. The influence she exercised over Ahab so dominated him that *"he sold himself to work wickedness in the sight of Jehovah"* (1 Kings 21:25-26).

Jezebel despised the worship of Jehovah and set out to utterly exterminate it. She prosecuted a campaign to rid the land of God's true prophets. 1 King 18:4 records the exploits of the God-fearing man Obadiah, governor of Ahab's house. When Jezebel slew Jehovah's prophets, Obadiah hid one hundred prophets, fifty in one cave and fifty in another, and fed them with bread and water. Her murderous campaign, however, was relentless.

Perhaps no story better illustrates the unprincipled character of the Ahab/Jezebel team than the theft of Naboth's vineyard (1 Kings 21). Though the vineyard was adjacent to Ahab's palace, it was Naboth's inheritance. Ancestral law (Lev. 25) among the Jews protected each family's inheritance lest the next generation be reduced to the status of pensioners. But Ahab had no regard for God's law or for the welfare of others. When Naboth refused to forfeit his family possession so that Ahab might have his herb garden, Ahab pouted. Jezebel, in turn, concocted a ruthless plot to have Naboth falsely accused of blasphemy and stoned to death. Her plan was executed and Ahab received his vineyard. But when he went to possess his vineyard, Ahab also received a very unwelcome visit from Elijah, whose prophecy of impending doom shook Ahab to the core of his being.

Elijah's Character: The "spirit" of the Prophets

Such unexpected visits from God's prophet evoked Ahab's consternation throughout his diabolical reign. Always, Elijah seemed to come from nowhere, to show up right at the point of crisis, and to utter the most staggering message of judgment. Then the prophet would depart into obscurity as quickly as he came. Try as he would, Ahab could never find him.

Such a time of extraordinary apostasy called for a display of extraordinary power and courage. To counter the momentum of idolatry, God sent Elijah the Tishbite to Ahab with the announcement, *"As the Lord God of Israel liveth, before whom I stand, there shall not be dew nor rain these years, but according to my word"* (1 Kings 17:1). Then as suddenly as he arrived, Elijah departed, to be seen no more for over three years. But just as he had prophesied, a 3½ year drought in which the land was devoid of dew and rain followed.

Elijah's name means "my God is Jehovah" and his career personified that definition. In a day when syncretism had given way to full-fledged idol worship, such an uncompromising commitment to the true and living God qualified Elijah to be the Lord's "man of the hour".

He is marked by an undaunted courage. Unintimidated before the face of a wicked king and an apostate people, Elijah spoke the Lord's message without equivocation. Even when Ahab accused him of "troubling Israel", Elijah retorted, *"I have not troubled Israel, but thou and thy father's house, in that ye have forsaken the commandments of the Lord and have followed Baalim"* (1 Kings 18:17-18).

He served as God's "covenant prosecutor", accusing king and people alike of breaking the law of God. His confrontation with the prophets of Baal on Mount Carmel (1 Kings 18) displayed not only an unflinching courage but a burning jealousy for the glory of God (1 Kings 19:10). He prosecuted the Divine lawsuit against the people of Israel, accusing them of complacency (1 Kings 18:21), infidelity, idolatry, and murder (1 Kings 19:10). He ridiculed the absurd practice of calling upon a lifeless god to answer prayer, making a public spectacle of the Baalite prophets (1 Kings 18:27). Elijah was the quintessential man of faith and prayer (Jas. 5:17-18).

His ministry marked the end of an era of Divine patience and the beginning of an era of purification. As such, Elijah set the pace for subsequent prophets who would confront a people hardened in unbelief with an uncompromising message of Divine judgment. The "spirit" of Elijah would live on in Amos, Hosea, Isaiah, Jeremiah, and even John the Baptist.

Yet Elijah was "a man of like passions as we are" (Jas. 5:17a). In spite of his tremendous courage and zeal, he had moments of weakness and personal pain. No doubt, this truly human man struggled with a tremendous sense of loneliness and ostracization. His lament on Mount Horeb, i.e. "...I only remain", suggests his feeling of abandonment. Who can doubt that the time spent by the brook with only ravens as his visitors and the public sentiment that he was responsible for the lengthy drought took a toll on his spirits? This feature would also be duplicated in the successors to Elijah's prophetic office. The road the prophets were called to walk was a lonely path.

But God marvelously sustained his faithful prophet. He fed him at the brook and by the widow, and spoke gently to the discouraged prophet under the juniper tree. He used him mightily to sustain the widow's oil and meal and raise her son to life. He honored his faith with a tremendous display of rain and fire from heaven. He mercifully gave him Elisha as a companion in his last days. So would God continue to bless and honor each of his faithful prophets who ministered in the tradition of Elijah.

Ahab's story ends in tragedy, but Elijah's in triumph. Ahab was killed in a battle with the Syrians by an arrow shot at random. Though the soldier aimed at nothing in particular, God directed the stray dart to the apostate king as its target (1 Kings 22:34). In the same place the dogs had licked the blood of Naboth, Ahab died a similar death (1 Kings 21:19).

Elijah, on the contrary, was taken to heaven in a chariot of fire (2 Kings 2:1-11). The prophet who lived in such abject loneliness and obscurity was ushered into his eternal home in a grand way. God spared his servant the pain of death, with the welcome message (no doubt), "Well done, thou good and faithful servant."

Elisha, Prophet of Grace

The prophetic tradition is a vivid illustration of the principle expressed in Isaiah 59:19: *"When the enemy shall come in like a flood, the Spirit of the Lord shall lift up a standard against him."* The failure of the monarchy opened the door for the "enemy's" advance; nevertheless, the Spirit of God sent prophets to call both king and people to repentance.

The prophetic ministry of Elijah, the covenant prosecutor, was the beginning of this Divine counter-assault. Elijah accused Israel (the northern kingdom) of failing to comply with the obligations of God's covenant. Upon his translation to heaven, the prophet's "mantle"[8] fell on Elisha, who continued the prophetic ministry of his predecessor. Elisha's prophetic career overlapped the dynasties of Omri and Jehu, concluding with his death *circa* 796 B.C. (merely some seventy-five years before the fall of the northern kingdom of Israel).

But even though Elisha continued the prophetic tradition of Elijah, yet his ministry was essentially different in tone from Elijah's. Elijah was like a burning meteor, flashing bolt after bolt of Divine justice upon sin. But Elisha, whose name means "God is my salvation", was like a placid moon, reflecting the brilliant light of Divine love and blessing. Elijah was the "fire, wind, and earthquake" of Divine communication, but Elisha, "the still small voice" of God's grace. F.W. Krummacher, an 18th century German theologian, writes:

> "Elisha was ordained to appear in Israel as an Evangelist, as the messenger of one whose feet were 'lovely on the mountains', whilst Elijah had to go forth as another Moses, to restore by his exertions a proper regard to those laws which had been despised and trodden under foot."

---

[8] The "mantle", a piece of cloth worn around the neck, symbolized prophetic authority.

Through Elijah, Jehovah had wounded and broken; now through Elisha, He would heal and bind up that which was broken.

To what Divine motive can we attribute the milder character of Elisha's ministry? It is due to the fact that the prophets were not only ordained to accuse Israel of her sins, but also to call out of this apostate society a remnant of godly and faithful servants to Jehovah. Elijah prosecuted the people for their crimes against God's holy law. Elisha's ministry, on the contrary, was primarily designed to call out a remnant for the Lord's name.

The Biblical narratives concerned with the prophetic career of Elisha provide a very detailed personal sketch of the man himself. Breaking from the style of historical analysis, the writer narrows his focus to biographical snapshots of this amazing servant of God. The picture that emerges is that of compassionate ministry. Perhaps the purpose of painting this lengthy personal portrait of mercy is to demonstrate that even in days of apostasy, God continues to deal with His faithful remnant in mercy.

The various episodes of Elisha's career serve to illustrate both the similarity and the dissimilarity between his and Elijah's prophetic calling. Yes, the two were similar. *"The spirit of Elijah rested on Elisha"* (2 Kings 2:15), in terms of the fact that he spoke with Divine authority and that God validated the prophet as His authentic servant through various miracles and signs. Further, both men were faithful to proclaim the Divine message and to act in the interests of the glory of Jehovah. But, though their respective ministries were essentially the same in message and aim, they were, generally speaking, distinct in tone and emphasis. Elijah reminds us of God's justice; Elisha, of God's grace and mercy.

Elisha Purifies the Spring at Jericho

The first official act of the prophet illustrates his "ministry of mercy". Elisha began his prophetic career at Jericho, a city cursed by God through his servant Joshua some five hundred years before (2 Kings 2:18-22). This city which was once so fertile and green was now a virtual wasteland. The primary source of their plight was the noxious water supply. The poisoned water was unfit for consumption and useless to the crops and vegetation.

Elisha met their overtures for help with compassion. But his plan to relieve the misery of that city was strange: *"Bring me a new cruse, and put salt therein"* (v. 20). A chemical compound that tended to produce the very opposite effect of fertility, i.e. salt, was employed for two reasons. First, salt had a medicinal value in the ancient world. Its use on this occasion symbolized healing. Second, its tendency to sterilize instead of fertilize indicated that the purification of the spring was totally the work of God—a supernatural and miraculous act.

When he cast the cruse into the bubbling spring, Elisha proclaimed, *"Thus saith the Lord, I have healed these waters; there shall not be from thence any more dearth or barren land"* (v. 21). What a grand display of God's mercy and love! The removal of this five-hundred year curse on Jericho was the first evidence that Elisha was a true man of God.

Judgment at Bethel

Elisha soon left Jericho for Bethel, a journey of approximately fifteen miles, or three days (2 Kings 2:23-25). Here, however, the prophet encountered a very different set of circumstances. Instead of humble petitioners such as those who dwelt at Jericho, Elisha met the tongues of scorn and derision.

Bethel was the religious seat of Jeroboam's idolatry. Here he had set up one of the two golden calves and established a surrogate "priesthood" to complete the separation between Israel and Judah (1 Kings 12:28ff). Jeroboam had turned the city whose name originally meant "house of God" into a city the prophets would subsequently call "Bethaven", meaning "house of vanity".

The prophet journeyed to Bethel, not for the purpose of cursing it, but rather, to call forth a remnant to repentance and covenant renewal. But before he could enter the city, a mob of "little children"[9], probably apprentices to the idolatrous priests of Bethel, began to mock him: "*Go up, thou bald head; go up, thou bald head*" (v. 23). "Go up" means "Ascend like Elijah", a statement that expresses their blasphemous unbelief of the prophet's translation to heaven. "Thou bald head" expresses their disdain for Elisha himself. Baldness was considered to be a disgrace and was a symptom of leprosy. The fact that Elisha was

---

[9] The Hebrew word implies young people between 15 and 18 years of age.

bald suggests that, unlike his predecessor, he did not possess a commanding physical presence. His appearance was not intimidating, and these youths were all too ready to capitalize on his physical limitations to express their utter disdain and disregard of the man himself.

But their taunts and jeers are more than an expression of personal disrespect toward Elisha. They are expressing their utter contempt for the cause that Elisha represents. Krummacher observes:

> "[This] is something more than a band of insolent boys; it is a hoard of young wretches who, already sold to the father of lies, have taken part against the kingdom of light and truth."

As such, these young men speak as the representatives of the entire city.

Elisha's authority as a man of God and future success as Jehovah's spokesman to the people was at stake. Were he to allow this wicked challenge to pass unmet, he would forever be branded as an imposter. The integrity of his calling and the glory of Jehovah's name demanded a response, just as the worship of the golden calves at the foot of Mount Sinai before and the lying spirit of Ananias and Sapphira after demanded a response.

In an Elijah-like display of heavenly authority, Elisha spoke a Divine imprecation. At once, two bears emerged from the wood, slaughtering forty-two of the blasphemers. It was a dreadful scene, but God vindicated the integrity of His prophet in a society marked by the grossest kind of impiety and irreverence. This episode serves to illustrate the spirit of the age in which the prophets lived and ministered the truth of God. It also teaches the very important principle that there are occasions when God's servants must stand firmly and courageously against evil, even though the overarching tone of one's ministry is one of consolation and encouragement. To sacrifice the glory of God on the altar of tolerance for evil is a breach of the first and a misunderstanding of the second of the two great commandments (cf. Mt. 22:37ff). May the Lord give us wisdom to make accurate judgments here.

Deliverance in the Wilderness of Edom

In the next scene, Elisha resumes the gracious display of mercy that characterizes his ministry (2 Kings 3:1-27). He is met by three kings—Jehoram (Ahab's son and the king of Israel), Jehoshaphat (the godly king of Judah), and the king of Edom—on their way to squash the Moabite rebellion. Their armies are fainting under the heat of the desert sun and the absence of water. In the extremity of their plight, Jehoram, the profligate king of Israel, begins to despair: *"Alas! The Lord hath called these three kings together, to deliver them into the hand of Moab"* (v. 10). But at Jehoshaphat's insistence, the three kings and their armies seek Elisha for counsel (v. 11).

What a rare turn of events in that day! The kings of Israel have long since ceased listening to God's true prophets. But now the three come to inquire of the Lord at the mouth of His servant. Like Elijah's victory at Mount Carmel, this scene of two idolatrous kings (Jehoram and the king of Edom) applying to God's servant for help depicts Jehovah's triumph over Baal.

Elisha recognized at once that the motives of Jehoram were selfish and carnal. In another display of prophetic courage and holy boldness, he responded to Ahab's son, *"Get thee to the prophets of thy father and...thy mother"* (cf. Jer. 2:27-28; Deut. 32:37-38). But for Jehoshaphat's sake, he complied with their request (v. 14).

Elisha then called for a minstrel, i.e. a harpist. As he played, the hand of the Lord came upon Elisha and he revealed a two-part message of good news: (1) a plan to relieve their thirst; (2) a promise regarding the victorious outcome of the battle.

As they complied with the command to "make this valley full of ditches", the desert yielded water to quench the army's thirst. When the Moabite army saw the sun reflecting red on the water, they presumed that the kings had fallen on each other and that the land flowed with the blood of the slain. They immediately took to the wilderness to finish the slaughter. Much to their chagrin, however, the combined armies of the three kings ambushed them and the power of Moab was broken. Hence, the prophet Elisha was mightily used of God again as an instrument of His delivering mercy.

Miracles of Mercy

Second Kings 4 through 8 records at least nine different miracles of mercy wrought by Elisha. These were acts of compassion in an age of violence and aggression. As such the

Biblical portrait of Elisha is a refreshing reprieve from the spirit of his age. On a practical level, his story teaches us the importance of ministering to the needy in a day when the majority displays a callous disregard for the glory of God. Regardless of how apostate society may be, there will always be a need for the ministry of mercy.

The first of these miracles was the *multiplying the widow's oil* (2 Kings 4:1-7). How heart-rending is the extremity of this widow of one of Jehovah's prophets! Deprived of her husband and left with a great indebtedness, she now faces the further plight of living her life bereft of her two sons. When she appealed for help to Elisha, he asked "What hast thou in the house?" She replied, "Nothing, save a pot of oil". He then advised her to borrow empty vessels from her neighbors and begin to fill the vessels with the oil. As she obeyed by faith (perhaps remembering the account of widow of Zarephath whose oil and meal was sustained by Elisha's celebrated predecessor), the widow set aside first one full vessel after another until finally, she had sufficient not only to repay her full debt, but to sustain herself and her two sons for many days to come.

The second miracle involved a mercy extended to another godly woman *in honor of her hospitality* (2 Kings 4:8-17). She is called a "great woman", for she was a woman marked by the heart of a servant. She and her husband built and furnished a room for Elisha's lodging as he traveled on his prophetic errands, but she was barren. Grateful for the generosity of this woman and her husband, Elisha promised that she would give birth to a son. The blessing she never dreamed possible was given at the precise time that Elisha had predicted.

When this child was yet young, however, he suffered what was apparently a sun stroke and died in his mother's lap. Elisha's third miracle of mercy involved *the resurrection of the great woman's son to life* (2 Kings 4:18-37). The woman called "great" because of her godliness, hospitality, and dependence on God, demonstrates also great gratitude to God for this special mercy.

The fourth miracle was an act of mercy to "the sons of the prophets", Elisha's young protégés in the ministry (2 Kings 4:38-44). In preparation for the feeding of this large group, someone had inadvertently mixed wild gourds into the stew. At once it was reported that the meal was poisoned. But Elisha knew an antidote: *"Cast meal into the pot"*. Thus the precious *food was decontaminated* and the sons of the prophets were abundantly fed.

Fifth was a miracle of mercy performed on behalf of an officer of the enemy army — *the cleansing of a leper* (2 Kiings 5:1-27). Naaman the Syrian was a very important military figure. He was "captain of the host of the king of Syria", Israel's arch-enemy at this juncture of its history. But this important person had a problem. Naaman was a leper. His maid, however, was an Israelite. When the god Rimmon could not cure him, his little maid advised him to apply to the prophet Elisha. Elisha's counsel to dip in Jordan seven times was insulting to Naaman, but when he submitted, his flesh was restored like that of a child. The Syrian captain tried to pay Elisha for his services, but the prophet refused the gift. Naaman henceforth committed himself to paying homage only to Jehovah, even though his civic responsibilities required him to frequent the house of Rimmon. This act of mercy toward someone outside the parameters of the Abrahamic Covenant is a powerful testimony to sovereign grace and to the breadth of God's covenant love (cf. Eph. 3:18). [10]

Elisha's sixth miracle was performed as an act of mercy to one of the "sons of the prophets" (2 Kings 6:1-7). While the prophets were building new quarters for their lodging, one of the men lost the head of his borrowed axe. He cried out for help, *"Alas, master! For it was borrowed."* When Elisha cast a stick into the water, the iron swam and he *recovered the borrowed property.*

The seventh episode cited involved a miracle in which Elisha foiled the military strategy of the Syrian army (2 Kings 6:8-23). Singlehandedly (that is, under the blessing of God), the old prophet *rescued Israel from her enemy.* The king of Syria had conspired to attack from a certain place. But Elisha warned the king of Israel to avoid the place. This happened several times (v. 10b). Finally, the king of Syria accused his servants of "leaking classified information" to the king of Israel (v. 11). His servant informed him that it was not they, *"but Elisha the prophet who tells the king of Israel the words that thou speakest in thy bedchamber"* (v. 12). The Syrian king, therefore, sent horses and chariots to

---

[10] According to Jesus, Naaman the Syrian is a trophy of sovereign grace (cf. Lk. 4:27).

surround the prophet in Dothan. When Elisha and his servant awoke the next morning, they were surrounded by the Syrian army. The servant despaired, but Elisha prayed, "*Lord, open his eyes, that he may see*". Surrounding the Syrian army, the servant saw God's chariots of fire. Then Elisha prayed that God would smite the army with blindness. He then led the entire army into the city of Samaria, the capital city of Israel. But instead of slaughtering the vulnerable enemy, Elisha counseled the king of Israel to feed the army and send them home. Thus Elisha demonstrated mercy not only to Israel, rescuing them from the enemy, but to the Syrian army itself, feeding them and allowing them to go free.

Further, Elisha mercifully *relieved the starving city of Samaria* and delivered them from the Syrians (2 Kings 6:24 – 7:20). When Elisha counseled the king to allow the Syrian soldiers to go free, it was not long until the enemy again besieged the city. The siege continued until the people within were on the verge of starvation (2 Kings 6:25). The king of Israel blamed Elisha's excessive display of mercy for Samaria's desperate plight, and he purposed to decapitate the prophet (2 Kings 6:31). When the king's delegation came to take Elisha, the prophet revealed that within twenty-four hours, food would be available in abundance (2 Kings 7:1). The unlikely prediction came true when, the next day, the Lord caused the Syrian army to hear a noise of chariots and horses so that they fled, abandoning their tents with food on the tables (7:6ff).

The final act of mercy was not a miracle, *per se*, but an episode that gives insight to the compassionate spirit that actuated the prophet. It again concerns the great woman of Shunem and is recorded in 2 Kings 8:1-6. Elisha revealed to her God's design to bring a seven-year famine upon the land. He warned her in advance so that she might sustain her family.

Steadfast Firmness

These various acts of compassion define the character of Elisha's prophetic career. But lest we should think that he was short on prophetic commitment to righteousness in that ungodly age, the Holy Spirit reveals another instance (in addition to the judgment at Bethel) in which he firmly stood his ground.

When Elisha's servant, Gehazi, pursued Naaman with the lie that his master had changed his mind concerning the talents of silver, Elisha rewarded the treachery with the dreadful sentence, "The leprosy therefore of Naaman shall cleave unto thee, and unto thy seed forever" (2 Kings 5:20-27). Gehazi departed from the prophet's presence a leper.

Indeed, Elisha did not fail to stand firmly for the glory of God. The over-arching compassionate character of his ministry, however, is recorded as an object lesson of the fact that the prophets were men whose love for the Lord (Elijah) was coupled with a love for the Lord's people (Elisha).

The Divided Monarchy

Chapter 10
THE LAST DAYS OF ISRAEL
2 Kings 9 – 17

The dynasty of Jehu (841-753 B.C.) marked the longest reign by a single family in the history of the Northern Kingdom. Jehu's royal family line breaks down as follows:

King	Dates (BC)	Length of Reign
Jehu	841-814	28 yrs
Jehoahaz	814-798	17 yrs
Jehoash	798-782	16 yrs
Jereoboam II	793-753	41 yrs
Zechariah	753	6 mos

The dynasty of Jehu ended just thirty years before Samaria and the Northern Kingdom's fall to Assyria in 722 B.C. Five random kings (Shallum, Menahem, Pekahiah, Pekah, and Hoshea) would reign over the final thirty years of Israel's history. Jehu's dynasty, therefore, marks the beginning of Israel's "last days". Second Kings 9 – 17 catalogs the respective terms of each of these Northern kings on the throne, a group that collectively *"did that which was evil in the sight of the Lord."*

Jehu, Instrument of Judgment (chs. 9-10)

Though Jehu was not a righteous king, he was, in fact, used by God as an instrument of judgment (2 Kings 10:29-31). It is difficult to determine whether his "zeal for the Lord" (10:16) was an actual concern for Jehovah's glory or the spirit of political revolution.

Under the express command of God (1 Kings 19:16), Elisha sent his servant to anoint Jehu as king over Israel. He was specially commissioned to punish the house of Ahab by executing Divine judgment upon it. This ministry involved avenging the blood of the prophets that Jezebel had slain, and purging the worship of Baal from Israel. Through this act of religious "cleansing", God issued the last call to repentance to Israel before Divine judgment descended upon the nation itself.

It is in this context that the bloody character of Jehu's extermination campaign must be interpreted. He was a flash of lightning against the dark night sky of a decadent society. Jehu was commissioned only after the nation persisted to rebel against God in spite of His many overtures to them. The 3 ½ year drought, display on Mount Carmel, and gentle character of Elisha's prophetic career had produced no positive effect on the people. The inception of Jehu's dynasty, therefore, marks the beginning of God's judgment on Israel for its national apostasy.

Jehu's ferocious revolution began with the assassination of Joram, the grandson of Ahab (2 Kings 9:14ff). His next act was the assassination of the wicked woman Jezebel, according to the word of the Lord (9:30-37). Seventy sons of the house of Ahab were then slain (10:1-11) and Jehu mounted his chariot and rode furiously for Samaria, the capital city of the Northern kingdom. There, he slew the Baal worshippers, burned the images of Baal, razed the house of Baalite worship, and "destroyed Baal out of

Israel" (10:18-28). Thus this perplexing figure executed his Divine commission to punish the house of Ahab and to begin the national judgment on Israel.

Syrian Incursions (ch. 13, 14:23ff)

Second Kings 10:32 clearly states that Jehu's revolution was the beginning of Divine judgment on Israel: *"In those days, the Lord began to cut Israel short."* The expression literally means "to cut off the ends" and speaks of the decline of the Northern kingdom. Divine judgment not only came from within Israel's borders, but also from without.

The Syrians, under Hazael's rule, "smote in all the coasts of Israel, from Jordan eastward, all the land of Gilead, of the Gadites, and the Reubenites, and the Manassites..." (10:32b). Hazael's military dominance of the tribes that had settled trans-Jordan was complete. Later, during the reign of Jehoahaz, Jehu's son, Syria made significant incursions into Israel and took many of its cities. Interestingly, there was a reprieve from Syrian dominance under Jehoahaz, but it was short-lived, for this kindness from God had no appreciable effect on the king or the nation (2 Kings. 13:4-7). Jehoash and Jereboam II[1] subsequently recovered them all, for the Lord had mercy on His covenant people (2 Kings 13:22-25; 14:25-28).

---

[1] It was during the reign of Jereboam II that Amos, Hosea, and Micah functioned as prophets of Jehovah. More on their respective commissions will follow later in this chapter.

147

Assyrian Dominance

Little more is heard in the narrative from Syria, Israel's perennial enemy. The discussion of the kings that reigned over Israel after Jehu's dynasty (i.e. during the final thirty years of her history) indicates that a new nation, the Assyrians, have assumed military dominance. During the reign of Pekah, the empire of Assyria would successfully besiege Samaria and Israel would fall (2 Kings 15:29).

The year was approximately 734 B.C. Pekah reigned over Israel and Ahaz reigned over the Southern kingdom of Judah. According to 2 Kings 16:5, Pekah allied himself with Rezin king of Syria to attack the Southern kingdom of Judah. Ahaz panicked, and in spite of the prophet Isaiah's warnings (Is. 7:1ff) he sent to Tiglathpileser king of Assyria for help (2 Kings 16:7-9). The invitation was just what Assyria wanted. The Assyrians invaded Dan and Naphtali (2 Kings 15:29) and though the full exile did not take place until twelve years later, many of the people were deported by the Assyrian emperor (Hos. 8:8-9).

In 722 B.C., the entire Northern kingdom fell to the Assyrians. It was in the ninth year of Hoshea, king of Israel that Assyria took Samaria "and carried Israel away into Assyria" (2 Kings 17:6), never to return to the land (Hos. 9:3).

The reasons for the fall of the Northern kingdom are enumerated in 2 Kings 17:7-23. Here the writer accuses Israel of idol worship, compromise with pagan cultures, immorality, resistance to Jehovah's prophets, Baal worship, sorcery, and pervasive disobedience to God's commandments.

The remainder of chapter 17 (vs. 24-41) describes the changes affected by Assyrian occupation of the Northern kingdom. The Assyrian king (Sargon II)[2] repopulated the cities of Israel with people from Babylon and several other Assyrian cities. These foreigners inhabited the homes of the Israelites, claiming their property for themselves. When God sent lions among them, the Assyrian occupants sent word that the God of the land was angry. Sargon, consequently, sent one of the priests home to teach them "the manner of the God of the land" (v. 27). Though he taught the new inhabitants "how they should fear the Lord," they still worshipped their pagan deities.

With foreigners occupying the majority of the promised land, it would not be long before Assyria would attempt to conquer the Southern kingdom of Judah as well. Chapter 18 records the continuing drama.

Israel's Pre-Exilic Prophets

After Elisha, God sent two more pre-exilic prophets to the Northern Kingdom of Israel—Hosea and Amos. Their written oracles are included in the section of the Old Testament called "the Minor Prophets."[3] Both Hosea and Amos prophesied in approximately 750 B.C., during the reign of Jereboam II. Hosea was a native to the Northern Kingdom, though Amos was a

---

[2] Shalmaneser had started the siege of Samaria, but died before he could finish it. Sargon II completed it and occupied the land.
[3] They are termed "Minor Prophets" by virtue of the length or size of their writings.

native Judean who traveled to Israel to fulfill his prophetic commission.

Hosea Incarnates His Message (chs. 1-3)

Hosea prophesied during a time of material prosperity and spiritual bankruptcy. Israel had been unfaithful to the covenant, attributing to idols the honor that belonged to Jehovah alone. Hosea's assignment was to prosecute the charge of infidelity, accusing Israel of "playing the harlot" (2:5) against God. The judgments he announced were realized in 722 B.C. when Samaria fell to the Assyrians.

But God called Hosea to incarnate as well as communicate His message. As an object lesson or illustration of the relationship between Jehovah and Israel, God commanded Hosea to marry a harlot named Gomer (1:2-3). In the marriage analogy, Hosea represents the covenant loyalty of God. Gomer, whether an infamous temple prostitute or simply a woman prone to infidelity, stands as a parody of the unfaithfulness of Israel to her heavenly Husband. The Old Testament scholar Willem VanGemeren writes:

> "The way of God with Israel is best reflected in Hosea's relationship with Gomer. Her infidelities represented Israel's apostasy, her children spoke of Yahweh's judgment, and Hosea's willingness to take Gomer back depicted Yahweh's love for Israel...Thus Hosea unveiled the details of his married life so all Israel would stand aghast at Gomer's adultery and at Hosea's

love for his adulterous wife. Yet his love for Gomer symbolically pointed to Yahweh's deep love for apostate Israel."[4]

The first child, Jezreel, was born legitimately to Hosea and Gomer (1:4). The next two children, however, were illegitimate (2:4-5). The girl was named *Loruhamah,* meaning "no mercy" (1:6), for God would no longer show mercy to the house of Israel. The son was named *Loammi,* meaning "not my people", denoting the covenant rejection and disenfranchisement of Israel.

The language of 2:2-4 is the legal formula for a Jewish divorce. Perhaps Hosea put away his wife for her adulteries, disowning her and disinheriting her children. But in chapter 3, God calls upon the prophet to reclaim his adulterous wife: "*Go yet, love a woman beloved of her friend, yet an adulteress, according to the love of the Lord toward the children of Israel, who look to other gods, and love flagons of wine*" (3:1). Hosea actually bought his own wife, redeeming her from the penury to which her immoral conduct had afflicted her, for fifteen pieces of silver and a homer and one-half of barley (3:2).

The dark scenes of Hosea 1-3 are balanced by the promise of restoration (1:10-11; 2:14-23). Hosea 2:14-15 outlines God's plan to bring His rebellious bride to repentance. Chapter 2:19-20, in contrast to 2:4, reads like the vows and promises of a wedding ceremony. The use of the words "lovingkindness" (Heb. *hesed* meaning covenant loyalty or steadfast love) and "faithfulness"

---

[4] Willem VanGemeren, *Interpreting the Prophetic Word*, p. 108.

indicate Jehovah's commitment to faithfully love His own even though they are unfaithful to Him. This double motif of judgment/hope is the hallmark of the prophetic message. Chapters 4-10, subsequently, are concerned to outline the reasons for Israel's rejection by God, and chapters 11-14, on the hope for restoration.

Hosea Indicts Israel (chs. 4-10)

As God's spokesman, Hosea prosecutes God's covenant lawsuit against Israel. The word "controversy" in 4:1 conveys the thought of a formal accusation or lawsuit. Beginning with this verse, Hosea states the case for the prosecution.

The charge was spiritual infidelity (4:17). Just as Gomer had played the harlot, so Israel "sold herself to lovers" (8:9). They sought counsel from the idols they had manufactured (4:12). Such infidelity brought upon them the sorest of judgments — Divine withdrawal and abandonment: *"They shall go with their flocks and with their herds to seek the Lord; but they shall not find Him; He hath withdrawn Himself from them"* (5:6; cf. v. 15; 9:12).

The root cause of Israel's demise was their rejection of the knowledge of God (4:6; cf. 5:4; 8:12; 11:3). Chapter four indicates that once they turned their backs on the knowledge of God, the nation began to decline dramatically. The consequences included moral depravity (v. 2), the failure of spiritual leadership (vs. 7-9), personal discontentment (vs. 10-12), and isolation from fellowship with God's people (v. 17).

Hosea compared Israel to a backsliding heifer—a stubborn and untamed cow that shook the yoke from its shoulders (4:16; 10:11). They were also like a silly dove who flies without discretion, looking to foreign alliances instead of the Lord for safety (7:11-12; 9:11). Other images include an unturned cake (7:8 – an image that speaks of their spiritual and moral complacency), an empty vine (10:1 – a metaphor employed to describe the absence of spiritual fruit), and an ungrateful and impenitent prodigal (11:3-7). Because Israel followed their own way, plowing wickedness and reaping iniquity, they ate a harvest of lies (10:13). Brief reforms proved to be as disingenuous and deceptive "as a morning cloud" (6:4).

The message of Hosea might be summarized in two verses —13:1 and 13:9: "*When Ephraim spake trembling [that is, when he acted in humility and godly fear], he exalted himself in Israel; but when he offended in Baal, he died*" (v. 1); "*O Israel, thou hast destroyed thyself; but in me is thine help*" (v. 9). The rebellious and self-willed pursuit of their own course, in other words, led to Israel's demise. Only by humble trust in Jehovah was there any hope for their future.

All in all, Hosea indicts the Northern kingdom with the charge of blatant rebellion to the Lord: "*But they like men [i.e. like Adam] have transgressed the covenant: there have they dealt treacherously against me*" (6:7). The startling scene of chapter 7 indicates just how far gone the nation was in its apostate condition: "*When I would have healed Israel, then the iniquity of Ephraim was discovered...*" (7:1). Like a surgeon who simply closes the patient when he sees the pervasiveness of the disease, so Israel has reached a point of no return.

They had sown the wind; now they would reap the whirlwind (8:7). God pledges to deal with them like "a moth" (5:12 – an image that suggests the silent destruction of the things we value) and "a lion" (5:14 – an image that speaks of a swift and savage judgment). He pronounces a "woe" upon them and pledges to snare them in his nets (7:12-16).

Jehovah's Faithful and Steadfast Love (ch. 11-14)

The only hope for such miserable sinners is the grace of God. In spite of Israel's infidelity, Jehovah is still faithful to His covenant. The God who had "loved Israel as a child" now pledges, in spite of her disobedience and unbelief, to mitigate the fierceness of His wrath: *"How shall I give thee up, Ephraim...how shall I make thee as Admah...[and] Zeboim? Mine heart is turned within me, my repentings are kindled together. I will not execute the fierceness of mine anger, I will not return to destroy Ephraim: for I am God and not man..."* (11:1, 8-9).

He promises to "ransom them from the power of the grave" and "redeem them from death" (13:14)—promises that find their ultimate fulfillment in the eschatological hope of the Messiah.

It is on the basis of God's covenant love that Israel is encouraged to repent (14:1). When their repentance is marked by the confession of sin, the forsaking of every foreign alliance, and the abandonment of the worship of idols, God pledges to forgive their sins: *"I will heal their backsliding, I will love them freely; for mine anger is turned away from him"* (14:4). Such a note of hope is given as an encouragement to the penitent sinner.

Amos, a "Lay" Prophet

Amos is also among the pre-exilic, literary prophets. He was not, like others, a career prophet, but was temporarily commissioned to carry God's message to the Northern kingdom. God called Amos to leave the fields of Tekoa in Judah where he was a shepherd and caretaker of sycamore trees, saying, *"Go, prophesy unto my people Israel"* (7:15).

Amos prophesied "two years before the earthquake" (1:1b; cf. Zech. 14:5). Uzziah was king in Judah and Jeroboam II reigned in Israel. It was a period of unparalleled material prosperity and leisure in Israel. From the perspective of many people in the Northern kingdom, these were "the best of times".

But from God's perspective, it was a time of social injustice and oppression. Though Israel was materially wealthy, it was morally bankrupt. The rich abused and exploited the poor, using the wealth they had accumulated to oppress those classified as the "have-nots."

Amos' Eight Oracles

Into this self-satisfied climate, Amos came with his message of impending doom: *"The Lord will roar from Zion, and utter his voice from Jerusalem..."* (1:2a). The Lion's roar that pierced the silence of affluence came from Zion and Jerusalem, not from the cult shrines of Bethel. As Amos crossed the border between the

Southern and Northern kingdoms and entered Bethel—the city
that epitomized the official state religion of Israel with one of the
two golden calves that Jeroboam had made (cf. 1 Kings 12:26-27)[5]
—he stated that Jerusalem, not Bethel, is the place from which
God speaks. The force of the point is unmistakable: *God did not
authorize the religious innovations of the Northern kingdom. Though
Israel had long since replaced the Divine pattern for worship that
Jerusalem symbolized, God still held them accountable to his original
revelation.*

The successive message of the prophet is indeed as
staggering as a lion's roar. Amos spoke of immorality, idolatry,
and injustice. His message reads like a catalog of human rights
violations.

He first condemned the sins of Israel's six neighboring
nations—Syria, Philistia, Tyre, Edom, Ammon, and Moab (1:3-
2:3). Even though each nation worshipped its own god, Amos
does not even pay cursory notice to that fact. Instead, he calls
them to account before the one, true, and living God over the
whole earth.[6]

He accuses each of committing multiple and repeated
atrocities—"*For three transgressions...and for four, I will not turn
away the punishment thereof...*". The charge against Syria and
Philistia (represented by their two principal cities, Damascus
and Gaza) is excessive cruelty (1:3-8). They went beyond that

---

[5] The other golden calf was in Dan on the northern border.
[6] One commentator writes, "Feel the weight of the monotheism of Amos".

which was necessary in warfare and showed no mercy to their enemies

Tyre and Edom are condemned for breaking treaties for self-interest and capitalizing on the misfortunes of others (1:9-12). Ammon and Moab are accused of despicable crimes against the helpless, Ammon against the future of Gilead and Moab against the past of Edom (1:13-2:3).

The people of Israel would have been initially sympathetic to Amos' message of judgment on these other nations. They would have even approved of his denunciation of Judah's lawlessness in 2:4-5, for they viewed their brethren to the south as opponents and rivals. But when Amos began the Divine diatribe against Israel (2:6ff)—the primary subject of the book— they must have felt very uncomfortable.

Amaziah, the priest at Bethel, certainly did not appreciate the unwelcome intrusion of the uncouth prophet from the South. He first sent a message to Jereboam II accusing Amos of leading a conspiracy against the king (7:10-11). Then Amaziah "flexed his political muscle", telling Amos to return to Judah as a more appropriate sphere of ministry (7:12-14). But Amos stood his ground, reminding Amaziah that he was motivated by the fact of God's call, not self-interest (7:14-15). His words of rebuttal, announcing God's rejection of this false preist, must have been particularly sobering to Amaziah (7:16-17).

The Sins of Israel

Amos' message of judgment against Israel highlights five major sins—each taking the form of a violation of human rights. The first sin was *economic oppression* (2:6-7a). The rich betrayed and cheated their brethren for economic gain, whether great ("for silver") or small ("for a pair of shoes").

Second, they were guilty of *denying justice to the poor* (2:7b). The rich ran the court system. When the poor appealed to the courts for justice, they were "turned away".

Third, he charges them with *gross promiscuity* (2:7c). The reference to trans-generational immorality, i.e. "father and son go in to the same maid", indicates just how pervasive a problem prostitution was in Israel. The phrase "to profane my holy name" may indicate temple prostitution, thus coupling the charge of immorality with idolatry.

The fourth sin was *depriving the poor of life's necessities* (2:8a). Keeping a poor person's garment past nightfall, according to Exodus 22:26-27, was strictly forbidden. To deprive him of his only means of warmth was especially cruel and inhumane.

The fifth sin was *extravagance gained at the poor man's expense* (2:8b). To strip the man who could not pay his debts of every possession as a means of financing an extravagant lifestyle was heartless and unmerciful.

The sins of this corrupt society are compounded by their ingratitude to God. He had given them every conceivable privilege and blessing (2:9-12). They were his covenant people, chosen out of all the nations of the world as his special inheritance (3:1-2). But now, because of their impenitence and disobedience, they would be judged (2:13-16). Their fellowship with God had been broken (3:3). Now, "the Lion" would roar in judgment (3:8).

The Day of the Lord

In spite of numerous judgments on a smaller scale, Israel still did not return to the Lord (4:6-11). *"Therefore,"* Amos says, *"prepare to meet thy God, O Israel"* (4:12). Amos' message is that judgment is imminent.

The nominally religious people of Israel centered their hopes on "the Day of the Lord"—the day in which Jehovah would punish sinners and balance the scales of justice. They fancied themselves righteous, thinking that it would be a day in which God would punish their enemies. But Amos pronounces a "woe" upon them for presumption: *"Woe unto you that desire the day of the Lord! To what end is it for you? The day of the Lord is darkness, and not light"* (Amos 5:18ff). They were wrong to take for granted that the Day of the Lord would be their day of triumph.

This phrase—"the Day of the Lord"—is one of the dominant motifs of the Prophets. It surfaces again and again (cf. Is. 2:12; 13:6ff; 22:5; 34:8; Jer. 46:10; Eze. 7:19; 13:5; 30:3; Joel 1:15; 2:1; 3:14; Zeph. 1:17ff; Zech. 14:1; Mal. 4:5). It is an eschatological expression describing any time the Lord intervenes in judgment. In Amos, it points to the fall of Samaria in 722 B.C.

This prophetic theme is picked up in the New Testament to describe the final judgment of the wicked (1 Ths. 5:1ff; 2 Pet. 3:10). In addition to the phrase "the Day of the Lord", New Testament writers also speak of "the day of Jesus Christ"—the happy day in which he returns for His people. The epochal event of the Second Coming will be both a day of doom to the wicked and glory to the righteous.

The Day of the Lord was ready to break forth upon the opulent, extravagant, and self-indulgent people of Israel (6:3-8). What would be the characteristics of this terrible day? Amos explains in five visions.

Amos' Five Visions

The first three visions are found in Amos 7:1-9: a swarm of grasshoppers (vs. 1-3), a fire (vs. 4-6), and a plumbline (vs. 7-9). These three visions reveal what God will not do, i.e. destroy Israel utterly, and what He will do, measure their sins against his own righteous standard. Obviously, the judgments His people do experience are less than their iniquities deserve. So, the first three visions teach that judgment would come in proportion to God's justice, but that it would not involve total annihilation.

The fourth vision concerns a basket of summer fruit (8:1-2). The basket of ripe fruit symbolizes the nation of Israel which was ripe for judgment: *"The end is come upon my people...I will not again pass by them [lit. spare them] any more"* (v. 2b). He pledges to "never forget" their evil deeds (v. 7). The judgment would be cause for great mourning (8:8-11). Worst of all, God's word would be withdrawn: "*I will send a famine...of hearing the words of the Lord: and they shall wander from sea to sea, and from the north even to the east, they shall run to and fro to seek the word of the Lord, and shall not find it*" (8:11-12). Perhaps there is no sorer judgment this side of the loneliness of hell than to be cut off from every Divine word of communication.

The fifth and final vision is of the Lord standing upon the altar (9:1ff). It is the most disconcerting of all. The Lord on the altar delivers the devastating message that judgment was not only imminent, but inescapable. There would be no place to hide (v. 2-4). Israel would be judged like the pagan nations, for there was no ethical difference between them, so far as the Lord was concerned (v. 7). He would judge them utterly, sifting them like grain in a sieve (vs. 8-9). Though they convinced themselves that they had gotten away with their sin, every sinful deed would be judged (v. 10).

Hope for the Future

Amos ends with a promise of restoration (9:11-15). Interestingly, the promise is framed in terms of the Davidic covenant, not in terms of the political structures that presently existed, i.e. Northern vs. Southern kingdoms (v. 11). James quoted this passage in Acts 15:16-17, applying the prophecy to the New Testament Church. At that time, Amos records, the old waste places would be rebuilt and the people would be blessed, never to be uprooted again. The Messianic overtones of these words are indubitable.

The Last Days of Israel

Chapter 11
THE GODLY KINGS OF JUDAH
931 – 586 B.C.

The Southern kingdom of Judah continued another 133 years even after Israel's demise. Though it, too, was in a state of moral and spiritual decline, yet Judah did not fail as rapidly as its brother in the north.

To what can we attribute Judah's comparatively prolonged existence even after the fall of Samaria? Unlike Israel, Judah enjoyed periodic covenant renewals under the influence of several godly kings. Godly leaders are conspicuously absent in the history of the Northern kingdom. But the Southern kingdom profited from the leadership of several men "who did that which was right in the sight of the Lord." These godly kings instituted religious reforms and called the people back to Jehovah in repentance. Like salt retards the process of decay in food, so the influence of these godly leaders checked and delayed the progress of Judah's declension. Let's consider the five most prominent of Judah's godly kings.[1]

Asa, Seeker of God
1 Kings 15; 2 Chr. 14-16

The first of these kings that "did that which was right in the sight of the Lord" was Asa (2 Chr. 14:2). We might call him "the

---

[1] Other godly kings of Judah include Joash (2 Chr. 24), Amaziah (2 Chr. 25), & Jotham (2 Chr. 27).

God-seeker", for over and again, the idea of "seeking the Lord" surfaces in the narrative of his reign (14:4, 7, 11; 15:2, 4, 12, 15; 16:12).

The first ten years of Asa's reign were occupied with various religious reforms and social quietness (14:1). He rooted out idol worship and *"commanded Judah to seek the Lord God of their fathers and to do the law and the commandment"* (2 Chr. 14:3-4; 15:8). Asa also "built fenced cities" and strengthened the military (14:6ff). When the enemy attacked, Asa sought the Lord in prayer saying, *"Lord, it is nothing with thee to help, whether with many, or with them that have no power: help us, O Lord our God; for we rest on thee, and in thy name we go against this multitude..."* (14:11). The Lord answered his prayer by giving Judah the victory over the Ethiopians.

In the eleventh year of his reign, the prophet Azariah encouraged him saying, *"The Lord is with you while ye be with Him; and if ye seek Him, He will be found of you; but if ye forsake Him, He will forsake you"* (2 Chr. 15:1). When all Judah saw that the Lord was with Asa, they *"entered into a covenant to seek the Lord...with all their heart and with all their soul"* (15:12). It was a very festive and happy occasion and a time of genuine spiritual revival. For the next twenty years, Judah enjoyed rest (15:15). Peace from war, material prosperity, personal godliness, and commitment to the worship of Jehovah prevailed (15:16-19).

In year thirty-six of Asa's reign, however, Baasha king of Israel moved against his brother in the South. Instead of seeking the Lord, Asa relied on the Syrians for support. When the prophet Hanani reminded him that *"the eyes of the Lord run to and fro throughout the whole earth to show Himself strong on behalf of them whose heart is perfect toward Him"* and rebuked Asa, saying, *"Herein thou hast done foolishly: therefore, from henceforth thou shalt have wars"*, Asa put Hanani in prison (16:9-10).

In year thirty-nine, he stumbled yet again. Plagued by a disease in his feet (perhaps gout), Asa relied on the physicians instead of the Lord (16:12). Though Asa was a godly king and God-seeker, his latter days were sadly marked by a personal, spiritual declension. At best, then, his godly leadership marked a mere temporary reprieve from disobedience for the Southern kingdom.

Jehoshaphat, Zealous Piety
1 Kings 22:41; 2 Chr. 17-20

Jehoshaphat reigned over Judah from 873 to 848 B.C. He was contemporary with Ahab, king of Israel. Like Asa, *"the Lord was with Jehoshaphat, because he walked in the first ways of his father David, and sought not unto Baalim; but sought to the Lord God of his father"* (2 Chr. 17:3-4).

Jehoshaphat is distinguished as the king whose *"heart was lifted up in the ways of the Lord"* (17:6). He was zealous for the service of God—"lifted up" not in personal pride or ambition, but "in the ways of Jehovah".

In the third year of his reign, he implemented a program of public religious instruction in Judah (17:7-9). By restoring the practice of teaching God's word in the public domain,

Jehoshaphat cultivated a renewed attitude of reverence for God, both in Judah and in the surrounding nations who witnessed the social reform (17:10).

King Jehoshaphat also removed the groves from the land and prepared his heart to seek God (19:3). He personally mingled with the subjects of his kingdom, urging them to return to Jehovah (19:4). Further, Jehoshaphat installed a system of judges and charged them, *"Take heed what ye do: for ye judge not for man, but for the Lord, who is with you in the judgment...deal courageously, and the Lord shall be with the good"* (19:5-11). Thus he implemented ethical righteousness in the ordinary affairs of Judah.

His complete dependence on God when the Moabites and Ammonites attacked Judah is exemplary. Standing in a large public gathering, the king prayed for God's deliverance, saying, *"We have no might against this great company that cometh against us; neither know we what to do: but our eyes are upon thee"* (20:12; cf. 20:1ff). Then he turned to the people and said, *"Be not afraid nor dismayed by reason of this great multitude; for the battle is not yours, but Gods...Ye shall not need to fight in this battle: set yourselves, stand ye still, and see the salvation of the Lord with you"* (20:15, 17).

The next morning, he took the people forward and said, *"Believe in the Lord your God, so shall ye be established; believe his prophets, so shall ye prosper"* and the whole army had a worship service right then and there (20:20-21). As they began to praise the Lord, a remarkable thing happened. Men of Seir, greedy for the spoils, sprang from hiding and ambushed the army of

Moab/Ammon. The army panicked and began to slaughter one another. Jehoshaphat and the people of Judah were three days gathering the spoils. On the fourth day, they "blessed the Lord" in the valley of Berachah ("blessing") and returned in a joyful parade to Jerusalem where another worship service was held in the house of the Lord (20:22-30).

The sole blemish on his pious career was the alliance Jehoshaphat made with wicked king Ahab. A marriage between his son and Ahab's daughter established an almost fatal union between the two kings. Had it not been for the merciful and providential intervention of God, Jehoshaphat would have been killed in one of Ahab's military campaigns (2 Chr. 18). The words of the prophet to Jehoshaphat upon his return to Jerusalem should give every believer pause before he allies himself to the world: *"Shouldest thou help the ungodly, and love them that hate the Lord? Therefore is wrath upon thee from before the Lord"* (19:2; cf. 1 Cor. 15:33; Ps. 1:1).

Beside this unholy alliance, Jehoshaphat stands as one of the most illustrious of Judah's kings. He was a truly "theocratic king", recognizing that his role as king was to assist his subjects to live in subjection to the nation's true King, the Lord of hosts. Jehoshaphat's greatness was the product of his personal godliness. He was a pious, spiritually-minded man, and God honored his devotion by bringing joyful revival to the entire kingdom.

Uzziah, Helped by Jehovah
2 Kings 15:1; 2 Chr. 26

Uzziah, also called Azariah (2 Kings 15:1), reigned from 787-735 B.C. His 52 years on the throne of Judah were the longest of any king. Though he was only 16 years old when he began to reign, Uzziah's career was marked by godliness and military reform.

He ruled over Judah at the same time that Jeroboam II reigned as king of Israel. Hosea and Amos, prophets to the Northern kingdom, and Isaiah, prophet to Judah, served during Uzziah's lengthy tenure as king of Judah.

Only two main details are recorded of him. The Chronicler mentions, first, the military campaigns and extensive defensive measures he took to fortify Judah against enemy invasion (2 Chr. 26:6-15), and secondly, the sin for which God struck him with leprosy (2 Chr. 26:16-21).

His name Azariah literally means "Jehovah helps", and he is distinguished by the fact that God helped him. Twice in 2 Chronicles 26, the writer indicates that he was "marvelously helped" by God and that his "name spread far abroad" (vs. 7, 15). God did help and strengthen him, "but when he was strong", Uzziah was lifted up in pride (2 Chr. 26:16). He overstepped the bounds of his God-given authority and sinned presumptuously. This act proved his destruction.

His sin was the usurpation of the office of the priesthood. Acting upon his authority as king, Uzziah presumed to burn incense in the place of the priest. When the priests challenged him saying, *"It appertaineth not unto thee, Uzziah, to burn incense unto the Lord, but to the priests the sons of Aaron...for thou hast trespassed"* (2 Chr. 26:18), the king became angry. At that moment, the Lord struck Uzziah with leprosy. He spent his last days quarantined in a leper colony.

How sad it was for such a godly king to die in relative disgrace! But even though Uzziah's long career ended in dishonor, Judah's real King, Jehovah, still reigned in holiness and glory. Isaiah's call to the ministry occurred the same year Uzziah died. He describes the encouraging scene as follows: *"In the year that king Uzziah died, I saw also the Lord, sitting upon a throne, high and lifted up, and his train filled the temple"* (Is. 6:1ff). Yes, Uzziah was a godly representative of Jehovah, but he was yet a man. Judah's hopes must rest in the true theocratic King, the thrice-holy Lord of hosts (Is. 6:3, 5).

Hezekiah, Religious Reformer
2 Kings 18-20; 2 Chr. 29-32

Hezekiah, the twelfth king of Judah, reigned from 729-700 B.C. He was, according to 2 Kings 18:5, the godliest and most impressive of Judah's kings—a man distinguished for his unique faithfulness: *"He trusted in the Lord God of Israel, so that after him was none like him among all the kings of Judah, nor any that were before him, for he clave to the Lord, and departed not from following Him, but kept His commandments."*

In the very first month of his reign, Hezekiah entered into a covenant with the Lord to repair the house of God and reopen the doors for public worship (2 Chr. 29:3-11). God's house had been sadly neglected during the reign of Ahaz. The project was completed in a mere eight days (29:17). Obviously, Hezekiah knew that religious reform and the rediscovery of worship is basic and fundamental to reform in society. A jubilant worship service on a grand scale followed the restoration project (29:20-36), which is even more remarkable in light of the fact that it was spontaneous and unplanned (29:36b).

In the second month of his reign, Hezekiah restored the Passover observance, *"for they had not done it of a long time in such sort as it was written"* (30:5b). He sent posts with letters throughout not only his own kingdom of Judah, but also the Northern kingdom of Israel, saying, *"Turn again unto the Lord God of Abraham, Isaac, and Israel, and he will return to the remnant of you...and be not like your fathers, and like your brethren, which trespassed against the Lord God...who therefore gave them up to desolation as ye see"* (30:6-9). As the messengers passed from city to city in Israel, they were laughed to scorn. A small minority in Israel, however, humbly obeyed Hezekiah's call to repentance. In contrast to the small success of this campaign in Israel, almost the entire Southern kingdom, responded to the word of the king with "one heart" and a very great congregation assembled in Jerusalem (30:10-13).

This one week convocation carried over for another entire week of teaching God's word and making confession to the Lord God of their fathers. There had not been such great joy in Jerusalem since the days of Solomon (30:21-27).

The result of these two weeks of rededication to Jehovah was a renewed commitment to worship God exclusively. The people went from city to city purging the entire land of every vestige of idolatry (30:1). Hezekiah himself destroyed Moses' brazen serpent, for the people had made it a superstitious relic of veneration (2 Kings 18:4).

Hezekiah continued his religious reformation by restoring the practice of giving. The priests and Levites had no source of livelihood beside the gifts of the people. Hezekiah commanded the people in Jerusalem to give the priests their portion "that they might be encouraged in the law of the Lord" (31:4). The people responded zealously, bringing corn, wine, oil, and fruit in such abundance that Hezekiah had to prepare special storehouses in the house of the Lord for the heaps of provision (31:5-11). Chapter 31 closes with the editorial comment, *"And in every work that he began in the service of the house of God, and in the law, and in the commandments, to seek his God, he did it with all his heart, and prospered"*.

Hezekiah began his reign just six years before the fall of the Northern kingdom to Assyria (2 Kings 18:9-12). During those six years of reformation and revival in Judah, Israel was gradually disintegrating. Eight years after the fall of Samaria, Sennacherib, king of Assyria, attempted to complete his campaign against the Jews. He began an expedition to conquer Judah as he had conquered Israel (2 Kings 18:13), and was successful in besieging several outlying cities.

Hezekiah feared that an Assyrian invasion of Jerusalem was imminent, and took great pangs to reroute the water supplies into Jerusalem as a preventative measure against a potential siege (2 Chr. 32:3-5). He spoke comforting words to the people saying, *"Be strong and courageous, be not afraid nor dismayed for the king of Assyria, nor for all the multitude that is with him: for there be more with us than with him: with him is an arm of flesh, but with us is the Lord our God to help us, and to fight our battles"* (2 Chr. 32:7-8). These words stabilized the people against fear.

Hezekiah was not himself, however, immune to fear. When the news first came that Sennacherib had taken the fenced cities, Hezekiah tried to conciliate him with the message, "I have offended; return from me," and whatever tax burden you impose upon me I will bear (2 Kings 18:14). Then Hezekiah took all the silver and gold from the house of the Lord and the treasures from his own house and gave it to the king of Assyria (18:15-16).

But Sennacherib was not distracted. He sent his deputy, Rabshakeh, with a large army, to Jerusalem. Rabshakeh sought to intimidate the people to surrender: *"What confidence is this wherein thou trustest?...But if ye say unto me, We trust in the Lord our God: is not that he, whose high places and whose altars Hezekiah hath taken away, and hath said to Judah and Jerusalem, Ye shall worship before this altar in Jerusalem?...Let not Hezekiah deceive you: for he shall not be able to deliver you out of my hand: neither let Hezekiah make you trust in the Lord, saying, The Lord will surely deliver us...Hath any of the gods of the nations delivered at all his land out of the hand of the king of Assyria?"* (2 Kings 18:17-35).

When Hezekiah received the report, he went into the house of the Lord and prayed. Isaiah the prophet sent the message back to the king, *"Thus saith the Lord, Be not afraid of the words which thou hast heard, with which the servants of the king of Assyria have blasphemed me"* (2 Kings 19:6). Rabshakeh later sent a letter to king Hezekiah, containing the same taunts and challenges. As soon as it was in hand, Hezekiah went to the house of the Lord "and spread it before the Lord", praying for God's deliverance (29:8-19).

God answered the kings prayer with a message through Isaiah, *"Thus saith the Lord concerning the king of Assyria, He shall not come into this city, nor shoot an arrow there...for I will defend this city, to save it, for mine own sake, and for my servant David's sake"* (19:20-34). That very night, the angel of the Lord slew 185,000 Assyrian soldiers as they bivouacked (19:35). Sennacherib returned to Ninevah, and shortly thereafter, was killed by his own sons as he worshipped in the house of his god Nisroc (19:37; cf. 2 Chr. 32:20-24).

During this pressure-packed episode, Hezekiah became gravely ill. When the prophet brought him the message that he would die, the king prayed for mercy (2 Kings 20; 2 Chr. 32:24-26; Is. 36-38). God answered his prayer, adding fifteen years to his life, and rolled the sun backward ten degrees on the sun-dial as a sign of his recovery.

In his prosperity, however, Hezekiah was lifted up in pride (2 Chr. 32:25-26). The Lord withdrew from him to test him (32:31). During this season, Hezekiah unwisely displayed all of the treasures and sacred furniture of the house of God to ambassadors from Babylon. Isaiah brought the message of coming judgment: *"Hear the word of the Lord. Behold the days come, that all that is in thy house...shall be carried into Babylon: nothing shall be left"* (2 Kings 20:16ff). Hezekiah responded, *"At least there will be peace and truth in my days"*.

Like the other kings of Judah, Hezekiah was just a man; nevertheless, he was unique in terms of his faithfulness to Jehovah and the extent of the revival in his day. He *"cleaved unto the Lord, and departed not from following him, but kept his commandments, which the Lord commanded Moses. And the Lord was with him"* (2 Kings 18:6).

The gains realized under Hezekiah's reign were lost during the tenure of his infamous son and successor, king Manasseh. Manasseh was, without a doubt, the most ungodly of Judah's kings. The fifty-five years that he sat on the throne were marked by unconscionable corruption.

Manasseh restored the "high places", promoted the worship of Baal, Asherah, and the practice of astrology, and placed altars to the host of heaven in the inner and outer courts of the Temple (2 Kings 21:3-5). He openly practiced the occult religions and participated in the worship of Molech together with its abominable rite of human sacrifice (2 Kings 21:6; cf. 23:10).

Further, he shed much *"innocent blood...till he had filled Jerusalem from one end to another"* (21:16). Under Manasseh's reign, the prophet Isaiah was sawn asunder as he took refuge in a cedar-tree (cf. Heb. 11:37). Josephus reports that Manasseh executed some of the righteous in Jerusalem every day.

Indeed, it was a time of such extreme moral degradation that God charged Manasseh with being more vile than the Amorites who once inhabited the land (21:9-10). The magnitude of his sins made severe judgment inescapable: *"Behold, I am bringing such evil upon Jerusalem and Judah, that whosoever heareth of it, both his ears shall tingle...And I will forsake the remnant of mine inheritance, and deliver them into the hand of their enemies...because they have done that which was evil in my sight..."* (21:12-15).

Two years after Manasseh's death, his grandson, Josiah, was inaugurated as king of Judah. He would be the last of Judah's godly kings before the promised exile to Babylon.

Josiah, Last of the Reformers
2 Kings 22-23; 2 Chr. 34-35

Josiah took the throne in 640 B.C., at a mere eight years of age. He reigned for approximately 31 years, until 609 B.C. Jeremiah was called by God to the prophetic office during Josiah's reign. The prophets Zephaniah and Nahum were also contemporary with Josiah.

In the eighth year of his reign—when Josiah was sixteen years old—he *"began to seek after the God of David his father"* (2

Chr. 34:3). In the twelfth year (at age 20), he set out to reform the nation of the gross departures of Manasseh's reign (22:3).

Josiah's reformation began with a plan to repair the Temple (22:4-6). In the course of the temple repairs, Hilkiah the high priest *"found the book of the law in the house of the Lord"* (22:8). This rediscovery of God's Law proved to be the catalyst for significant national reform.

How telling is this scene! God's word had slid into obscurity and disuse during the previous generation. When the word of God is forgotten—whether in the life of an individual or a society of people—moral and spiritual conditions will inevitably decline. The rediscovery of that word often proves to be the first step in revival and renewal.

Why was God's law lost in the temple—the very place it should have been prominent? Deuteronomy 31:25-26 directed that the Book of the Law should be deposited in the innermost sanctuary of the Tabernacle or Temple. It was the place of safe-keeping until the next occasion for its use in Divine worship. The discovery of this book and the scribe's apparent unfamiliarity with its significance on this occasion, however, bespeak the sad state to which the true worship of Jehovah had sunk during the past 50+ years (22:10).

When the book was read to Josiah, the king was literally stunned. He responded in a shocking display of humble penitence, tearing his garment (22:11). He immediately made request for an explanation of this unexpected message. The prophetess Huldah returned the alarming news that judgment was coming, though Josiah, *"because [his] heart was tender"*, would not see it during his lifetime (2 Kings 22:14-20).

Motivated by a new awareness of the will of God and renewed zeal for his glory, Josiah set out on a program of national reformation. His reforms began with a campaign to abolish idolatry (2 Chr. 34:4-7). Second Kings 23:4-20 describes in vivid detail the radical steps he took to purge the land of false gods. He first removed all the symbols of idolatry from the Temple and burned the various vessels that were used in the worship of Baal (23:4). He also deposed the non-Levites who were functioning in the office of priest (23:5). He took the image of Asherah that had been erected in the house of the Lord and ground it to powder (23:6). Then he took the legitimate priests who had participated in grove worship and declared them unfit for further service (23:8). He extended his campaign into Israel, cleansing the entire land of every last vestige of idolatry (23:19-20).

Next, Josiah organized a solemn observance of the Passover (23:21). Second Chronicles 35 describes this memorable occasion —a Passover celebration such as the nation had not experienced since the days of Samuel (2 Chr. 35:18).

Indeed, Josiah was a godly leader. The writer of Kings characterizes his personal piety in the most glowing of terms: *"Like unto him there was no king before him, that turned to the Lord with all his heart, and with all his soul, and with all his might, according to all the law of Moses; neither after him arose there any like him"* (2 Kings 23:25). The Chronicler adds another impressive stroke to his godly portrait. In his summary of the influence Josiah had on the people he ruled, the Chronicler says: "*And all his days, they departed not from following the Lord, the God of their fathers*" (2 Chr. 34:33b).

But, in spite of his commitment to godliness, God did not withdraw his threat of judgment: "*Notwithstanding the Lord turned not from the fierceness of his great wrath, wherewith his anger was kindled against Judah, because of all the provocations that Manasseh had provoked him withal*" (2 Kings 23:26). Why? Why did not Josiah's reforms avert Divine judgment?

The implication is that Josiah's personal repentance and commitment to Jehovah was genuine, but the nation's was superficial. Yes, they followed his lead and "departed not from following the Lord" all Josiah's days, but the nation itself was not genuinely broken for its sin. Josiah's reforms, therefore, exercised a temporary benefit on the nation, but produced no lasting benefit. In a matter of four short years after his death, Nebuchadnezzar would make his first trip to deport the people of Judah to Babylon. Within a short twenty-three years, Jerusalem would be leveled to the ground and Judah, led into captivity.

Chapter 12
JUDAH'S PRE-EXILIC PROPHETS

Though previous passages have hinted at the Messianic character of God's plan, it is in the prophecy of *Isaiah* that this dominant plot of the Old Testament, for the first time, clearly emerges.

Isaiah

Isaiah has been termed "the evangelical [or gospel] prophet" because his book teaches that *God's ideal of a theocratic kingdom would ultimately be realized through the coming and career of the Messiah.*

Earthly kings, established to function as Jehovah's servants or agents of the theocracy, had failed to develop a society that lived consistently under Divine authority, dedicated to God's glory. The Messianic King, however, "would not fail, neither be discouraged" in his quest to "set judgment in the earth" (Is. 42:4). "Immanuel" would come supernaturally to establish the kingdom of God (Is. 7:14; 9:6). Jehovah's *special* "Servant" would win the victory in the war against sin (Is. 40:1ff). He would reign in righteousness and beauty (Is. 32:1; 33:17; 9:7) as the King, under whose sovereign sway even the Gentiles would take refuge (Is. 2:2; 11:10; 42:1,6-7; 49:6; 56:6-7; 60:3).

This Messianic emphasis in Isaiah's message is developed within the context of historical narrative. Isaiah paints the historical portrait of Judah's demise as the dark background against which the brilliant images of Messianic promise and hope shine forth. The historical city of Jerusalem would be destroyed (Is. 64:10-11), but Messiah would restore and revive Zion as "the city of our solemnities, a quiet habitation" (Is. 33:20-22; 62:1-2). Isaiah loved the old city of Jerusalem, but looked ahead hopefully to the "new" Jerusalem or Messianic kingdom as the eschatological hope of the ages.

The Life and Times of Isaiah

Isaiah was called to be God's prophetic spokesman to Judah in approximately 740 B.C., the year that king Uzziah died (Is. 6:1-8). His career continued through the reigns of Jotham, Ahaz and Hezekiah, concluding in approximately 700 B.C. (Is. 1:1).

He lived, therefore, to see the fall of Israel (722 B.C.) and the subsequent campaign of Sennacherib, king of Assyria, against Judah. The southern kingdom would, in fact, continue another 114 years after Isaiah's death. His prophecy, however, announces the certainty of Judah's impending demise.

Isaiah functioned as counselor to king Hezekiah. It was Isaiah who brought the message that God would deliver Jerusalem from the Assyrian invasion (Is. 36-37), that Hezekiah's life would be extended after his illness (Is. 38:1-22), and that Judah would eventually be carried away to Babylon (Is. 39:6). He was a faithful spokesman for God, whether his oracle was one of judgment or hope.

Structure of *Isaiah*

The book of *Isaiah* has been called "the little Bible". Like the sixty-six books of the Bible, Isaiah contains sixty-six chapters. The first thirty-nine chapters, like the thirty-nine books of the Old Testament, are primarily concerned to expose sin. The tone dramatically changes from confrontation to comfort, however, beginning with chapter 40, just as the note of gospel hope begins with the fortieth book of the Bible, i.e. Matthew.

The book may be generally outlined as follows:

I.	The Apostasy of, Coming Judgment on, and Hope of Judah (Is. 1-12)
II.	God's Judgment on the Nations (Is. 13-23)
III.	The Day of the Lord (Is. 24-27)
IV.	Oracles of Judgment/Hope to God's People (Is. 28-35)
V.	Hezekiah's History (Is. 36-39)
VI.	Jehovah's Righteous Servant (Is. 40-53)
VII.	The Future of the Restored Kingdom (Is. 55-66)

Themes of *Isaiah*

Three primary themes (or motifs) dominate Isaiah's message: the "Day of the Lord" or judgment motif; the "Servant" or deliverance motif; and the "Restoration" or hope motif. Let's consider them in that sequence.

The Day of the Lord. The vision of the holiness of God on the occasion of Isaiah's prophetic commission (Is. 6:3) set the tone for his basic message. This thrice-holy God would hold both the nations and His covenant people accountable for their sins. His judgments were certain. Every disobedience to His holy Law would receive a just recompense of reward.

Isaiah accuses Judah of pervasive apostasy: *"The whole head is sick, and the whole heart faint. From the sole of the foot even unto the head there is no soundness in it; but wounds, and bruises, and putrifying sores..."* (1:5b-6). Judah was proud and idolatrous (2:5-22), brazen and ostentatious (3:8-9, 16ff), self-willed and hypocritical (4:1), and spiritually barren and ignorant (5:1-7, 11-16). Their values were topsy-turvy (5:20; cf. 29:16). They were proud, immoral, and unjust (5:21-23); therefore, God's anger was kindled against His people (5:24-25).

The nations or kingdoms of this world are also under Divine censure. Isaiah has a message of impending judgment for Babylon, Assyria, Philistia, Moab, Damascus, Ethiopia, Egypt, Edom, Arabia, and Tyre (chs. 13-23). "The day of the Lord is coming", says the prophet. *"It shall come to pass in that day, that the Lord shall punish the host of the high ones that are on high, and the kings of the earth upon the earth. And they shall be gathered together as prisoners are gathered in the pit, and shall be shut up in the prison, and after many days shall they be visited"* (24:21-22).

How should we explain the fact that portions of this description of the coming "day of the Lord" seem to point to the final judgment at the second coming of Christ (cf. 24:17-20; 26:19)? This is an example of "prophetic foreshortening" in which the Holy Spirit blends in the same context the immediate historical application with the more long-term, Messianic application. The apocalyptic language of Isaiah 24-27 has a primary application to the judgments that were coming on Judah and the nations of that day (34:1ff). But the "day of the Lord" described in this passage has an ultimate application to the final "day of judgment" at the Redeemer's return.

What form would the "day of the Lord" judgments take so far as Judah was concerned? Judah would be taken to Babylon (39:6). God would distress Jerusalem with heaviness and sorrow (29:2ff). He would give them *"the bread of adversity and the water of affliction"* (30:20a). In His anger with Judah, the Lord would *"pollute [His] inheritance and give them into [the Chaldeans'] hand"* (47:6).

Jehovah's Righteous Servant. In addition to the promised threat of judgment, *Isaiah* develops a "deliverance" motif. Deliverance from Babylon is the theme of chapters 40 through 48. These chapters reveal that God would raise up His special "Servant" to do His bidding and bring deliverance to His people.

Historically, that man was the Medo-Persian named Cyrus. The fact that the Lord calls this leader by name at least 150 years before Cyrus was born and that the predictive prophecies of his career were so meticulously fulfilled is an amazing testimony to the Divine inspiration of the Bible (Is. 44:28; 45:1). Isaiah predicts that Cyrus would come as a mighty conqueror to destroy Babylon, rescue the captives of Israel, and issue the edict to restore Jerusalem and the Temple. Though he did not know the Lord (Is. 45:4-5), Cyrus' would be used by God to accomplish His greater purposes (Is. 45:6; 46:9-11).

Prophetically, the identity of Jehovah's "Servant" points forward 700 years to the Messiah. The four "Servant Songs" of Isaiah comprise a prophetic portrait of the One who would come to accomplish that which no other person could accomplish. The first of these Songs, Isaiah 42, describes the meek and humble character of God's Servant. The second, Isaiah 49, speaks of the commission of God's Servant "to bring Jacob again to him" (v. 5). The third, Isaiah 50, describes the obedience of God's Servant to the task He would be given. The fourth and final Song, Isaiah 52:13 – 53:12, concerns the sufferings of God's righteous Servant as the means by which deliverance would be accomplished.

This "Servant" is none other than the Messianic King whom New Testament believers know as the Lord Jesus Christ. The New Testament contains eighty-five direct quotes from Isaiah 53, showing the fulfillment of each detailed prophecy in the sufferings and death of Jesus Christ. He is the One through whom God would "comfort" His people (Is. 40:1ff), and "magnify the law and make it honorable" (Is. 42:21). He is the "Branch" who will judge the poor with righteousness (Is. 11:1-5), the "Redeemer who shall come to Zion" (59:20), the Child of Israel's hopes whose name would be called, "Wonderful, Counselor, the Mighty God, the Everlasting Father, the Prince of Peace" (Is. 9:6).

The Restored Kingdom. The third dominant theme of *Isaiah* is the hope of restoration. This "Servant" of Jehovah would not only deliver God's covenant people from bondage, but He would also set up a glorious, theocratic kingdom.

Isaiah is replete with the language of spiritual renewal (Is. 2:1-4; 4:2-6; 12:1-6; 25:6-9; 26:1-4; 30:19-26; 32:1-4, 13-20; 33:17-22; 35:1-10; 40:9-11; 42:16; 43:19-21; 44:2-5; 45:22-25; etc.). Though deliverance from such a formidable captor would seem impossible, and the restoration of Jerusalem more impossible still, the Lord would *"comfort His people and have mercy upon His afflicted"* (Is. 49:12-16, 24-26).

He would call them to "awake" from spiritual slumber, don their "beautiful garments" and rejoice in His redemption (Is. 52:1-10). Though He forsook them for a small moment, He would gather them with great mercies and everlasting kindness (Is. 54:7-8). The future glory of Zion would be inaugurated with the advent of the Messiah and even Gentiles would come to that light (Is. 60:1-5). Even former persecutors would be converted to the truth and worship with the people of God (Is. 60:14). No more would His people be termed "Forsaken" or "Desolate", but "Delightful" and "Married" (Is. 62:2-4).

This beautiful language must be interpreted in terms of the perfect Kingdom that Messiah would inaugurate. No wonder the prophet Isaiah is called "the gospel prophet!"

Jonah & Nahum

Unlike God's call to prophesy to His covenant people, some of the prophets before the exile were commissioned to carry a message of judgment to the surrounding nations. Among these prophets were Jonah, and Nahum.[1] While Isaiah and Jeremiah were sent to Israel and Judah, these prophets spoke to nations outside the covenant community. Jonah and Nahum brought God's message to Ninevah, the capital of the Assyrian empire.

God of the Nations

The fact that these nations were largely pagan and that the citizens worshipped idol gods is extremely significant. Why would the God of the Hebrew patriarchs send his prophets to nations that did not even acknowledge Him? On what basis could Jonah or Nahum speak authoritatively to people who worshipped Baal, Astarte, Chemosh, or Molech? Their right to address these pagan societies was grounded in the fact that Jehovah is "the God of the nations" (Ps. 22:28).

The structure of the book of Genesis, as we have previously noted, reveals that the God who established a special covenant with Israel is the very same God that created the world. Yes, it is true that the Old Testament is the story of God's relationship to Israel, but that story does not begin until Genesis 12. The previous eleven chapters set the broader stage of "world history" on which the more specific scenes of "sacred history" are developed.

Before the Spirit of God reveals Him as the God of the Hebrews, in other words, He reveals Him as the God of all nations. Though these nations have not received God's

---

[1] Obadiah's prophecy is also an example of a commission to call a non-Israelite nation to an account before God. He delivered his prophecy to the nation of Edom. The precise era of Obadiah's prophetic career, however, is unknown.

covenant blessing or special revelation, they have received God's creation blessings (e. g. natural life, breath, food, water, etc. – Mt. 5:45) and the general revelation of His moral law, both in nature and in the conscience; therefore, they are accountable to their Creator for every violation of His law (cf. Rom. 1:18ff), for *"He is kind unto the unthankful and to the evil"* (Lk. 6:35b; cf. Ps. 145:9, 14-17).

It was by virtue of this truth that Paul approached the heathen philosophers with their pantheon of false gods at Mars Hill, saying, *"God that made the world and all things therein, seeing he is Lord of heaven and earth, dwelleth not in temples made with men's hands, neither is worshiped with men's hands, as though he needed anything, seeing he giveth to all life and breath and all things... for in Him, we live, and move, and have our being..."* (Acts 17:24-28). He proceeded to indict the Athenians for the sin of idolatry and to announce that God will "judge the world in righteousness" on His appointed day (v. 31).

Is Paul justified to intrude into this polytheistic culture with his monotheistic message? Did he really have any reason for concern when he saw the city wholly given to idolatry (v. 16)? Wouldn't it be more appropriate to adopt a "to-each-his-own" mindset and exercise pluralistic tolerance? Instead, he patently dismisses the entire pantheon as irrelevant, and shines the spotlight of his message on the one and only God over the whole earth—the God to whom they must render account. He, only, is the true and living God.

The inclusion of the books of Jonah and Nahum in the canon of Old Testament Scripture serves to remind us of the truth that the God of Israel is also the God of all nations. Though all do not yet acknowledge Him, yet all men are, nonetheless, accountable to Him. Our God, in other words, is a global God! Every other god is a sheer fabrication of carnal imagination (cf. 1 Cor. 8:6).

Both of these men prophesied God's word to the ancient city of Ninevah, the capital of Assyria. Jonah prophesied in *circa* 750 B.C.; Nahum, approximately one hundred years later in 650 B. C. Both books are concerned with one message – the coming judgment on Ninevah.

The sin of man, even in foreign lands, is an offense to God, Creator of all mankind, and calls for judgment. The prophetic note of Jonah and Nahum highlights the principle of man's universal accountability to God. The two books portray a God who is both sovereign over the nations and holy in His dealings with them.

The Goodness and Severity of God

But they also describe a God who is good and longsuffering (Nah. 1:3, 7). In His mercy, God postponed the destruction of Ninevah for over one hundred years when they responded penitently to Jonah's preaching. The book of Jonah is the record of the prophet's personal struggle with the fact of God's goodness to these enemies of Israel.

The Assyrian Empire and its capital city of Ninevah was dominant during the reigns of Jeroboam II and Hezekiah, the kings of Israel and Judah respectively. It was the Assyrians who conquered Israel in 722 B.C., then threatened to invade Judah during the reign of Hezekiah.

God's call to Jonah to go to Ninevah with a message of impending judgment, therefore, was an especially unpalatable task. Jonah did not like the Assyrians—with good reason. Their savage cruelty to enemy armies was legendary. John MacArthur writes:

> "Assyrian rulers of this era were ruthless men who boasted of their own brutalities. They liked to torture their victims with slow, cruel means of death, and they were known for building monuments to their conquests out of mutilated human remains."[2]

Ninevah, itself, had been founded by Nimrod (Gen. 10:8-12) and was a citadel of false religion. It is not surprising, then, that Jonah rebelled against God's call. He wanted to see God's judgment satisfied on these wicked sinners. If he obeyed God and preached against their sins, they might repent and be spared from judgment. Jonah's reason for fleeing God's commission to him is stated in 4:2: *"I knew that thou art a gracious God, and merciful, slow to anger, and of great kindness, and repentest thee of the evil."*

Just as he had expected, the city did repent *en masse*. Over 500,000 people "believed God", clothed themselves in sackcloth

---

[2] *The Love of God*, p. 59.

and repented of their evil ways (3:5-10). It was the most extensive moral reformation in history.

But Jonah was angry. He wanted to see God's judgment on these wicked sinners. As his story concludes, God gives Jonah a powerful lesson about Divine compassion, goodness, and mercy. He rebuked Jonah's lack of love for the Ninevites. He reminded him that Ninevah was filled with many "innocents", i.e. more than 120,000 people who *do not know their right hand from their left hand* – 4:11). He showed him the hypocrisy of exercising greater concern over a gourd vine than he did over the little children of Ninevah.

Perhaps, as some Bible students have observed, the book of Jonah also serves as a precursor for God's program to bring the Gentiles (heathen nations) into the fellowship of gospel blessings. Peter's reaction to the commission to preach to the Gentile Cornelius is not unlike Jonah's reluctance to preach to the men of Ninevah (see Acts 10). Further, Jesus himself referred to this historical event to denounce Israel's unbelief (Mt. 12:38-41). If such is indeed a legitimate explanation of the Divine intent of the book, Jonah's story aims to correct Israel's delusion that she alone would enjoy the privileges of Divine worship and favor.

Nahum & God's Inflexible Justice

More than one hundred years later, however, God sent another prophet to Ninevah, a city that was more wicked and ruthless than ever. His name was Nahum and he prophesied the final doom of that infamous city.

Nahum teaches that the God whose goodness and longsuffering are so evident in *Jonah* is also uncompromising and relentless in His wrath toward rebellion and wickedness. Throughout the prophecy, Jehovah is depicted as a God of inflexible justice.

Nahum's prophecy was probably spoken during the reign of godly king Hezekiah. The first chapter is a hymn of triumph, expressing the impending fall of the city that had perpetrated such persecution on the people of God. Chapter 2 describes the downfall of Ninevah, and chapter 3, the reasons for God's judgment on this city.

This prophecy of God's judgment on Assyria was partially fulfilled when the angel of the Lord slew 185,000 Assyrian soldiers in one night (2 Kings 19:35-37). The nation never recovered from this blow. Later, Ninevah and the Assyrians were assimilated into the Babylonian Empire. The final destruction of Ninevah came when the city was overwhelmed by the armies of the Medes and leveled forever. Even today, the city is in ruins.

The fate of Ninevah is a testimony to God's covenant faithfulness to His people: "*He that toucheth you toucheth the apple of His eye*" (Zech. 2:8). Though Assyria was the "rod of His anger" to discipline His people (Is. 10:5), they themselves would suffer Jehovah's punitive wrath for their proud impenitence (Is. 10:12).

Micah

The prophet Micah, a contemporary of Isaiah, ministered during the reigns of Jotham, Ahaz, and Hezekiah, kings of Judah (Mic. 1:1). The scope of his prophetic career stretched from approximately 735 to 700 B.C., embracing the fall of the Northern Kingdom in 722 B.C.

Similarities and Differences

Since Micah ministered during the same time period as Isaiah and Amos, it is not unusual that the language of their respective prophecies parallel (cf. Mic. 4:1ff and Is. 2:1ff; Mic. 2:1-2 and Amos 2:6-7). Unlike Isaiah, however, who was of noble birth and circulated among the aristocracy, Micah came from a rural background, the village of Moresheth-gath in the hill country of Judah. He was a "country preacher", like Amos, while Isaiah lived and ministered in the big city of Jerusalem. Micah was, consequently, familiar with the poor of Judah. The list of small towns in 1:10-15 and the effect that the coming judgment would have on them bespeaks his humble origins.

Micah differed from the prophets who had preceded him in another, more striking, way: *his message of impending judgment was heeded*. As a result of his preaching, Judah repented and Jerusalem was spared. Judgment was postponed for one hundred years.

A century after Micah, Jeremiah also prophesied the destruction of Jerusalem. When the authorities demanded his death for treason, Jeremiah appealed to the fact that the people of Judah had responded penitently to Micah's similar message one hundred years earlier:

> Micah the Morasthite prophesied in the days of Hezekiah, king of Judah, and spake to all the people of Judah, saying, *Thus saith the Lord of hosts; Zion shall be plowed like a field, and Jerusalem shall become heaps, and the mountain of the house as the high places of a forest.* Did Hezekiah king of Judah and all Judah put him at all to death? Did he not fear the Lord, and besought the Lord, and the Lord repented him of the evil which he had pronounced against them? (Jer. 26:18-19).

Jeremiah appeals for his life against the charge that his prediction of coming judgment constitutes treason by reminding the people that Micah also prophesied the destruction of Judah. Instead of wanting to kill him, the people repented and the disaster was delayed. A century after Micah, the memory of his successful ministry was used by God to spare Jeremiah's life.

Analysis of Micah's Prophecy

The book of Micah consists of three main addresses, each introduced by the word "hear" (1:2; 3:1; 6:1). The first section, chapters 1 and 2, is a pronouncement of judgment on Israel and Judah. The second division, chapters 3 through 5, is a denunciation of the ruling classes for perverting justice. The third address, chapters 6 and 7, is a description of Jehovah's lawsuit, i.e legal case, against his people.

In each prophetic address, however, Micah strikes the note of hope and restoration. At the end of section one, deliverance is promised to the remnant (2:12-13). The bulk of section two announces the future hope of the Messianic kingdom (chs. 4-5). The book concludes with an oracle of comfort grounded in God's pardoning grace (7:8-20).

This two-fold emphasis is evident in the various prophecies of the book. Micah predicts the fall of Samaria (1:6-7), the invasion of Judah by Assyria (1:9-16), the fall of Jerusalem and destruction of the temple (3:12; 7:13), the Babylonian exile (4:10), the return of the exiles and restoration of the nation (4:1-8, 13; 7:11, 14-17), and the advent of the Messiah in Bethlehem (5:2). The outline of Micah with its emphasis on both *judgment* and *restoration*, then, looks like this:

I. Oracle of Coming Judgment (1-2)
   A. The Sins of Israel and Judah (1:2 – 2:11)
   B. Deliverance Promised to Remnant (2:12-23)
II. Oracles Concerning the Theocratic Kingdom (3-5)
   A. Failure of the Theocratic Officers (3)
   B. Promise of the Messianic Kingdom (4-5)
III. Oracles Concerning Guilt and Hope (6-7)
   A. The Lord's Case Against Israel (6)
   B. Restoration and Forgiveness (7)

The *Judgment* Motif

The prophecy of Micah begins with a poetic description of Jehovah's descent from heaven in sweeping judgment upon his people (1:2-4). In imagery designed to startle his audience, Micah describes the destabilizing effects of this Divine assault on disobedience.

The attack would commence at Samaria, i.e. the Northern kingdom of Israel (1:5-8), and would proceed to the Southern kingdom of Judah (1:9): *"Her [i.e. Samaria's] wound is incurable; for it is come unto Judah; he is come unto the gate of my people, even to Jerusalem"*. Since the sin of Samaria had spread south to Jerusalem, the judgment that befell the Northern kingdom would also touch the Southern.

Chapter one concludes with an appeal to Jerusalem to take responsibility for the smaller towns and villages around her, like a parent would assume responsibility for his/her children (v. 16). Then the prophet reveals an unthinkable prospect: *"...for they are gone into captivity* [i.e. exile] *from thee"* (v. 16b). Exile meant slavery and the cessation of Judah as a nation.

Chapter two reveals the reasons that judgment was imminent. The wealthy were exploiting the poor for financial gain (2:1-5), and false prophets opposed the truth by saying that the Spirit of the Lord does not get angry and send judgment on people (2:6-7). They mistreated other people, robbing men of their garments, women of their homes, and children of their inheritance (2:8). The only prophets they would have were those who would sedate their consciences with lies (2:10).

In chapter three, Micah blames the leaders for perverting justice (3:1, 9). How frequently is it the case that the leaders cause the people to err! The judges were corrupt (3:1-4). They justified the wicked and condemned the righteous. They were like cannibals, consuming those they were responsible to defend (v. 3). The prophets were corrupt (3:5-8). They would only minister to those who paid them. The rulers were also corrupt (3:9-12). They sought public prosperity through the most cruel and inhumane means (v. 10).

Chapters six and seven record the Lord's "controversy", i.e. lawsuit, against his people. It is a legal indictment against them for forgetting past mercies (6:3-5), for religious hypocrisy, violence, and dishonesty (6:6-7, 12). Religion was formal; idolatry was rampant; judges accepted bribes; people were promiscuous; and the rich took advantage of the poor. The social and moral chaos was such that people could not even trust their very closest relatives (7:5-6).

They were willing to do everything except what God required. He had not commanded them to offer thousands of rams, ten thousand rivers of oil, or their children as sacrifices for their sin (6:6-7): *"What doth the Lord require of thee, but to do justly, to love mercy, and to walk humbly with thy God"* (6:8).

This important verse stresses God's claims in regard to the way we treat others and our attitude toward the Lord. God requires his people to do right, to be equitable, just, and honest in their dealings with others. He also requires them to show mercy toward others. One may practice "strict justice" in his dealings with others, but we who are recipients of God's mercy must always temper our conduct toward others with gentleness, kindness and compassion. Finally, God requires a daily conduct that is characterized by humility. How can those of us who are sinners be anything but humble before Him?

The *Restoration* Motif

In the midst of this overwhelming indictment and prophecy of judgment, Micah brings a message of hope and comfort. The first section ends with the promise that the remnant would be gathered from exile and restored by "the breaker", a reference perhaps to the Messianic Deliverer (2:12-13).

Chapter four describes a future era when the kingdom of God would enjoy international dominion, glory, and peace: *"But in the last days...the mountain of the house of the Lord shall be established in the top of the mountains, and it shall be exalted above the hills; and people shall flow unto it...for the law shall go forth of Zion, and the word of the Lord from Jerusalem. And he* [i.e. Messiah] *shall judge among many people and rule strong nations afar off; and they shall beat their swords into plowshares, and their spears into pruninghooks..."* (4:1ff).

The promises of restoration that pervade chapter four are then explained in terms of the coming of the Messianic King. This very specific prophecy, spoken some 700 years before Christ, actually pinpoints the very city in which he would be born: *"But thou Bethlehem-ephratah, though thou be little among the thousands of Judah, yet out of thee shall he come forth unto me that is to be ruler in Israel..."* (5:2).

Yes, Judah would have a King who would reign forever. He would be a Shepherd-King, providing for the needs of His people (5:4). This new era of the kingdom of God under the Davidic Messiah would be a time of personal refreshing, social influence, and spiritual victory (5:7-8).

197

Chapter seven reveals the basis of their hope for restoration —the pardoning grace of God: *"Who is a God like unto thee that pardoneth iniquity, and passeth by the transgression of the remnant of his heritage...He will turn again, he will have compassion upon us; he will subdue our iniquities; and thou wilt cast all their sins into the depths of the sea"* (7:18-19). The name "Micah" means "Who is like Jehovah?" This passage answers, "No one!" Our God is incomparable in terms of his majestic holiness (Ex. 15:11) and in terms of his marvelous grace (Mic. 7:18). Otherwise, no sinner would ever have cause to hope for restoration. Since, however, He "delights in mercy [*hesed*]", there is hope for sinners.

Habakkuk

The preservation of a godly remnant in the midst of general apostasy is one of the recurring themes of the minor prophets (cf. Zeph. 3:12-13; Mal. 3:16-18). The book of Habakkuk offers an individual perspective on the kinds of challenges and questions faced by that remnant while living in a society under the judgment of God.

The fall of Ninevah and the Assyrian empire to the Babylonians, predicted by the prophet Nahum, occurred in 612 B.C. at the battle of Carchemish. Between that event and the fall of Jerusalem to the Babylonians in 586 B.C., the prophet Habakkuk ministered to the people of Judah.

These were days of unprecedented spiritual and moral decadence. The reforms under godly king Josiah just twenty-five years earlier had already faded and the people of Judah had reverted to their former sinfulness. The unprincipled Jehoiakim, son of Josiah, now sat on the throne (cf. Jer. 22:18-19). The book of Habakkuk opens with the prophet's complaint to God concerning Judah's ungodliness.

The Prophet's Perplexity (Hab. 1)

Habakkuk's name means "the wrestler." The book that bears his name is not technically a prophecy, i.e. a message God gave him to deliver to the people, but a personal journal revealing Habakkuk's own inward struggle with the circumstances of the day. As such, it offers the Bible student valuable, practical insight to pastoral questions such as, "Why does God appear to be silent; how can a good God allow evil to triumph over good; and, how can the godly live in an ungodly world without either losing heart or compromising their convictions?".

Unlike the historical narratives of Kings and the prose of the other literary prophets, the book of Habakkuk shines the spotlight on one man's personal experience as he tried to make sense of events in his day. Though he does not know it, Habakkuk is witnessing the demise of the Southern kingdom of Judah.

In chapter one, "the wrestler" grapples with two very difficult questions—"How long?" and "Why?" He is perplexed at, first, God's apparent inactivity, and second, His apparent injustice.

First, Habakkuk complains about Divine silence in the face of spiritual and moral apostasy: *"O Lord, how long shall I cry, and thou wilt not hear! Even cry out unto thee of violence, and thou wilt not save?"* (1:2). The prophet is justifiably grieved at the social oppression, exploitation of the weak, perpetual controversy, and perversion of justice that he witnessed in Judah (1:3-4). He asks, "Lord, why don't you do something?"

In 1:5, the Lord answers, "I am doing something." Though it appeared the Lord was remote and disconnected from the scene, he was, in fact, both aware of and actively involved in the situation. But instead of relieving Habakkuk's concerns, God's message only compounds the prophet's perplexity: *"Behold ye among the heathen, and regard, and wonder marvelously: for I will work a work in your days, which ye will not believe, though it be told you."* What God says next truly perplexes the prophet: *"For lo, I raise up the Chaldeans [Babylonians], that bitter and hasty nation, which shall march through the breadth of the land, to possess the dwelling places that are not theirs"* (1:6). The ruthlessness of the Babylonians is described in vivid terms in verses 7-11.

Habakkuk must now wrestle with a new question, namely, "How can a good God employ a nation even more wicked than Judah as the instrument of judgment on his covenant people?" Now, he must grapple with the problem of God's apparent injustice.

How does Habakkuk deal with these questions? First, he goes to God in prayer and reminds himself of the character of God (1:12-13). What an important practical lesson is here! When the mind is filled with questions, it is helpful to reaffirm the certainties of the Divine nature. Habakkuk finds comfort in the attributes of God—His eternity, holiness, covenant faithfulness, and omnipotence.

Secondly, Habakkuk resolves to wait for God to answer: "*I will stand upon my watch, and set me upon the tower, and will watch to see what he will say unto me…*" (2:1). He wants an explanation for apparent injustice. He is troubled by the problem of evil's apparent triumph. Habakkuk is confounded at the prospect that truth is on the scaffold, while wrong is on the throne.

The Lord's Answer (Hab. 2)

God does answer him, but somewhat vaguely: "*The vision is yet for an appointed time, but at the end it shall speak, and not lie: though it tarry, wait for it; because it will surely come, it will not tarry*" (2:3). The words mean, in essence, "You will understand it by-and-by, Habakkuk." Seldom does God explain his actions to his servants in this world, but assures them that all will be well in time.

In the meantime, he answers their struggles and perplexities by bidding them to trust him: "*The just shall live by his faith*" (2:4b). All the hard questions that burden their minds—the apparent Divine delays and the seeming Divine inconsistencies —together with all of the challenges of living a godly life in an ungodly environment are resolved when one is content to entrust them all to the One who is all-wise and all-knowing. "*The just shall live by faith.*"

God gives Habakkuk two great assurances to support his faith: (1) The Assurance of Future Glory (2:14); (2) The Assurance of Present Sovereignty (2:20). The promise that, indeed, *"the earth shall be filled with the knowledge of the glory of the Lord, as the waters cover the sea"* (2:14) served to remind the prophet of the larger picture. In the grand scheme of things, no present event or circumstance will distract God from his master plan. Habakkuk's world was certainly not "full of the knowledge of the glory of the Lord", but God's purposes will not be thwarted.

The present assurance that God is in sovereign control—that he is, indeed, on his throne—gave Habakkuk the needed basis for trusting Him. *"The Lord is in his holy temple: let all the earth keep silence before him"* (2:20). With the certainty of such a sovereign God ruling the world, the godly remnant existing in these uncertain circumstances could cope with life in this world. The just shall live by faith.

The Lord's answer includes still another feature. Not only does he say to the prophet "Trust me", he also says, "Justice will be served." Though Babylon would temporarily dominate God's people, its day of judgment would come.

Habakkuk 2:4-20 contains the pronouncement of four "woe's" (oracles of doom) on Babylon (vs. 9, 12, 15, 19) for her sins. God's message is, "Even though I will employ the ungodly Chaldeans as my instrument of chastisement on Judah, they will be held accountable for their own sins." Ultimately, the scales of justice would balance.

The Prophet's Praise (Hab. 3)

Habakkuk responds to the Lord's speech with a psalm of praise in chapter 3. He reviews Jehovah's acts in history and exults in this God of such awesome power.

The book concludes with a memorable confession of faith, and surprisingly, a note of joy: "*Although the fig tree shall not blossom, neither shall fruit be in the vines; the labor of the olive shall fail and the fields shall yield no meat; the flock shall be cut off from the fold, and there shall be no herd in the stalls: yet I will rejoice in the Lord, I will joy in the God of my salvation*" (3:17-18). The prophet admits that though every staple of life were removed, the Lord who changes not would still be the source of his joy and happiness.

How thrilling is this book! It began with a sigh and ended with a song. In chapter one, Habakkuk questioned God's justice. In chapter two, he rested in God's sovereignty. In chapter three, he rejoiced in God's salvation. He started in the lowlands, but finished on the mountain-top (3:19). He began with fear and fretting, but ended in faith.

Like Habakkuk, the godly remnant of his day and ours struggles to make sense of apparent Divine delays and dispensations of providence. We cry, "How long, O Lord?". This book reminds us that he reigns, that he will ultimately prevail, and that we can live godly lives in an ungodly world when we walk by faith and not sight.

Zephaniah

The prophet Zephaniah ministered God's word to Judah in approximately 630 B.C., during the reign of godly king Josiah (Zeph. 1:1). Like his contemporaries, Jeremiah and Habakkuk, his prophetic career was one of the last of Judah's prophets, dating some fifty-odd years before the Babylonian exile.

Zephaniah ministered early in Josiah's reign, prior to the reforms he initiated. Jerusalem was marked by a cosmopolitan atmosphere (1:18). Religious syncretism (1:5), human exploitation (1:8-9), spiritual lethargy (1:12), personal arrogance (3:2), and the profanation of Divine worship (3:4) characterized the day. Perhaps the preaching of Zephaniah exercised an influence to spur young king Josiah to initiate the religious reformation for which he was later distinguished.

In the words of Matthew Henry, the book of Zephaniah *"foretells the general destruction of Judah and Jerusalem by the Chaldeans, and sets their sins in order before them, which had provoked God to bring their ruin upon them, calls them to repentance, threatens the neighboring nations with the like destructions, and gives encouraging promises of their joyful return out of captivity in due time..."*[3] Two themes are prominent in the book: *The Day of the Lord* (1:7-10, 14-16, 18; 2:2-3; 3:8, 11, 16), and *The Idea of a Remnant* who will be protected in the day of the Lord (2:3, 7; 3:12-13, 18-20).

---

[3] *Matthew Henry's Commentary: Volume 4 (Isaiah to Malachi)*, p. 1371.

The Day of the Lord

The "day of the Lord" is an eschatological expression that speaks of *any time the Lord intrudes into human affairs, either in judgment or deliverance*. The people of Judah assumed that in their case, the "day of the Lord" would be a time of blessing. Zephaniah challenges that assumption, saying,

> That day is a day of wrath, a day of trouble and distress, a day of wasteness and desolation, a day of darkness and gloominess, a day of clouds and thick darkness, a day of the trumpet and alarm against the fenced cities, and against the high towers. (1:15-16)

"Judgment is coming," says the prophet, and it is coming soon (1:7, 14). God would indeed manifest his presence, but it would take the form of a theophanic judgment, not blessing (1:7; 3:5). The description of this "day" in chapter one is sobering.

First, the prophet indicates that it would be a judgment like *Noah's Flood* (1:2-3a). The imagery suggests total destruction. Secondly, it would be a judgment like *the plagues of Egypt* (1:4-6). The expression "I will stretch out mine hand" alludes to the book of Exodus, when God "stretched out his hand" in the judgment of the ten plagues (cf. Ex. 6:6; 7:5; 8:5; etc.). Thirdly, it will be a judgment like *the conquest of Canaan* (1:7-18), when homes were invaded (v. 9), both city and country were filled with lamentation (v. 10), and the military fortifications were besieged (v.16). Clearly, the "day of the Lord" is a time of war and Jehovah himself is the conquering warrior.

The Divine motive in judgment is the jealousy of God (1:18). "Jealousy" describes God's righteous concern for the glory of his name and feeling when his people pursue other gods (cf. Ex. 20:5; 34:14). It is a virtue, not a vice, in God, for he alone deserves to be glorified (Is. 42:8; 43:21).

Zephaniah 2 expands the "day of the Lord" motif to the nations, a fact that anticipates the ultimate "day of the Lord" at the final judgment (cf. 2:11; 3:8). The prophet announces God's plan to punish the Philistines (2:4-5), Moabites and Ammonites (2:8-10), Ethiopians (2:12), and Assyrians (2:13-15). Interestingly, the city of Ninevah fell within two decades of Zephaniah's prophecy.

Zephaniah's message is clear. Judah could expect a final judgment of epochal proportions. The wrath of Jehovah would be averted no more.

The Protected Remnant

The prophet Zephaniah develops yet another theme in his prophecy, i.e. the protection and deliverance of a godly remnant. Jehovah would preserve a witness for his name (*"I will leave in the midst of thee..."* Zeph. 3:12; cf. 2:3b), even in the cataclysm of coming judgment, and deliver them from exile and restore the kingdom to them in his time (3:14-17, 20).

The idea of the remnant is a common theme in the prophets. It describes a smaller, spiritual entity within the larger national body of Israel (cf. Is. 10:20-22). In even more specific terms, the remnant describes the true worshipers of God.

What are the characteristics of this godly remnant? First, they are *meek and humble* (2:3). They have a sense of their own weakness and dependence on the Lord. Second, they *do what he commands* (2:3). Their ethic is defined by justice, equity, and truth. Third, they are *people of prayer* (3:10). Even in circumstances when they are geographically estranged from the house of God, they still make supplication to God. Fourth, they are *afflicted and poor* (3:12). They are sensible sinners, aware of their own spiritual poverty and bankruptcy. They are despised and rejected by society, yea, even persecuted for righteousness sake. Fifth, they are *sorrowful* (3:18). They know what it is to mourn over their own sinfulness and the misery that sin has brought into the world. They are burdened by the reproach that sin has brought on the cause of God and truth. Sixth, they are *committed to holiness* (3:13). Finally, they *trust in the name of the Lord* (3:12b). Because they recognize their own helplessness, they turn beyond themselves in reliance upon God.

The Lord promises to take special care of this remnant (3:13b). He will protect (2:3b) and preserve (3:12) them. He will purify their lips (3:9). He will deliver them from captivity, conquer their enemies, gather them home, and restore their reputation among men (3:19-20). No wonder the prophet calls upon the remnant to reply in praise: *"Sing, O daughter of Zion; shout, O Israel; be glad and rejoice with all thy heart, O daughter of Jerusalem. The Lord hath taken away thy judgments, he hath cast out thine enemy: the king of Israel, even the Lord, is in the midst of thee: thou shalt not see evil anymore"* (3:14-15)!

Jeremiah

Jeremiah, often called "the Weeping Prophet", was the last of Judah's prophets before the Exile. His prophetic career began in 627 B. C. and continued for forty-one years, encompassing the respective reigns of Judah's final five kings – Josiah, Jehoahaz, Jehoiakim, Jehoiachin, and Zedekiah.

The book that bears Jeremiah's name is arranged as follows: Chapters 1-20 contain specific prophecies concerning Judah; Chapters 21-45 describe historical events leading up to and embracing the fall of Jerusalem; Chapters 46 to the end of the book contain his prophecies against the nations.

A Personal Portrait

Within the more formal development of Jeremiah's message, however, another very interesting feature of the book emerges— a portrait of the prophet as a person. The autobiographical material of this book pictures the prophet as a passionate and persecuted servant of God, and evokes the thoughtful reader's empathy and admiration. Jeremiah the person stands as an example of faithfulness to the call of God despite relentless opposition to every successive generation. Three particular traits distinguish Jeremiah among the prophets: his unenviable commission to minister without any hope of success, his uncommon passion for God's glory, and his unrequited love for the people to whom he ministered.

An Unenviable Commission

Jeremiah's commission to be Jehovah's prophet came in the thirteenth year of Josiah's reign (627 B.C.; see 1:2; 25:3). His name means "Jehovah appoints", a perpetual reminder of God's special plan for his life even prior to his birth (1:5).

The young man felt unqualified for such an important role, but God charged him to fearlessly speak the truth in the confidence of the Lord's abiding and saving presence (1:7-8). Then God "touched [his] mouth", enabling the prophet with Divine giftedness, and equipping him with the information necessary to fulfill his calling (1:9)[4].

Next, the Lord informed Jeremiah of the two-fold nature of his commission: *"I have this day set thee over the nations and over the kingdoms, to pluck up and to break down and to destroy, and to throw down, to build, and to plant"* (1:10). These words indicate that though his ministry would be ultimately constructive, i.e. "building and planting", it would be primarily destructive (plucking up and breaking down). Jeremiah's principle task would be to root out and dismantle the sins of his disobedient society. Yes, he did announce the new era of blessing, but the majority of his commission concerned the proclamation that the old era was coming to an end.

The very nature of his calling was frequently unpleasant. Jeremiah would be required to remain celibate (16:1-2), a Divine

---

[4] This "information" is expressed in the two visions of 1:11-16 — the vision of the "almond tree" indicating that the time was ripe for judgment, and the vision of the "boiling pot", indicating that judgment would overflow on Judah from the north.

condition that undoubtedly compounded the sense that he was alone, and to wear a yoke upon his neck like a prisoner as an object lesson of the coming bondage of Judah (27:2).

Then the Lord revealed to Jeremiah the most foreboding news yet. Even more distressing than the hardships that would accompany his prophetic commission would be the lack of success he would experience for all his labors. Jeremiah's ministry would be rejected (1:17-19).

God does not hold out to his servant even a remote prospect of marginal success. From the very beginning of Jeremiah's career, the Lord made it plain that his would be the unenviable task of announcing that God's longsuffering had come to an end to a people who refused to hear that message.

Jeremiah appears, consequently, as a man of paradox. He is torn between his love for God's people and his concern for God's glory. He agonized over the coming desolation, yet was committed to the bold and faithful proclamation of God's word. One author says, "[Jeremiah] struggled with the God he served, and God prevailed."[5]

The personal struggle and tension he felt is expressed in various complaints, or lamentations, to God (see 8:18-9:2; 12:1-7; 15:10, 15-21; 17:14-18; 20:13-18). These soliloquies reveal a thoroughly "human" prophet who deeply felt the sting of personal criticism, misrepresentation, rejection, slander, and loneliness.

---

[5] VanGemeren, *Interpreting the Prophetic Word*, p. 297.

An Uncommon Passion

The Biblical portrait of this man reveals a person who was no mere "professional" prophet. Jeremiah did not consider his calling as something purely formal. It was not simply "a job" to him. Jeremiah really cared. His concern for God's glory was genuine. In fact, the language he employs indicates an extremely passionate man.

It was this concern for the honor of God's name and the integrity of God's truth that prevented Jeremiah's resignation. Chapter 20:7-12 describe the prophet's decision to quit preaching: *"I said, I will not make mention of him, nor speak anymore in his name'.* The daily pressure of ridicule and reproach had taken a toll on his spirit. He was ready to give up.

But, to his chagrin, he couldn't quit. God had made it impossible for Jeremiah to resign, for *"his word was in [Jeremiah's] heart as a burning fire shut up in [his] bones".* The longer he delayed to preach, the fire raged within, for Jeremiah *"heard the defaming of many..."* That expression describes the rampant dishonor that was being done to the name of God by false prophets. Jeremiah could listen to their falsehoods for only so long. The glory of God demanded a counter-voice for the truth.

An Unrequited Love

Though Jeremiah was accused of desiring harm to God's people, the truth was the very contrary. He loved the people of Judah. He had compassion for them, like a shepherd has compassion on lost sheep (see 50:6, 17).

He demonstrated his love for God's people by weeping over their backslidden plight (13:15-17; 14:17). He also made intercession for them (14:7), though the Lord in his wrath prohibited further prayers of intercession, the space for repentance being past (14:11-12; cf. 15:1-6). Jeremiah, nonetheless, hopes for the day when the people would turn back to the Lord (14:19-22).

But Jeremiah's love for the people to whom he ministered was unrequited. They did not share such tender affections for this man. He was seen, instead, as a thorn in their sides.

His friends and family at Anathoth betrayed him, considering the prophet an embarrassment to them (11:18-21). The personal conspiracy against Jeremiah was strong (18:18-23).

Even though his calling and message was challenged by the people, the false prophets grew in popularity. The growing indifference of the people to God's truth and willingness to accept the false message of "Peace, peace" from these men broke Jeremiah's heart (23:9ff). Men like Hananiah sought to discredit Jeremiah's message with a counter-message of peace (28:1ff).

Indeed, Jeremiah was almost a lone voice for truth. During the reign of Jehoiakim, Jeremiah was brought to trial for treason. A gathering of religious leaders comprised of the the priests and the prophets agreed, *"This man is worthy to die; for he hath prophesied against this city, as ye have heard with your ears"* (26:11). In his own defense, Jeremiah appealed to a similar prophecy uttered by Micah a century earlier—a message the people of his day had humbly believed and obeyed (26:18ff).

Later, however, king Jehoiakim cut Jeremiah's written prophecies with his penknife and burned them in the fire (36:23). But God gave him instruction to dictate the prophecies again—a testimony to the indestructibility of God's word.

Finally, Jeremiah was accused of defecting to the Babylonians and imprisoned for treason (37:13-21). Though the princes urged the king to put him to death, God preserved him from death through the intervention of Ebedmelech, the Ethiopian (38:4-13).

Jeremiah is both a tragic and a heroic figure: tragic in his personal sufferings, yet heroic in his commitment to the Lord and empathy for the people who rejected him. Willem VanGemeren poignantly summarizes this personal portrait of Jeremiah:

> ...The prophet's suffering is a means of identifying himself with the suffering, disgrace, and alienation of the godly in exile...His distress is vicarious...He is a pilgrim in his own land, awaiting God's desolation and the renewal of his kingdom on earth. Accordingly, Jeremiah became a paradigm for all who suffer and await the fullness of restoration...Jeremiah remains an encouragement to the godly remnant in any age that the only way 'to withstand the erosive effects of timidity, anguish, helplessness, hostility, loneliness, despair, misunderstanding, and failure' is in communion with God and in hope of the coming restoration.[6]

---

[6] *Interpreting the Prophetic Word*, pp. 296-297.

Jeremiah's Message

Like the prophets before him, Jeremiah brought a two-dimensional message. He proclaimed both that judgment was imminent and that revival was certain. The note of judgment, however, dominated his message (cf. 1:10).

Jeremiah dared to speak the unpalatable truth that Judah should surrender to the enemy for judgment could not be averted. But the nation had long since lost any sense of accountability. The nation was incorrigible and impenitent (2:23; 6:16-17; 8:5-7; 17:23; 19:15; 22:21). So far as they were concerned, the prospect of Babylonian captivity was unthinkable. The sheer suggestion that the temple would be destroyed constituted, at least in their minds, treason and treachery.

The Case Against Judah

"Backsliding" is a key word of this book, appearing some thirteen times. Jeremiah charges Judah as a "backsliding nation" (8:5). Even in the face of Israel's judgment, Judah, Israel's "treacherous sister", did not turn to the Lord with her whole heart, "but feignedly" (3:10). In fact, Judah had "done worse than the fathers" (7:26; 16:12). Ethically speaking, there was no difference between them and the pagan nations around them (9:25-26; cf. 4:22).

In general terms, Judah's sins were two. First, they had *"forsaken [the Lord] the fountain of living waters"*. Second, they had replaced him with self-manufactured gods: *"...they have hewn them out cisterns, broken cisterns, which can hold no water"* (2:13).

They trusted in the "arm of flesh" instead of hoping in Jehovah, "the fountain of living waters" (17:5-13). They chose the idols of the heathen over the true and living God (10:2-16).

Jeremiah chapter 5 outlines the sins that warranted exile. Twice in this chapter, the Lord interrupts the list to ask, *"Shall I not visit for these things, and shall not my soul be avenged on such a nation as this?"* (5:9, 29; cf. 9:9). Among the evidence presented against Judah was her hypocrisy (v. 2), obstinacy (v. 3), idolatry (v. 7; cf. 11:13), promiscuity (v. 8), unaccountability (v. 12), inhumanity (vs. 26, 28), dishonesty (v. 27), and apostasy (vs. 30-31). The penalty for these high crimes would be exile: *"Lo, I will bring a nation upon you from far...and they shall eat up thine harvest...they shall impoverish thy fenced cities, wherein thou trustedst, with the sword..."* (vs. 15-19). In the aftermath of Divine judgment, Jerusalem would be the poetic equivalent of the universal chaos that existed prior to the ordering of creation (4:23-28).

In chapter six, the nation is further prosecuted for covetousness, religious deception, lack of contrition, and rebellion (6:13-17). So impenitent were they that even their elaborate offerings were rejected by God (v. 20). Again, Jehovah warns: *"Behold, a people cometh from the north country, and a great nation shall be raised from the sides of the earth...they are cruel, and have no mercy...and they ride horses, set in array as men for war against thee, O daughter of Zion"* (6:22-23).

So apostate was Judah that they blamed God for their sins (7:8-10). They even burned their sons and daughters in the fires of Tophet and set their idolatrous statues in the house of God (7:30-31; cf. 19:4). At this time, Judah was so disobedient and rebellious that *"truth,"* God says, *"is perished, and is cut off from their mouth"* (v. 28).

Who is to Blame?

The culpability and blame for Judah's wickedness is placed at the feet of her leaders. Over and again in Jeremiah's prophecy, Jehovah incriminates the priests and prophets for being concerned about their own popularity instead of God's law (5:31; 8:8-11; 14:13-16).

Jeremiah 23 is a devastating diatribe against the false prophets of Jeremiah's day. Though they occupied a very important and influential office, these "pastors destroyed and scattered God's sheep" (v. 1). The land was "full of adulterers", says Jeremiah, because "both prophet and priest are profane" (vs. 10-11). Indeed, the people will seldom rise higher than those who lead them.

Instead of faithfully declaring God's truth and turning their hearers away from evil, these prophets spoke "a vision of their own heart" (23:16). They endorsed the sins of the people, saying, "No evil shall come upon you" (v. 17). But the Lord says, "I know exactly what is going on. I am a God at hand; not merely a God who is far away" (see vs. 21-32).

The Specifics of Coming Judgment

In chapter 25, the prophet delivers a very specific prophecy of the coming judgment. Not only does he identify the conquering king, but he also specifies the length of captivity. *"Because ye have not heard my words, behold, I will send and take all the families of the north, saith the Lord, and Nebuchadnezzar the king of Babylon, my servant, and will bring them against this land...and this whole land shall be a desolation, and an astonishment; and these nations shall serve the king of Babylon seventy years"* (25:8-11).

Verse 12 states that after seventy years, God will make Babylon "perpetual desolations", indicating that the reference to Nebuchadnezzar as God's "servant" should be interpreted in terms of the king's unwitting, not voluntary, obedience. Nebuchadnezzar would be used, in other words, as Jehovah's instrument of judgment, but he and his kingdom would still be called to account for their sins. This is a striking example of the theological principle termed "the law of second causes."

Announcing the New Era

Jeremiah not only announced the end of the old era, but also the beginning of the new. He spoke of a day when the people would return.

Chapter 50:17-20 strikes this note of hope in a summary of the nation's history:

> "Israel is a scattered sheep; the lions have driven him away: first the king of Assyria hath devoured him; and last this Nebuchadnezzar king of Babylon hath broken his bones.

Therefore, thus saith the Lord of hosts, the God of Israel; Behold, I will punish the king of Babylon and his land, as I have punished the king of Assyria. And I will bring Israel again to his habitation...In those days, and in that time, saith the Lord, the iniquity of Israel shall be sought for, and there shall be none; and the sins of Judah, and they shall not be found: for I will pardon them whom I reserve."

Israel's hope for restoration was grounded not in the prospect of moral reform or their pledge to repent, but in the pardoning grace of God. Grace, God's initiative to favor the undeserving, would be the foundation of the promised new covenant.

Jeremiah 29-33 concentrates on the more positive note of the prophet's message. Intended as Divine encouragement to those who were suffering in captivity, these chapters are replete with precious promises. The theme of the passage is poignantly expressed in 31:17: *"There is hope in thine end, saith the Lord, that thy children shall come again to their own border."* A new covenant was coming, not like the covenant with Moses, but a covenant in which God would deal with his people by virtue of an inward work of grace in the heart.

A Letter to the Captives (Jer. 29)

A review of the historical background is necessary to the interpretation of Jeremiah's letter to the captives in Jeremiah 29. The Babylonian captivity actually took place in three stages. Second Kings 24-25 details this process. Nebuchadnezzar made his first trip to Jerusalem during the reign of Jehoiakim, probably in 605 B. C. Intimidated by the threat of conquest, Jehoiakim "became his servant" and paid tribute, i.e. taxes, to Babylon for the next three years (2 Kings 24:1).

After Jehoiakim rebelled against this arrangement, Nebuchadnezzar made yet another visit to Jerusalem. The year was approximately 598 B.C. and Jehoiakim's son, Jehoiachin (called "Coniah" in Jer. 22:24ff) was on the throne of Judah. This time, Nebuchadnezzar "besieged" the city and Jehoiachin surrendered to him without a fight. Jehoiachin's family, servants, military officers, and most talented craftsmen and workers were moved to Babylon. *"None remained, save the poorest sort of the people of the land"* (2 Kings 24:10-17). Of the estimated 50,000 people living in Jerusalem at that time, some 10,000 to 11,000 left the city for Babylon. The treasures of Solomon's temple were also confiscated and carried away, just as the Lord had said (v. 13; cf. Is. 39:6). Nebuchadnezzar installed Zedekiah to act as a deputy king in Jehoiachin's stead.

The final visit of Nebuchadnezzar to Jerusalem took place in 586 B. C. during the eleventh year of Zedekiah's reign. Zedekiah had attempted to gain independence from Babylon and Nebuchadnezzar decided to put a stop to the rebellion, once and for all (see 2 Chr. 36:13). Nebuchadnezzar and the Babylonian army leveled Jerusalem to the ground and carried the remainder of the people of Judah into captivity.

Jeremiah's letter to the captives in chapter 29 was composed between the second and third steps in this exile process (29:2). His message to them is, "Settle down in Babylon and plan on staying for awhile" (see vs. 5-7).

What is the significance of such a command? They must have wondered why the prophet would advise them to pray for the peace and prosperity of Babylon during their stay and to build houses and raise families in that foreign land. First, this counsel suggests a very important practical principle: *God intends for people to live where they are, not where they wish they were.* Life happens in the realm of today's reality, not in the sphere of yesterday's memories or tomorrow's dreams. Though present circumstances may be less than what you had expected, settle down, plant a garden, get involved, and pray for the Lord's blessings to abide upon the place where you dwell, *"for in the peace thereof shall ye have peace"*, says the Lord (29:7).

Secondly, the Lord intimates by this command that He is not finished with the nation. Though Judah was suffering God's judgment for their sins, yet they would not be disowned as His covenant people. A hint of future hope glimmers in the words, *"Take wives and beget sons and daughters...that ye may be increased there, and not diminished"* (29:6). Why would God counsel them to maintain interest in the population of the nation if he had no future plans for them?

All doubts that He did have future plans for the nation dissolve with the promise in verses 10-14: *"For thus saith the Lord, That after seventy years be accomplished at Babylon I will visit you, and perform my good word toward you, in causing you to return to this place. For I know the thoughts that I think toward you...thoughts of peace, and not of evil, to give you an expected end..."* How comforting these words must have been to them! At the very moment they were suffering Divine displeasure, they are given this "good word" of future hope.

A New Covenant (Jer. 30-31)

The prophet embellishes the happy prospect in chapter 30 by adding the promise of the nation's reunification to the promise of restoration from exile: *"I will bring again the captivity of my people Israel and Judah, saith the Lord: and I will cause them to return to the land that I gave to their fathers, and they shall possess it"* (30:3; cf. v.4). Of course, Israel and Judah had been divided since the death of Solomon, i.e. for approximately 320 years. Furthermore, Israel had ceased to exist as a nation some 125 years earlier. Yet God promises to reunite the kingdom.

If the prophecy of reunification is not surprising enough, God also promises to restore "David their king" unto them (30:9), though he has been dead for at least 350 years. Further, covenant language is employed to speak of the renewed relationship between Jehovah and the nation: *"And ye shall be my people, and I will be your God"* (30:22); *"At the same time, saith the Lord, will I be the God of all the families of Israel, and they shall be my people"* (31:1). The God who loved them and drew them into a covenant relationship with Himself would renew His vows to the "virgin of Israel" (31:3-4). He would conduct them home like a Father caring for his firstborn (31:9) and like a Shepherd gathering his flock (31:10).

What do all of these strange, but precious, promises mean? How should we interpret the pledge to restore David as their king and to bring both Judah and Israel back together in a united Zion?

Obviously, these promises depict a new era in which the theocratic ideal would finally be realized in the Messiah. Besides Jeremiah, the prophets Isaiah, Ezekiel, and Hosea also spoke of a time when David would again reign over Israel (Is. 55:3-4; Eze. 34:23-24; 37:24; Hos. 3:5). Since the Bible knows nothing of the Hindu concept of reincarnation, such references can only make sense in terms of a Messianic King who would proceed from David's lineage.

Though Jeremiah's words have a historical application, therefore, in terms of the return of the captives from Babylonian exile, they also possess a more profound prophetic significance beyond the imminent application. These are words that find their ultimate fulfillment in the new, or Messianic, covenant—a covenant, like the old, of worship and service, but unlike the old in the sense that the compulsion for obedience would not be principally external but internal (31:31-34). In the new era, God's people would worship and serve Jehovah not by means of the law written on stone tablets, but by means of the law written in the heart. Mount Zion (or Calvary) rather than Mount Sinai would be the theocratic center of the Messianic kingdom.

Jeremiah, in other words, predicts the return of the nation from Babylon and the resumption of Divine worship and blessings in the land of promise. But his prophecy says too much to apply to these political circumstances alone. These grand and glorious words echo the hope of God's people through the ages

—the hope of a Messianic King who would subdue every foe, gather the entire covenant family from the least to the greatest unto Himself, and be the object of their everlasting worship and obedient service in the ultimate theocratic community. In the coming Messiah, God's plan to establish a theocratic kingdom would be realized, once and for all.

An Object Lesson (Jer. 32)

Chapter 32 transports us from the mystical considerations of the heavenly kingdom back to the mundane circumstances of Jeremiah's prophetic ministry. As in other sections of the book, Jeremiah is once again called to model the message he had preached.

God counsels Jeremiah to buy a field in Anathoth (33:6-8). At once we are surprised, for a real estate investment in Judah at the very moment the nation was in process of being deported to Babylon does not seem very wise. But the Lord intends to illustrate the message of restoration. He instructs the prophet to put the deed in an earthen vessel for safe-keeping, for "*Houses and fields and vineyards shall be possessed again in this land*" saith the Lord (33:14-15).

Though his faith struggles to hope for restoration in lieu of the ominous scenes of judgment, Jeremiah prays, reminding himself that God is the Creator and that nothing is too hard for Him (32:17). God answers his prayer, saying, "*Buy thee the field for money, and take witnesses; for the city is given into the hand of the Chaldeans*" (32:25), but "*Behold, I will gather them out of all countries...and will bring them again unto this place..."* (32:37), for *"I am the Lord, the God of all flesh: is there anything too hard for me?"* (32:27). Omnipotence is not intimidated by the apparently daunting challenge of restoration.

An Abundance of Prosperity (Jer. 33)

Not only would the nation be returned home and reunited in a new covenant of peace, but it would experience revival and spiritual renewal. Prosperity and health would return to Jerusalem. Chapter 33 begins with the thrilling promise of Divine abundance: *"Call unto me, and I will answer thee and show thee great and mighty things, which thou knowest not"* (33:3).

Such promises of renewal pervade the entire chapter: *"Behold, I will bring it health and cure, and I will cure them, and will reveal unto them the abundance of peace and truth"* (33:6); *"It shall be to me a name of joy, a praise and an honor before all the nations of the earth, which shall hear all the good that I do unto them: and they shall fear and tremble for all the goodness and for all the prosperity that I procure unto it"* (33:9); *"Again there shall be heard in this place...the voice of joy, and the voice of gladness, the voice of the bridegroom, and the voice of the bride, saying Praise the Lord of hosts: for the Lord is good and his mercy endureth forever"* (33:11).

Once more, in this jubilant passage of spiritual renewal, the prophet returns to the Messianic theme (33:15ff). This suggests to us that renewal and revival, peace and prosperity, health and happiness, are ultimately defined in terms of the Messiah and his Kingdom, not a mere physical return to a geographic fatherland.

Chapter 13
THE BABYLONIAN CAPTIVITY
2 Kings 25; Jeremiah 39; Lamentations

The Old Testament story of Israel, the covenant community of God, is a story revolving around three primary places: Egypt, Canaan's Land, and Babylon. Israel dwelt in Egypt from about 1900 to 1500 B.C. and in Canaan for the next nine hundred or so years. In 586 B.C., Nebuchadnezzar, king of Babylon, besieged Jerusalem, destroyed Solomon's temple, and carried the Jews into Babylon as exiles.

The kingdom of Babylon was, at that time, a dominant world empire. Geographically, it was located in modern Iraq. Assyria had fallen to Babylon at the battle of Carchemish in 605 B.C. and Nebuchadnezzar had extended Babylonian control into Ashkelon, a city in ancient Philistia, the region known today as the Gaza Strip, in 604 B.C. After a brief yet unsuccessful raid on Egypt in 601 B.C., Nebuchadnezzar targeted Jerusalem. After a brief revolt, King Jehoiachin of Judah and 10,000 of his nobles were deported to Babylon in March of 597 B.C. Zedekiah was installed as a puppet king, and Judah became a satellite kingdom, paying heavy tribute, i.e. taxes, to Babylon. About a decade later when Zedekiah revolted, Nebuchadnezzar launched another, final campaign against Jerusalem. It was a brutal and devastating assault culminating in the fall of Judah and destruction of the city of God.

The Historical Details

Nebuchadnezzar's army blockaded the city for eighteen months until the people ran out of food (2 Kings 25:1-3; Jer. 39:1-2). The severe famine spawned unthinkable atrocities. Jeremiah describes the bone-chilling scenes of starvation and disease:

> "...the children and the sucklings swoon in the streets of the city. They say to their mothers, Where is corn and wine? When they swooned as the wounded in the streets of the city, when their soul was poured out into their mothers bosom...Shall the women eat their fruit, and children of a span long?...The young and the old lie on the ground in the streets...the tongue of the sucking child cleaveth to the roof of his mouth for thirst: the young children ask bread, and no man breaketh it unto them They that did feed delicately are desolate in the streets: they that were brought up in scarlet embrace dunghills" (Lam. 2:11-12, 20-21; 4:4-5).

After eighteen months of growing extremity, the city was attacked. In his *Antiquities of the Jews*, the historian Josephus, describes how the enemy army built huge mounds or embankments and launched "darts" or missiles over the walls. As soon as "the city was broken up" and enemy officers invaded, king Zedekiah attempted to escape by tunneling beneath the city walls and fleeing under the cover of darkness. He was quickly captured, forced to witness the execution of his own sons, blinded, bound, and carried off to Babylon (Jer. 39:4-7; 2 Kings 25:4-7; cf. Eze. 12:12-13).

Nebuchadnezzar's army then proceeded to burn the temple that Solomon had built for the worship of Jehovah and to level the city to the ground (Jer. 39:8; 2 Kings 25:9). The priests ministering in the house of the Lord were slain (2 Kings 25:21), the approximately 60,000 people who remained in the city except the very poorest were taken to Ramah and screened for deportation to Babylon (2 Kings 25:11-12; Jer. 39:9-10; cf. Jer. 31:15), and the remaining items of brass furniture that had been used for Divine service in the temple were confiscated. Jerusalem was left a smoking ruin. For the second time in their history, God's covenant people would be slaves in a heathen kingdom for years to come.

How shocking are these events! How surprising that the apparently indomitable kingdom of Judah would fall to the enemy! *"The kings of the earth and all the inhabitants of the world, would not have believed that the adversary and the enemy should have entered into the gates of Jerusalem"* (Lam. 4:12).

A Poetic Perspective

The book of Lamentations is Jeremiah's poetic perspective on the fall of Jerusalem. Written in "limping meter", the cadence of a funeral dirge, Lamentations strikes the mournful note of abject humiliation and hopelessness. The book is comprised of 5 chapters, each consisting of 22 verses, except for chapter 3 (which has 66, or 22 x 3).

Written from a first-person vantage point, Lamentations reads like an eyewitness account of Jerusalem's devastation. One can almost see the weeping prophet stumbling through the burning rubble that was the city of God, and reliving the stunning events of the past days and hours.

An eerie and lonely silence, where once the sounds of life were heard, now prevails: *"How doth the city sit solitary, that was full of people!...The ways of Zion do mourn, because none come to the solemn feasts: all her gates are desolate: her priests sigh, her virgins are afflicted, and she is in bitterness"* (1:1, 4). The prophet reflects on happier days, but the present reality draws him back to the devastating consequences of Judah's sins: reproach, desecration, and abandonment (1:7-9).

In desperate agony, he cries to the curious bystander, *"Is it nothing to you, all ye that pass by? Behold and see if there be any sorrow like unto my sorrow, which is done unto me, wherewith the Lord hath afflicted me in the day of his fierce anger"* (1:12). The prophet laments the brutal deaths of Judah's soldiers and the broken dreams of a nation without a rising generation (1:15). He pictures Zion as a beggar, earnestly pleading for compassion only to meet with stony and calloused silence (1:17).

Jeremiah's poetic documentary proceeds to attribute Jerusalem's demise not to Babylon, but to Jehovah: *"How hath the Lord covered the daughter of Zion with a cloud in his anger, and cast down from heaven unto the earth the beauty of Israel, and remembered not his footstool in the day of his anger!...The Lord hath done that which he had devised; he hath fulfilled his word that he had commanded in the days of old: he hath thrown down, and hath not pitied: and he hath caused thine enemy to rejoice over thee..."* (2:1ff, 17).

228

Though Lamentations 1 and 2 express a kind of personal detachment, as if Jeremiah is reporting a news story, the emotional tension is elevated to the level of personal calamity in chapter 3. It is as if the prophet Jeremiah now feels the whole weight of this catastrophe upon his own shoulders: *"I am that man that hath seen affliction by the rod of his wrath...Surely against me is he turned...He was unto me as a bear lying in wait, and as a lion in secret places. He hath turned aside my ways, and pulled me in pieces: he hath made me desolate..."* (3:1-17). Jeremiah feels to be the very incarnation of Divine judgment, the personification of God's wrath.

In his apparent hopelessness and despair, however, he suddenly recalls a hopeful fact. Though the city was destroyed and the people banished to Babylon, the nation had not been totally annihilated. The people were yet alive: *"This I recall to my mind, therefore have I hope. It is of the Lord's mercies that we are not consumed, because his compassions fail not. They are new every morning: great is thy faithfulness"* (3:21-23). Like a catapult to his spirits, this thought opens a window of encouragement to the prophet. He embarks on a series of fruitful meditations concerning God's gracious character and covenant fidelity, and resolves to cry for pardon again unto God in the heavens (3:24-66).

This interlude of hope is followed in chapter 4 by further reflection on the siege of the city. The song of mourning concludes with a prayer for Divine mercy in Lamentations 5.

Who can disaffectedly read Jeremiah's concluding confession?

> "Our skin was black like an oven because of the terrible famine. They ravished the women in Zion, and the maids in the cities of Judah. Princes are hanged up by their hand: the faces of the elders were not honored. They took the young men to grind, and the children fell under the wood. The elders have ceased from the gate, the young men from their music. The joy of our heart is ceased; our dance is turned into mourning. The crown is fallen from our head: woe unto us, that we have sinned! (Lam. 5:10-16).

Who can read his final plea without learning that the true meaning of humble repentance is an attitude that both hopes in God's goodness and submits to His severity: *"Turn thou us unto thee, O Lord, and we shall be turned; renew our days as of old. But thou hast utterly rejected us; thou art very wroth against us"* (Lam. 5:21-22)?

The Nation in Babylon

The sad story of Judah's exile is summarized in 2 Chronicles 36:15-21. The Chronicler explains the reason for the length of the Babylonian Captivity in verse twenty-one: *"To fulfill the word of the Lord by the mouth of Jeremiah, until the land had enjoyed her Sabbaths: for as long as she lay desolate she kept Sabbath, to fulfill threescore and ten years."*

What does this mean? The law required Israel to cease agricultural operations and allow the land to remain fallow

230

every seven years. The nation, however, had failed to observe these sabbatical years. Since the ministry of Samuel and the beginning of the Prophetic office some 490 years earlier, 70 sabbatical years had passed. To achieve compliance with His own law and honor his prescribed sabbaticals for the land, God thrust the people from the land for 70 years. The practical application of this principle is unmistakable: *The Lord has ways of achieving his purposes and will not allow injustice to prevail forever.*

Songs in the Night

Two particular Psalms capture the somber scene of the nation in exile. Psalm 126 reflects on a past deliverance from bondage—probably slavery in Egypt—then prays for a new deliverance: *"Turn again our captivity, O Lord, as the streams in the south"* (v. 4). It is likely that the present "captivity" is a reference to the fact of Babylonian exile.

The last two verses of Psalm 126 describe a scene in which the present toil can be endured only by the hope for restoration: *"They that sow in tears shall reap in joy. He that goeth forth and weepeth, bearing precious seed, shall doubtless come again with rejoicing, bringing his sheaves with him"* (vs. 5-6). My, how these exiles longed for home in that foreign land!

Psalm 137 is more specific still. Written by some anonymous poet, it describes the mourning of the exiles in Babylon: *"By the rivers of Babylon, there we sat down, yea, we wept, when we remembered Zion. We hanged our harps on the willows in the midst thereof. For there they that carried us away captive required of us a song; and they that wasted us required of us mirth, saying, Sing us one of the songs of Zion. How shall we sing the Lord's song in a strange land?"* (vs. 1-4). Though the Babylonians made sport of the captives, cajoling them to perform one of their cherished songs of worship, the Jews could do nothing but weep for that which they had lost. The forlorn question, "How shall we sing the Lord's song in a strange land?", expresses a sense of alienation and despair that echoes the experience of the broken-hearted sinner who is suffering for his disobedience to the Lord.

The Psalmist proceeds to describe the intense emotion of homesickness and their vow to remember their identity: *"If I forget thee, O Jerusalem, let my right hand forget her cunning. If I do not remember thee, let my tongue cleave to the roof of my mouth; if I prefer not Jerusalem above my chief joy"* (vs. 5-6). That challenge to retain their rich heritage and sense of covenant identity as the people of God would be no small feat in this foreign environment. How easy it would be to accommodate the spirit of the age and to conform themselves to the Babylonian culture!

The Rise of the Pharisees

Would the Babylonian captivity mean the end of Israel as a nation? One group was determined to prevent that very real possibility. To meet the challenge of non-conformity, a godly remnant of Jews in Babylon covenanted together to preserve the patriarchal traditions. They called themselves "the separated ones".

These godly men saw the need to provide a means by which the captives might "stay in touch" with their heritage. They began to teach the Scriptures to the young lest the faith of Israel be forgotten. Regular classes for religious instruction were organized. Regular times of prayer were observed. Great pangs were taken to insure that Jewish dietary laws and restrictions were followed.

Of course, the commitment to develop such a sub-culture of holiness in this pagan environment produced certain tensions. When conscience would not permit them to partake of the Babylonian's non-kosher diet or when edicts required them to bow in worship before the image of Nebuchadnezzar, they faced terrifying recrimination. But they must have reasoned, "We are here because our ancestors compromised with the spirit of the age; therefore, it's high time that we begin to live as a separated people, come what may." They were willing to give their lives for the preservation of their heritage and God honored the devotion of these "separated ones" by shutting the mouths of lions and protecting them from even the slightest damage in the fiery furnace.

These "separated ones" later came to be known as "Pharisees". Though the New Testament portrait of the Pharisees is a less-than-flattering picture of perfectionism, rigidity, and pretentiousness, such was not always the case. This sect began as a group of noble purpose, heroic resolve, and godly commitment. In lieu of the historical background of the origin of Pharisaism, it is plain to see that the New Testament story of their religious hypocrisy and opposition to Christ is a classic example of "good gone wrong".

The two exilic prophets whose literary contributions are included in the Old Testament canon, Ezekiel and Daniel, were likely members (though the group was probably not yet formally organized) of this class known as "the separated ones". It is likely that the three Hebrews—Hanani, Mishael, and Azariah, also known by their Babylonian names of Shadrach, Meshach, and Abednego—were also numbered among these earliest "Pharisees".

Though Christians today would not want to duplicate the kind of self-righteous and legalistic spirit that characterized the Pharisees of Jesus' day, yet the challenge facing us, i.e. to faithfully serve Christ in an environment antagonistic to faith, is the same as the challenge that faced these Jews in Babylon. Since the gospel calls us to live counter-culturally (cf. Rom. 12:3), the record of these devout Israelites in captivity is an example worth heeding and emulating.

Spiritual "Babylon"

In a thoroughly Biblical sense, the contemporary believer must still contend with the influence of "Babylon". This is the very label Scripture apocalyptically assigns to the fallen world-system (or as Augustine termed it, the "City of Man") in which the Christian seeks to live out his faith.

The book of Revelation speaks at length about "Babylon the great, the mother of harlots and abominations of the earth" (Rev.

17:5). She is depicted as the great opponent of the kingdom of God, a "woman drunken with the blood of the saints and with the blood of the martyrs of Jesus" (17:6). She rides upon the back of the "beast", imagery designed to suggest that the fallen world-order is controlled by the devil (17:7; cf. 1 Jno. 5:19; Eph. 2:2; 2 Cor. 4:4; Lk. 4:5-6). She is the delight of merchants and kings, for they have been enriched and empowered by their allegiance to her. Indeed, Bible prophecy spiritualizes this historical antithesis between Babylon and Jerusalem to describe the contrast between the "kingdoms of this world" and the "kingdom of God", the very theme of the Old Testament.

From henceforth in Scripture, the name "Babylon" will stand as a representative symbol of all that is in opposition to the kingdom of God. No wonder God calls upon his people to "come out of her...and be not partaker of her plagues" (Rev. 18:4; cf. 2 Cor. 6:16).

The Babylonian Captivity

Chapter 14
THE EXILIC PROPHETS
Ezekiel; Daniel

E zekiel was one of two literary prophets God raised up while the nation was in Babylonian exile. He was among the ten thousand leading citizens taken to Babylon during the second deportation (597 B.C.). He was approximately 25 years old at the time. Some four years later (~593 B.C.), God called Ezekiel to serve as His prophet as he sat by the river Chebar in Babylon (1:1). We know by the carefully dated chronological prophecies in his book that he ministered in this capacity for the next twenty-two years, or until 571 B.C.

Ezekiel's Theme

The first eleven years of his career, Ezekiel predicted the fall of Jerusalem (chs. 1-24). While Jeremiah preached the message in the city of Jerusalem itself, Ezekiel pronounced the same message from a distance. During the final fifteen years of his ministry, however, Ezekiel's message focused on the renewal of the kingdom of God (chs. 33-48), the transformation of the nation as a truly theocratic community, and the restoration of covenant blessings under the rule of the Davidic Shepherd-King (Eze. 34).

One recurring thought in Ezekiel's prophetic message acts as a unifying theme in the book: *the glory of the Lord.* Ezekiel builds his message around the central theme of *God's purpose to be glorified through the glorious self-disclosure of His great name.*

237

The Vision of Jehovah's Glory

Ezekiel's ministry began with a vision of the glory of the Lord (1:28). The vision begins with a an approaching storm cloud (1:4). Suddenly, out of the cloud, he saw four living creatures, or cherubim (1:5). The wonder of these composite creatures was compounded by another scene of omnidirectional wheels, moving like a gyroscope. The motion of the wheels and the cherubim were perfectly synchronized, so that "when those went, these went; and when those stood, these stood" (1:21).

At once, Ezekiel heard a voice beyond the immediate scene and saw a spectacle more majestic yet. The throne of the universe was inhabited by a man who gave the appearance of fire and brightness (1:25-27). He translates the vision in verse 28: *"This was the appearance of the likeness of the glory of the Lord. And when I saw it, I fell upon my face, and I heard a voice of one that spake."*

This vision sets the pace for the rest of the book. That Jehovah revealed his glory to the prophet in Babylon bespeaks at least three thoughts: (1) God's presence is free and sovereign. He is not restricted to the temple in Jerusalem. (2) God's judgment is free and sovereign. He will not negotiate the glory of His name with a disobedient people. Ezekiel is concerned to vindicate God's glory in the judgments upon Judah for her sins; (3) God's grace is free and sovereign. He intends to manifest His glory again in the restoration of His covenant people.

Glory (Heb. *kabod*) might be defined as God in self-display or self-disclosure. It is a composite attribute, encompassing everything that God is. *Kabod* means "weighty; heavy"[1] and speaks of something that makes a substantial impression. It is awe-inspiring and majestic.

The desire to see the glory of the Lord was the passion of Moses' heart. His request for the beatific vision, *"Show me thy glory"* (Ex. 33:18), was answered by a verbal, not a visual, revelation. Like Moses, we also view the glory of God by faith, i.e. by testimony, not by sight.

When Old Testament saints did receive a visible manifestation of Divine glory, it was, invariably, an overwhelming experience. At the completion of Solomon's temple, the cloud, a visible manifestation of God's presence, *"filled the house of the Lord, so that the priests could not stand to minister because of the cloud: for the glory of the Lord had filled the house of the Lord"* (1 Kings 8:10-11; cf. Ex. 40:34). When Isaiah saw Jehovah's glory in the temple, he cried out in conscious awareness of his own corruption (Is. 6:1-5). And when Ezekiel saw this vision of the glory of God, he sat in silent astonishment for seven days (Eze. 3:15).

The Departure of Jehovah's Glory

Ezekiel spent the first eleven years of his prophetic ministry announcing, like a watchman on the city walls (3:17; 33:1ff), the

---

[1] Note how 2 Cor. 4:18 contrasts the lightness of affliction when compared to the weightiness of coming glory.

coming judgment on Jerusalem (chs. 1-24). His message is simply, "Jehovah manifested his glory to the nation, but they did not glorify Him. Now, He will abandon them to the consequences of their sins."

The striking description of the departing glory of Jehovah from the temple and the city of Jerusalem itself in chapters 10 and 11 is a stunning and shocking message. God has written "Ichabod"[2] over the nation, the prophet says. The covenant blessings of Divine protection and provision have been revoked. Jehovah's presence has been removed. Israel and Judah were a "rebellious house" (2:3ff; 12:21ff; 14:1ff; 20:1ff) and the glory of God demanded justice. Scripture unequivocally affirms that God will indeed be glorified in the act of judging iniquity (cf. Rom. 9:17).

The Renewal of Jehovah's Glory

Yet here is also a message of hope. God aims to be glorified not only in the punishment of sin, but in the pardon of it. The glory of the Lord, in other words, embraces not only His glorious holiness (Ex. 15:11) but also His glorious grace (Rom. 9:23). Ezekiel's final prophecies are messages of comfort and encouragement to the exiles (chs. 33-48).

The prophet has a dual purpose. He wants both to remind the exiles of the sins that incurred such judgment and to sustain the faithful remnant with the hope of future blessedness. And he

---

[2] The glory has departed.

ties both motifs to this common anchor – Jehovah's concern for His own glory.

This fact is evident in the most frequent phrase of the book. Over sixty times, Ezekiel highlights God's purpose to be known and glorified by the phrase, *"They shall know that I am the Lord..."* (6:7, 10, 14; 7:4; 12:15-16; 33:29; 36:11, 37-38; 37:13; 38:23; etc.).

This formula speaks of Jehovah's purpose to disclose (or reveal) His glory as the chief end in all that He does. And it is the basis of Israel's hope for covenant renewal (20:42, 44). The prospect of future grace, in other words, is grounded in the Lord's supreme self-regard to the glory of His own name.

Notice how the Lord defines His motives in future blessings on the nation in terms of His concern for His own "holy name": *"I do not this for your sakes, O house of Israel, but for mine holy name's sake, which ye have profaned among the heathen, whither ye went. And I will sanctify my great name...and the heathen shall know that I am the Lord, when I shall be sanctified in you before their eyes"* (36:22-23; cf. 39:7, 21-29).

The vision of the valley of dry bones (Eze. 37) is a powerful allegory of God's sovereign purpose to revive and restore the nation. In Babylon, the potential of restoration looked to be as hopeless as this valley of very dry bones. But such abject and desperate circumstances are no strain on Divine power. With such a glorious God in control, there is hope even in the most apparently hopeless situation.

Of course, Ezekiel's prophecy of the nation's renewal has an immediate, or historical, fulfillment. But, like so many other passages in the prophets, it also has an ultimate, eschatological fulfillment in the Messianic kingdom.

The passage in Ezekiel 34, for instance, describing the reign of the Davidic Shepherd-King as the One through whom Jehovah would shepherd his people is clearly a Messianic reference. Also, the image of the river flowing from the presence of God, transforming everything in its path (Eze. 47) is strikingly similar to the imagery of the "river of life" that flows from the New Jerusalem in Revelation. Finally, the promise of Jehovah's perpetual presence in the "new" Jerusalem with which the book concludes says too much to exclusively apply to the arena of physical history.

Obviously, Ezekiel's eschatological emphasis is consistent with the developing plot of the Old Testament concerning God's great purpose to establish a truly theocratic community in which He is known and acknowledged as the sole object of worship. In such a kingdom, He alone will be glorified.

Daniel and "The Kingdom of God"

In addition to Ezekiel, Daniel was Divinely commissioned to prophesy the word of the Lord during the Babylonian captivity. The book that bears his name is of strategic importance to the development of the Biblical plot. What has been, heretofore, an implicit theme, lurking just below the surface of historical events, is now spelled out in very explicit and clear terms.

Perhaps more than any other single book in the Old Testament canon, *Daniel* serves to synthesize the various parts of the Old Testament message into a theologically coherent whole. Everything prior to this point has been "rising action"—a musical crescendo, if you please. *Daniel* is the literary "climax" or musical *fortissimo* (if I may mix metaphors). The book of *Daniel*, in other words, provides a rational, or theological, grid for interpreting the significance of the historical events that have gone before. It resolves the apparent disparity of historical events and ties them together in terms of a common theme. What is that theme? In a word, that unifying theme is *the kingdom of God* (2:44; 4:3, 34; 6:26; 7:14-22, 27), or *the sovereignty of God* (2:37; 4:17, 25, 32-35; 5:21).

Of course, we have already made the point, over and again, that the Old Testament is a story describing *God's purpose to establish a truly theocratic kingdom for His name*. Further, we have seen how the Holy Spirit has developed this plot in increasingly specific terms. Second Samuel 7, a passage in which Jehovah covenants to establish David's son as the king over His people forever, is a case in point. But *Daniel* moves beyond the realm of veiled inference[3] to the realm of explicit and unambiguous reference. This book, then, with its message of *God's supremacy over all earthly kingdoms* is a sort of theological summary for the narratives of the Old Testament.

---

[3] Of course, passages that describe the fulfillment of the Davidic Covenant in the Messianic Kingdom are not ambiguous to those of us who consider them retrospectively, i.e. in lieu of NT understanding. Viewed prospectively, however (as one observes the unfolding of the OT plot), there is some ambiguity. My point is that the book of Daniel serves to interpret that which was, at best, implicit, in very explicit terms, so that there is no longer any doubt concerning the primary theme of the OT.

Kingdoms in Conflict (Dan. 1)

Daniel's prophecy begins with a description of his exile to Babylon. He was part of the first deportation, being taken to Babylon in 605 B.C., "in the third year of the reign of Jehoiakim, king of Judah" (1:1). According to 1:3-4, Daniel was among the youths of nobility. His prophetic career continued throughout the duration of Babylonian exile, spanning the respective reigns of Nebuchadnezzar, Belshazzar, and Darius the Mede (or Cyrus; cf. 6:28). His last dated prophecy was given "in the first year of Darius the Mede" (9:1; 11:1), or 536 B.C.

Impressive Jewish teens like Daniel were brought to Babylon as part of Nebuchadnezzar's program to transform them into cultured Babylonian statesmen. Ashpenaz, the head of the king's royal academy, was commissioned to indoctrinate them in Babylonian culture, perhaps with a view to using them as liaisons between Babylon and Judah (1:3-4). This academic program would last for three years (1:5).

Daniel, together with Hananiah, Mishael, and Azariah, was among the young adults enrolled in this program. To facilitate cultural integration, their names were changed. Their Jewish names contained either the syllable *el* (for God) or *iah* (for Jehovah). Their Babylonian names honored the gods of Babylon. Daniel (my God is judge) was given the Babylonian name Belteshazzar (Baal[4] will protect). Hananiah's name (Jehovah is

---

[4] Baal was the sun god.

gracious) was changed to Shadrach (Aku[5] inspires). Mishael (Who is like God?) was renamed Meshach (belonging to Aku). Azariah (Jehovah helps) became Abednego (servant of Nebo[6]).

It is apparent that the Babylonian society was a strange mixture of secularism and paganism. The Babylonians prized science, philosophy, history, and other academic disciplines (1:4), but they also practiced astrology and magic, and worshiped the sun, moon, planets, and elements of the earth, i.e. fire, water, wind, etc. This secular/pagan duality parallels popular trends in the modern world and may be the reason that the fallen world order is identified as "Babylon" in the book of Revelation.

As one of king Nebuchadnezzar's courtiers, Daniel soon faced a crisis. Any pious Israelite would find such circumstances challenging. How far could he go to comply with Nebuchadnezzar's program without compromising his convictions? How could he be a faithful subject of God's kingdom while living in a Babylonian kingdom that required him to violate the very first commandment? How could he sing Jehovah's song in a strange (foreign) land?

This antithesis between the kingdom of God and the kingdoms of men is the primary motif of Scripture. The kingdom is His special project in the earth and is presented in Scripture in terms of contrast to the world. The Biblical message is that there are really only two kingdoms in the world: the kingdom of God

---

[5] Aku, or Venus, was the moon god.
[6] Nebo was the god of science and learning.

and the kingdom of men. God's kingdom is His new society in contrast to the fallen world system, a heavenly dominion as opposed to a mere earthly or human form of government. It is a counter-cultural concept describing a way of life that fundamentally differs from conventional structures.

The two kingdoms, consequently, are locked in perpetual conflict. The kingdoms of this world are antagonistic to the kingdom of God. Because our King makes certain claims upon the lives of His people, we will frequently find ourselves in conflict with the culture in which we live.

Daniel felt keenly this tension. When the king appointed a certain daily fare for Daniel and the other noble youths (1:5), Daniel conscientiously objected. Perhaps the diet would require him to violate the dietary laws God had prescribed in Leviticus. His conscience would not permit him to submit at this point. As one of the original "Separated Ones" (the group that eventually became known as the 'Pharisees'), *"Daniel purposed in his heart that he would not defile himself with the portion of the king's meat, nor with the wine which he drank; therefore he requested of the prince of the eunuchs that he might not defile himself"* (1:8).

Daniel lived counter-culturally in the kingdom of Babylon. He did not attempt to change the Babylonian culture, but to maintain his own fidelity to the Lord. Though he served a human king, Daniel consciously and deliberately committed himself to obeying the King of heaven and earth.

And God took care of Daniel: *"Now God had brought Daniel into favor and tender love* [lit. sympathy] *with the prince of the eunuchs"* (1:9). Like Joseph before him, Daniel was befriended and respected by a foreign official. Though Ashpenaz was skeptical of Daniel's request for a diet restricted to vegetables, he gave Daniel and his friends a ten-day trial. At the end of the trial period, they were healthier than everyone else (1:10-16). This program continued for three years, during which time God blessed them to make remarkable academic and physical progress (1:17).

When the program was completed, the king found these young men "ten times better" in all matters of wisdom and understanding than all his magicians and astrologers (1:20). These impressive and pious servants of the true God were superior to all the kings courtiers. Even in unpleasant circumstances, the principle is still true: *"He that honoreth me, I will honor, saith the Lord"* (1 Sam. 2:30).

God's Kingdom and World History

The theme of Daniel 2-7[7] is *God's sovereignty, i.e. absolute authority, over the nations.* Repeatedly, God is called the "most High" (*El-Elyon*) and the "King of heaven" in this section of Daniel's prophecy. Chapters two and seven are parallel, each describing the contrast between the four "world kingdoms" and the universal superiority of the kingdom of God. The message of Daniel is that world history is a story of five kingdoms—four political, vulnerable, and temporary and one spiritual, invincible, and everlasting.

---

[7] One of the few OT sections written in Aramaic.

The Exilic Prophets

Nebuchadnezzar's Dream (2:1-36)

Daniel, the young Hebrew courtier to the Babylonian king, distinguished himself by his piety before the prince of the eunuchs. Now God would give him further influence before Nebuchadnezzar himself.

Nebuchadnezzar's dreams night after night troubled him (2:1). To add to his general sense of uneasiness, he could not recall the details of these dreams (2:5). He commanded his magicians, sorcerers, and astrologers, under threat of death, to use their respective arts to both make known the content of his dreams and to interpret its significance (2:2-12). When they voiced complaint at the unreasonableness of the charge, Nebuchadnezzar decreed that all the wise men in Babylon should be slain.

Daniel and his fellows were numbered among the wise men. When the captain of the king's guard proceeded to implement the king's decree, Daniel appealed to Nebuchadnezzar himself for a brief stay of execution. He promised to reveal the dream and the interpretation (2:13-18).

When God revealed the matter to him in a night vision, Daniel praised the God of heaven. His benediction is a celebration of Divine sovereignty: *"Blessed be the name of God forever and ever: for wisdom and might are his: and he changeth the times and the seasons: he removeth kings, and setteth up kings...He revealeth the deep and secret things: he knoweth what is in the darkness, and the light dwelleth with him..."* (2:20-23).

248

When Daniel appeared before Nebuchadnezzar, he carefully ascribed glory to God: *"There is a God in heaven that revealeth secrets...But as for me, this secret is not revealed to me for any wisdom that I have more than any living..."* (2:25-30). Then he described the things that Nebuchadnezzar had seen in his dream.

Nebuchadnezzar had dreamed of a giant colossus. This figure was a composite image. The head was of gold, the torso of silver, the midsection of brass, the legs of iron, and the feet of both iron and clay. Daniel proceeds to describe how the king saw a little stone smite the statue in the feet so that the entire image toppled and crumbled. The wind blew the pieces away and the little stone that smote the image grew to a mountain that filled the whole earth (2:31-35).

The Meaning of the Colossal Image (2:37-43)

Nebuchadnezzar's Colossus describes four "world empires" or earthly kingdoms. Notice that though the image is made of composite materials, it is a single entity, suggesting the thought that all earthly kingdoms are essentially the same. Whatever the particulars, every earthly kingdom is something purely physical and political. The kingdom of God, however, is depicted as an entity separate and external to the Colossus. It is the "stone cut out of the mountain without hands" that smites the Colossus and dominates in its stead. The point is identical to the Lord's teaching: *"My kingdom is not of this world"* (Jno. 18:36).

Each of the kingdoms represented by the metals of Nebuchadnezzar's image is a "world" empire (cf. 2:39). This does not mean, however, that each exercised global dominance, but rather that the sway of each was expansive. Babylon and Persia, for instance, ruled every land between the rivers Tigris (in modern day Iraq) and Nile (in modern North Africa). Greece increased its territorial dominance even further, and Rome, further still.

The composite image also suggests the thought that one empire would succeed another in world history. Regardless of the apparent dominance of each respective kingdom, another would rise to conquer and replace it. No earthly power will continue forever.

Notice also the deteriorating value of the metals represented in the image. The head of the image is composed of the most precious metal, i.e. gold. The following kingdoms are represented by metals of lessening value, i.e. silver, then brass, then iron, and finally iron mixed with clay. Probably, this declining value of the elements comprising the Colossus indicates the decrease in absolute authority exercised by each successive kingdom.

Daniel explains the image beginning in verses 37-38: "*Thou, O king...art this head of gold.*" Nebuchadnezzar's kingdom—the Babylonian Empire—is represented by the head of gold. After Babylon, Daniel says, "another kingdom inferior to" the Babylonian would arise. This kingdom, represented by the breast and arms of silver, was a coalition of Medes and Persians, often called the Medo-Persian Empire. The third kingdom, represented by the belly and thighs of brass, refers to the Grecian

Empire under the rule of Alexander the Great. The fourth and
final kingdom, represented by the legs of iron, speaks of the
mighty Roman Empire (2:39-40).

An intriguing prophetic detail is added to the description of
the Roman Empire. Though it would successfully subdue and
break its enemies (v.40), the Roman Empire would eventually
deteriorate. Verses 41-42 describes its decline: *"And whereas thou
sawest the feet and toes, part of potters' clay and part of iron, the
kingdom shall be divided; but there shall be in it the strength of the
iron, forasmuch as thou sawest the iron mixed with miry clay. And as
the toes of the feet were part of iron, and part of clay, so the kingdom
shall be partly strong, and partly broken* [lit. brittle]".

The mixture of clay with the iron indicates inherent
weakness. Every earthly kingdom, or political empire, is
inherently weak by virtue of the human element that comprises
it. The Roman would be especially so in lieu of the various
divisions and subdivisions it would experience.

The Coming Dominance of God's Kingdom (2:44-45)

Daniel then explains the significance of the little "stone" that
smote Nebuchadnezzar's Colossus. *"And in the days of these kings,
shall the God of heaven set up a kingdom, which shall never be
destroyed: and the kingdom shall not be left to other people, but it shall
break in pieces and consume all these kingdoms, and it shall stand
forever"* (2:44).

Notice the specific time table given for the inauguration of
God's kingdom – *"...in the days of these kings."* The point is

obvious. In the days of the Roman Empire, especially when it began to decline, God would set up His kingdom. Interestingly, Jesus of Nazareth appeared on the stage of history preaching, "The kingdom of heaven is at hand" during that very era. Though Jesus' announcement of God's kingdom was viewed with suspicion by the kings of his day, it is evident that the kingdom he intended to establish was essentially spiritual, not political.

Daniel's prophecy describes four characteristics of God's kingdom that distinguish it from the political kingdoms of men. *(1) It will be invincible – "…shall never be destroyed"*. Unlike the empires of Babylon, Persia, Greece, and Rome, the kingdom of God would never fall to enemy conquest. *(2) It will have no successor – "…shall not be left to other people"*. God's kingdom will never slip into irrelevance. It will not be replaced by a successor like Babylon was replaced by Persia, etc. *(3) It will achieve universal dominance – "…it shall break in pieces and consume all these kingdoms"*. The kingdom of God is aggressive in character. It aims to dominate. Though it will never fall to a rival kingdom, God's kingdom will, in fact, overcome every rival. Jehovah the King intends to be the object of universal worship. His program will not be complete until every earthly monarch dismounts his throne and bows the knee in acknowledgment that Jesus Christ is the "only Potentate, King of kings, and Lord of lords" (1 Tim. 6:15). *(4) It is an everlasting kingdom – "…and it shall stand forever"*. Unlike the transitory kingdoms of men, the kingdom of God will last forever.

The little stone cut out of the mountain, Daniel explains in 2:45, will smite the Colossus in the feet and topple it. Interestingly, the Roman Empire fell shortly following the advent of the Lord Jesus Christ some two millennia ago. Since that time, no further "world empires" have emerged. Now, the gospel of the kingdom calls men to a life of separation from the kingdoms of men (2 Cor. 6:16; Rev. 18:4). One day, the last trumpet will sound and the angel will say, *"The kingdoms of this world are become the kingdom of our Lord and of His Christ, and he shall reign forever and ever"* (Rev. 11:15).

Illustrations of Jehovah's Supremacy

Stories from the exile comprise the midsection of Daniel's prophecy: the account of Shadrach, Meshach, and Abednego in the fiery furnace (ch. 3); the story of Nebuchadnezzar's insanity (ch. 4); the story of Belshazzar's feast (ch. 5); and the account of Daniel in the den of lions (ch. 6). Though numerous practical lessons are taught in this concentration of narratives, one dominant characteristic ties them together. Each story illustrates the principle that *"the most High rules in the kingdoms of men"*. An emphasis on God's supremacy and the superiority of His kingdom to the kingdoms of men is the common theme of each story.

The four stories may be grouped under two heads of practical application. Daniel 3 and 6 convey the practical lesson that God honors the faith exhibited by His servants. Daniel 4 and

5 teach the practical truth that God judges the pride and presumption of those who would rival Him.

God Honors Faith (Dan. 3 & 6)

The narratives of Daniel 3 and 6 have a very clear pastoral purpose. The Holy Spirit intends to use the experiences of Shadrach, Meshach, Abednego, and Daniel as models of conviction and non-conformity. Though the writer does nothing more than state the facts of the case, it is apparent that these stories are meant to inspire confidence and encourage the readers to faithfulness, even in the most adverse of circumstances.

Each story develops the same basic plot of tension between the kingdom of God and the kingdoms of men. That tension might be expressed by the question, "What should a person do when obedience to man's law means disobedience to God's?" Both the three young Israelites and Daniel exhibited uncommon valor in the face of great opposition. They are paragons of faith and courage—examples of godliness and devotion while living in exile. These heroic examples of triumphant faith in the face of unimaginable pressures have sparked similar confidence in the hearts of God's servants when they, too, faced the pressure of persecution.

Faith that Survives the Fire (Dan. 3): Perhaps Daniel's interpretation of the king's dream fueled Nebuchadnezzar's pride. Nebuchadnezzar's decision to build a gold replica of himself harks back to the Colossal image of chapter 2 and the words, *"Thou, O king, art this head of gold."* When the statue was constructed it was over 90 feet high.

At the dedication of the image, an edict was issued that demanded worship of the image, under threat of death, at the given signal. This story, consequently, is immortalized as a symbol of the tyranny of despotic governments.

Of course, obedience to this edict would necessarily force the Jews in Babylon to violate the very first commandment, *"Thou shalt have no other gods before me."* When Shadrach, Meshach, and Abednego refused to comply, they were summoned to appear before the king.

Their courageous and confident confession of faith before Nebuchadnezzar is a summary definition of Divine sovereignty. Notice the dual dynamic of trust in God's ability and submission to God's will: *"If it be so, our God whom we serve is able to deliver us from the burning fiery furnace, and he will deliver us out of thine hand, O king. But if not, be it known unto thee, O king, that we will not serve thy gods, nor worship the golden image which thou hast set up"* (3:17-18).

Faith affirms God's ability, but denies His liability. The sovereign King of heaven and earth has the power to deliver but is not obligated to do so. The three Hebrews express confidence in His power, contentment in His will, and commitment to His law.

And God honored their faith. Though Nebuchadnezzar was furious at their insubordination, he had no right to lay claim to their worship. In an insane paroxysm of anger, he heated the ovens to excess and cast the bound youths into the fire. But the fire had no power over them. Not a hair was singed. Instead, the king saw them moving about in the midst of the fire with a fourth companion, "like unto the Son of God" at their side. God's presence with his children in the midst of the fire is a reality that makes the sorest trial bearable (cf. Is. 43:2).

Nebuchadnezzar responded to this amazing deliverance by issuing a new edict forbidding criticism of the God of Shadrach, Meshach, and Abednego, *"for there is no other God that can deliver after this sort"* (3:29), and by promoting the three Hebrews to position of power and influence.

Faith that Calms every Fear (Dan. 6): The narrative of chapter 6 develops the same dynamic though the circumstances are different. Like the three Hebrew youths, Daniel is compelled to obey a law that would violate his conscience. And like them, again, he decides to obey God rather than man. As a consequence of his civil disobedience, Daniel is persecuted. But once again, God delivers his servant from oppression.

Darius, the Mede, is now the ruler of Babylon. The year is approximately 536 B. C. and Daniel is approximately 80 years old (cf. 9:1).[8]

Darius installed a new governmental structure to the kingdom in which authority was delegated to 120 princes (6:1). These 120 would answer to three presidents who would in turn

---

[8] This Darius is either the same person known as Cyrus, the Medo-Persian, or Cyrus' father Ahasuerus (6:28). He assumed control of Babylon in 536 B.C.

report to Darius. Daniel, in lieu of his "excellent spirit", was the chief of these three presidents (6:2-3).

To have a Hebrew in such a position of honor and power irritated the native Babylonian princes. They conspired to disenfranchise Daniel. The sinister plot involved an appeal to Darius to make a decree forbidding prayer to any God except king Darius for thirty days. The flattered king unwisely issued the edict.. He would later rue the naiveté that led to such a hasty decision.

When Daniel learned of the decree, he calmly maintained his habit of devotional activity. Undaunted by the threat of persecution, he prayed thrice each day with windows open, "as he did aforetime" (3:10). The conspirators reported his activity and reminded Darius that "the law of the Medes and the Persians" was irreversible. Daniel must be cast into the den of lions.

That night, Darius could not sleep, but Daniel rested calmly. He was more secure in the lion's den than Darius was in his palace. Darius tossed in anxiety on his bed, but Daniel enjoyed perfect peace in his God.

At first light, Darius called into the mouth of the cave: *"Daniel, O Daniel, servant of the living God, is thy God, whom thou servest continually, able to deliver thee from the lions?"* (3:20). Daniel replied, *"O king, live for ever. My God hath sent his angel, and hath shut the lions' mouths, that they have not hurt me: forasmuch as before him innocency was found in me; and also before thee, O king, have I done no hurt"* (3:21). Then Darius commanded that Daniel's accusers be cast into the same pit, upon the fulfillment of which the lions consumed them all (3:24). The king, subsequently, decreed that everyone in his kingdom *"tremble and fear before the God of Daniel, for he is the living God, and steadfast forever, and his kingdom that which shall not be destroyed."*

Daniel's deliverance is attributed to his faith (3:23). His faith gave him a calm and poised spirit in the midst of trial. He believed in a God who takes care of His servants (cf. Is. 54:17; Ps. 34:22; Deut. 32:36; Ps. 86:2, 4, 16; Ps. 91:14-16; Jno. 12:26). He would have sooner died obeying God's word than lived in disobedience to God's will. Daniel's God is the Sovereign God who takes the wise in their own craftiness and vindicates those who put their trust in Him. With such a God on the throne of His kingdom, who would not "dare to be a Daniel"?

God's sovereignty is not only displayed in the way He deals with His servants, but also in the way He deals with all men. The narratives of chapters 4 and 5 display the sovereignty of God in the affairs of men. He makes His mighty power known not only in the remarkable deliverances wrought in the lives of His people, but in the stunning judgments visited upon men. Daniel 4-5 affirms a very important practical truth: *God invariably judges those who would presume to rival His glory.*

God Judges Proud Rivals (Dan. 4-5)

Nebuchadnezzar's Insanity (Dan. 4). Though Nebuchadnezzar, king of Babylon, has twice acknowledged the power of the God of the Hebrews, his pride and feeling of self-importance is yet unbroken. But God intends to teach the proud monarch an unforgettable lesson.

The king dreamed yet again. In his dream, Nebuchadnezzar saw a great and lofty tree (4:10-12). But like the colossal image of chapter 2, the tree was felled so that nothing but the stump remained. On the ground, the tree became a man whose heart was transformed into the heart of an animal.

Once again, Nebuchadnezzar sought the interpretation from Daniel. Daniel explained that the lofty tree represented Nebuchadnezzar in his influence and power. The cutting down of the tree bespoke Nebuchadnezzar's fall from his glorious estate and a period of humiliating insanity.

Some time passed before the dream was realized. One day, the king proudly surveyed the glory of his kingdom: *"Is not this great Babylon, that I have built for the house of my kingdom by the might of my power, and for the honor of my majesty?"* (4:30). Suddenly, the boasting monarch was struck with madness.

Nebuchadnezzar's "understanding", i.e. rationality, ability to reason, was withdrawn. He imagined himself to be a beast. No longer did he sit on the throne of his kingdom, but walked about in the pasture on his hands and knees, as if he were an animal. This continued for a season of "seven times" — probably seven months, or perhaps seven years. During this episode of mania and lunacy, the king of the mighty Babylonian empire grazed in the pasture like an ox. He slept in the field instead of the royal palace and when morning dawned, his body was wet with the dew of heaven. Like an animal, he did not observe the protocol of basic hygiene. His nails grew like bird claws and his hair like eagle's feathers.

Imagine the embarrassment of the Babylonians when a foreign dignitary asked, "Where is your king?" and they were forced to reply, "See that fellow in yonder pasture walking on his all-fours? That's the king of the mightiest empire in the world." Surely no sinner is so proud but God can humble him.

At the end of this period of Divine judgment, Nebuchadnezzar's sanity was restored. Suddenly, he saw everything clearly. He realized for the first time in his life that he was not invincible, neither was his kingdom impregnable.

His confession, recorded in 4:34-35, is arguably the clearest and most thorough statement of Divine Sovereignty in the whole of Scripture: "*And all the inhabitants of the earth are reputed as nothing: and he doeth according to his will in the army of heaven, and among the inhabitants of the earth: and none can stay his hand, or say unto him, What doest thou.*" In the aftermath, the king of Babylon was restored to the glory of the throne. No longer, however, did he cherish his former illusions of grandeur: "*Now I Nebuchadnezzar praise and extol and honor the King of heaven, all whose works are truth, and his ways judgment: and those that walk in pride he is able to abase*" (4:37).

Belshazzar's Last Feast (Dan. 5). Two generations later, Nebuchadnezzar's grandson (cf. Jer. 27:7) ruled Babylon as coregent with his father Nabonidus. An unscrupulous and indulgent man, Belshazzar organized a great feast for a thousand of his lords. It would prove to be his "last hurrah."

Apparently, the sacred vessels taken from the temple in Jerusalem had been safely kept in the temple treasury at Marduk. In a drunken stupor, however, Belshazzar called for them to be brought to his party. In a daring act of sacrilege, he would use these sacred vessels for the entertainment of his guests.

As they drank wine from the golden vessels, Belshazzar and his guests *"praised the gods of gold, and of silver, of brass, of iron, of wood, and of stone"* (5:4). Suddenly, an uninvited and unexpected Visitor intruded: *"In the same hour came forth fingers of a man's hand, and wrote...upon the plaster of the wall of the king's palace"* (5:4). Belshazzar was literally terrified by the apparition.

He shouted for the magicians to interpret the handwriting on the wall. But like his grandfather's dream, the vision was unintelligible to Babylon's spiritual advisors. Belshazzar's wife remembered that Daniel had interpreted the king's dream years before and suggested that he be called.

When Daniel was summoned before the king, he refused every offer of compensation. Instead, he faithfully recounted the story of Nebuchadnezzar's pride and God's sore judgment upon him. Then, Daniel made personal application of his message: *"And thou his son, O Belshazzar, hast not humbled thine heart, though thou knewest all this; but hast lifted up thyself against the Lord of heaven...and the God in whose hand thy breath is, and whose are all thy ways, hast thou not glorified"* (5:22-23).

Daniel proceeded to interpret the dreadful sentence written on the wall. *"MENE: God hath numbered thy kingdom, and finished it. TEKEL: Thou art weighed in the balances, and art found wanting. PERES: Thy kingdom is divided, and given to the Medes and Persians"* (5:26-28). That very night, Belshazzar was slain and Darius the Mede assumed power over the once mighty Babylonian empire.

How telling are these two narratives! The sovereignty of God means that He possesses absolute authority, transcending everything and everyone. As the transcendent One, He will tolerate no rival. Though his people necessarily suffered his chastening rod for these many years in Babylon, the pride of the Babylonian empire would not escape His judgment. He will have all the glory, for He is God and beside Him there is no other.

The Messianic Kingdom (Dan. 7-12)

In chapters 1-6, Daniel has been concerned to picture God's protection of those who maintained fidelity to Him in a hostile society. Now, Daniel 7 marks a transition from history to prophecy. The theme of the book, however, does not change. Chapters 7 through 12 further develop the same theme, namely, *God's purpose to establish His Kingdom in the earth*. The focus, however, is different. Instead of describing historical events, the last half of Daniel's prophecy is primarily eschatological, i.e. oriented toward the future.

And one important detail is added. These chapters indicate that *God's purpose to establish His kingdom in the earth will be fulfilled only through the Messiah.*

Daniel 7-12, then, with its Messianic tone and apocalyptic genre, is the climax of the Old Testament. All has been building in rising action to this thought, i.e. God's plan to establish His sovereign rule through the coming Messiah. Daniel's point is that God's people are to live in anticipation of God's King who would establish God's Kingdom. The note of antithesis, however, is still present here, just as it was in the earlier chapters of the book. Daniel 7-12 reveals an ongoing conflict between the Kingdom of God and human kingdoms, though God's Kingdom will triumph in the end. Daniel wants his readers to view human events (such as the rise of the wicked king who would persecute the saints in 11:36-45[9]) eschatalogically—that is, as the outworking of Antichrist's agenda to assault the Kingdom of God.

The book of Daniel, therefore, may be summarized in terms of three emphases. Old Testament history professor Willem Van Gemeren writes:

> "The message focuses on the sovereignty of the Creator-Redeemer over the kingdoms of this world, on the suffering and perseverance of the saints during the wars among the kingdoms of this earth, and on their final reward. Difficult as it may be to fit all the pieces together, the general scope of Daniel, like that of Revelation, gives a kingdom perspective...[It is intended] to inspire confident hope in the final establishment of the everlasting kingdom of God."[10]

---

[9] Probably a reference to Antiochus Epiphanes (175-164 B.C.), a ruthless persecutor of the Jews.
[10] *Interpreting the Prophetic Word*, p. 342.

For all who prayerfully yearn for the coming of His kingdom, yet live in a world ruled by human pride, political power plays, and self-preservation, Daniel's message that God will establish His kingdom through the sovereign reign of His own Son is a hopeful note indeed.

Three passages are especially significant in lieu of the Messianic motif of these chapters:

The King's Ascension (Dan. 7)

"The Ancient of Days" is pictured in 7:9 as the great King enthroned over the universe. His throne is mobile, like a chariot, indicating the dynamic nature of His sovereignty. He sits as the Judge of all flesh (7:10).

Suddenly, the Son of Man (a Messianic title) is ushered before Him to receive the reward for His completed covenantal assignment: *"And there was given him dominion, and glory, and a kingdom, that all people, nations, and languages should serve him..."* (7:14; cf. Rev. 5:6-14; Acts 2:36; Phi. 2:9-11; Eph. 1:20-23; 4:8-10). His dominion is universal in scope and perpetual in duration.

The Messianic Kingdom is subsequently given to *"the saints of the most High"* who will *"possess the kingdom forever, even forever and ever"* (7:18; cf. Lk. 22:29-30). They enter into this kingdom through much tribulation now, for the coming Antichrist ("the little horn" of v. 20) makes *"war with the saints"* (7:21), speaking *"great words against the most High, and wearing out the saints of the most High"* (7:25). This spiritual conflict continues until the

"Ancient of Days" comes and the saints "possess", in the ultimate sense, "the kingdom" (7:22, 27).

The Risen King, therefore, will finally conquer every foe that arises from the kingdoms of men, including the infernal power behind them, the Antichrist (cf. 1 Cor. 15:24-25). Though human kingdoms may appear to dominate the saints, yet the Messiah reigns as King even now, and will fully and finally establish His Kingdom when he returns the second time.

The Prophecy of 70 Weeks (Dan. 9)

Another passage of significance to the coming Messiah is Daniel 9:20-27, Daniel's prophecy of 70 Weeks. This prophetic portion is important because it provides a time structure for dating Messiah's anticipated advent. When will this King come? This amazing prophecy gives a specific answer to that question.

Daniel knew that the Babylonian captivity would last 70 years (cf. Jer. 25:11-12). Now, as that 70 year period of exile draws to a close, Daniel prays for the restoration of the kingdom (9:17-19). Suddenly, Gabriel flew swiftly, touched Daniel, and proceeded to explain God's answer to his prayer (9:21-22).

He explained that the establishment of God's Kingdom would not be simultaneous with the restoration of the people from Babylon. Instead, it would be realized in the coming of the Messianic King (9:25-26). Using the 70 year gauge, the angel reveals that 69 sevens (or 483 years) from the "commandment to restore and to build Jerusalem" (a reference to Nehemiah's permission to restore the walls of Jerusalem in 445 B.C.) "unto

Messiah the Prince" would elapse. This amazing prediction dates the onset of Messiah's short ministry at approximately 28 A. D. "After" the 69th "week", presumably in the 70th, Messiah would be "cut off, but not for himself" (9:26), a reference, no doubt, to the substitutionary death of the Lord Jesus Christ. Through his death, Messiah will "seal up sins, make reconciliation for iniquity, and bring in everlasting righteousness" (9:24). During this period, Jerusalem will also be destroyed (9:26-27).

Though it is not possible to exactly pinpoint the historical dates described by this prophetic language, yet the general time frame is beyond question. With a two or three year margin of error, we can be confident that Daniel's prophecy of the 70 Weeks places the crucifixion of Christ near 30 A. D. Is it any wonder then that such a crowd of Jews from various geographical locations had converged on the city of Jerusalem on the Day of Pentecost? Who can doubt that they had been counting prophetic "weeks"?

The Time of the End (Dan. 12)

The final passage of significance to the Messianic plot of Daniel's kingdom perspective is found in the final chapter of the book. Daniel 12 reveals events at "the time of the end" (12:4), when the Kingdom of God will be realized in the ultimate sense. Then, every foe will be vanquished and every competitor silenced (11:45b).

Verses 1 and 2 contain the clearest statement of the doctrine of the resurrection in the entire Old Testament. The specific events of the "time of the end", however, are "closed up and sealed" (12:9). Daniel's questions are not all answered. He is only told that the righteous will be tested, the wicked will persist in wickedness and ignorance, and the wise will understand.

The book ends with a very comforting promise: *"But go thy way till the end be: for thou shalt rest, and stand in thy lot at the end of the days"* (12:13). Though Daniel, now in his 80's, would never likely see Jerusalem again, he would nonetheless enter into his eternal inheritance when Messiah returns the second time. Then he will hear, *"Come ye blessed of my Father and inherit the Kingdom prepared for you from the foundation of the world"* (Mt. 25:34).

The Exilic Prophets

Part 3

The
Chronistic History

(or Post-Exilic Era)

Timeline of Post-Exilic Period

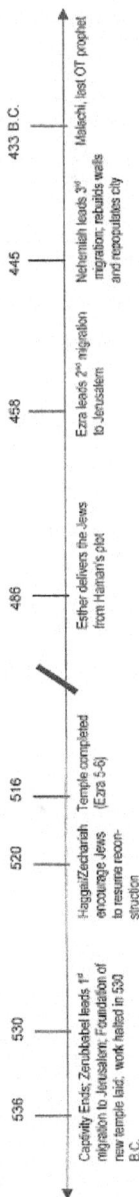

536	530		520	516		486		458		445	433 B.C.

Captivity Ends; Zerubbabel leads 1st migration to Jerusalem; Foundation of new temple laid; work halted in 530 B.C.

Haggai/Zechariah encourage Jews to resume reconstruction

Temple completed (Ezra 5-6)

Esther delivers the Jews from Haman's plot

Ezra leads 2nd migration to Jerusalem

Nehemiah leads 3rd migration; rebuilds walls and repopulates city

Malachi, last OT prophet

Cyrus, the 1st Persian king	Cambyses, 2nd king	Darius I, 3rd king of Persia	Xerxes, 4th king of Persia	Artaxerxes I, 5th king of Persia, reigned from 464 to 423 B.C.

270

Introduction to Part 3

The fall of Babylon and restoration of the Jews marks the third major division in Old Testament history. Many modern Old Testament scholars refer to this period as the nation's "Chronistic History". The Chronistic, or post-exilic, period refers to events that transpired between 536 and 400 B.C. and corresponds to the books of Chronicles, Ezra, Nehemiah, and Esther. The dominant theme is *Israel's restoration as a theocracy*. The Chronicler wrote his history to give guidance and direction for restoring the nation during the post-exilic period. The prophecies of Haggai, Zechariah, and Malachi also belong to this period.

This objective to rebuild and renovate Jewish society explains the apparent redundancy of Chronicles to the book of Kings. It is true that 1st and 2nd Chronicles consists of a record of the pre-exilic kingdom, just as 1st and 2nd Kings. One might wonder why Chronicles is necessary seeing that it simply repeats the history of Kings. The answer is intriguing.

Kings was written before but Chronicles after the Babylonian captivity. Kings was written to explain to the people *why* God had judged the nation and sent it into exile for 70 years. Chronicles, on the other hand, was written to remind the people of their identity as a theocratic community and to encourage them to rebuild Jerusalem and the temple so that life and worship might be resumed. Interestingly, Chronicles includes a note of hope that is missing in Kings. For example, Manasseh's sins are spotlighted in Kings, but nothing is said of his repentance. The Chronicler, however, records both his sins and his repentance, emphasizing God's grace to the penitent man. One can readily see that such examples of Divine grace were intended to give hope to the returning exiles as they set out to rebuild their lives from the ruins of Divine judgment.

Chapter 15

RESTORATION OF THE THEOCRACY
Ezra, Nehemiah, Esther

The God of Israel is also the God of the Nations. He governs the world He created with perfect and exact justice. Though He had used Babylon as His instrument of judgment upon Israel, she was, nonetheless, culpable for her own sins. Now He would take punitive measures on Babylon for all her atrocities against His people and the other nations (Jer. 51:7, 24-25, 34-35, 49; Ps. 137:8-9).

The Fall of Babylon & Release from Captivity (Jer. 51)

At the time of the Jewish deportation to Babylon in 586 B.C., Jeremiah had prophesied of God's plan to conquer the Babylonian empire and to restore Israel to her homeland. Jeremiah 51 records this happy, yet sobering, message:

> "For Israel hath not been forsaken, nor Judah of his God... though their land was filled with sin against the Holy One of Israel. Flee out of the midst of Babylon, and deliver every man his soul...for this is the time of the Lord's vengence; he will render unto her a recompense...Babylon is suddenly fallen and destroyed...forsake her, and let us go every one into his own country: for her judgment reacheth unto heaven, and is lifted up even to the skies...Behold, I am against thee, O destroying mountain, saith the Lord, which destroyest all the earth: and I will stretch out mine hand upon thee, and roll thee down from the rocks, and will make thee a burnt mountain...Babylon shall

become heaps, a dwellingplace for dragons, an astonishment, and a hissing, without inhabitant...And I will punish Bel in Babylon, and I will bring forth out of his mouth that which he hath swallowed up: and the nations shall not flow together any more unto him: yea, the wall of Babylon shall fall...Ye that have escaped the sword, go away, stand not still: remember the Lord afar off, and let Jerusalem come into your mind..." (Jer. 51:5-9, 25, 37, 44, 50).

By what means would Divine judgment come upon the mighty mountain that was the Babylonian empire? It would come by means of the Medes (Jer. 51:11, 28). Just as Babylon had been the instrument of judgment in God's hand against the nation of Israel, so the Medes would be God's "battle ax" against Babylon (Jer. 51:20ff).

Some fifty years later, the prophecy found its fulfillment when Daniel interpreted the handwriting on the wall at Belshazzar's palace. God's dreadful sentence of judgment against the king of Babylon consisted of three parts: (1) Your reign is over; (2) Your character is deficient; (3) Your kingdom has been given to the Medes and Persians (Dan. 5:25-28). That very night, Belshazzar, king of Babylon, was assassinated and Darius the Mede took the throne (Dan. 5:30-31).

The Role of Cyrus

Darius, the new governor of Babylon, was probably vice-regent to Cyrus, the king of Medo-Persia. Darius continued in this post from 538 to 536 B.C., when Cyrus assumed the throne himself. The conquest of Babylon meant that Cyrus now claimed the world for Persia (modern day Iran). The Medo-Persian empire would subsequently stretch from India to Egypt and Thrace, including all of Western Asia, and rule for the next 204 years, or until 334 B. C. It has been suggested that the fall of Babylon was the defining moment in the historical shift from Eastern to Western dominance in the civilized world.

Who was this man Cyrus? He was the product of a royal marriage between Cambyses, a Persian, and Mandane, the daughter of the last king of Media. Some 150 years before his birth, Isaiah had prophesied of him as an unwitting "servant" of Jehovah, i.e. someone the Lord would use to accomplish His purposes, even calling him by name (Is. 44:28; 45:1-4). Hence, Cyrus is an object lesson of a very important aspect of Divine providence known as "the principle of second causes".

As a Persian, Cyrus was probably a Zoroastrian monotheist. His religious training would have naturally predisposed him to favor the Jews over the polytheistic Babylonians. His decision to free the Jews and restore them to their inheritance, however, was not due to any natural predisposition. Scripture attributes this act, one unparalleled in history, to nothing short of the providence of God:

> "Now in the first year of Cyrus king of Persia...the Lord stirred up the spirit of Cyrus king of Persia, that he made a proclamation throughout all his kingdom, and put it also in writing saying, Thus saith Cyrus king of Persia, All the kingdoms of the earth hath the Lord God of heaven given me; and he hath charged me to build him a house in Jerusalem,

which is in Judah. Who is there among you of all his people? The Lord his God be with him, and let him go up" (2 Chr. 36:22-23).

Thus Cyrus was not only the Jews' emancipator, but counselor and encourager. He also pledged himself to be their helper. He both wrote to the appointed governors neighboring Judea to request their assistance on behalf of the returning exiles and restored to the Jews all the remaining temple vessels that Nebuchadnezzar had originally seized in the exile (Ezra 1:1-11). Cyrus' letter to his appointed governors in Syria concerning his decree to give the Jews leave to rebuild Jerusalem also gives a detailed account of these sacred vessels.[1] In that epistle, Cyrus also commissioned Zerubbabel, the governor of the Jews, to rebuild the temple, and the priests to resume their official duties of Divine worship. He wrote: "The priests shall also offer these sacrifices according to the laws of Moses in Jerusalem; and when they offer them, they shall pray to God for the preservation of the king and of his family, that the kingdom of Persia may continue."

Remarkably, only 42,360 Israelites determined to return to Jerusalem from Babylon under the leadership of Zerubbabel in 536 B.C. (Ezra 2). The 70 years in Babylon had taken its toll on Israel's sense of identity and a great number of Jews chose to remain in Babylon. Two other groups eventually migrated homeward—a group under the leadership of Ezra in 457 B.C.,

---

[1] Flavius Josephus, *Antiquities of the Jews*, Book XI, pp. 228-229.

and one under Nehemiah in 444 B.C. Babylon subsequently became an important center for Jewish learning until the city itself declined near 300 years before Christ.

> *Hail the day so long expected,*
> *Hail the year of sweet release;*
> *Zion's walls are now erected*
> *And her watchmen publish peace.*
> *Swell the sound ye kings and nobles,*
> *Priests and people, rich and poor,*
> *Babylon is fallen, is fallen, is fallen;*
> *Babylon is fallen to rise no more.*
> *- Unknown*

The post-exilic books of Ezra and Nehemiah were originally one book called 1 and 2 Ezra. The two volumes form a single history of the post-exilic efforts of the returning exiles to rebuild the temple and the city of Jerusalem.

The group of 42,000 Israelites who migrated home under Cyrus' edict of restoration was the first of three such migrations. Though this initial group was enthused about going home and well-intentioned about the rebuilding of the temple, they did not proceed far before the work was halted.

No sooner had they celebrated the Feast of Tabernacles and laid the foundation for the new temple (Ez. 3), that they met with opposition. The *"adversaries of Judah and Benjamin"*, probably a reference to Samaritans, *"hired counselors against them, to frustrate their purpose"* (Ez. 4:1-6), and wrote a letter of accusation against the Jews to send to Ahasuerus[2] (or Cambyses), king of Persia. They argued that Jerusalem had a reputation as a "rebellious and bad city" (4:12), that the people would refuse to pay taxes so that the king's revenue would be damaged. They insisted that Cambyses search old records to learn of Jerusalem's long history of insurrection, rebellion, and sedition, lest they complete their project and rise to revolt against Persian control (4:15-16).

Cambyses was swayed by the accusation and issued a decree to stop the rebuilding project (4:17-24). Everything came to a grinding halt for the next sixteen years, i.e. 536 to 520 B.C., and a spirit of apathy prevailed among the people.

Not long after Darius I took the throne of Persia in 522 B.C., he rediscovered Cyrus' original edict and the work was resumed (Ez. 5-6). He commanded the opponents both to leave the Jews alone and to provide them with whatever materials they needed (6:7-10). The prophets Haggai and Zechariah provided the spiritual incentive by challenging the apathy of the people with the question, *"How long will you dwell in your ceiled houses while the Lord's house lieth waste?,"* and Zerubbabel and Joshua the high priest orchestrated the mechanics of the project. By 516 B.C., a rebuilt temple stood in the very place that Solomon's temple had been destroyed some 70 years earlier in 586 B.C. The dedication of the new temple and the first observance of the feast of the

---

[2] A common title of many Persian kings. It is the Hebrew translation of the Persian title *Khshayarsha*. Though he is called by the title *Ahasuerus*, *Cambyses* was his actual name, just as the Persian king in the time of Esther is called *Ahasuerus*, though *Xerxes* was his name.

278

Passover in the new house of worship was a joyful occasion indeed (6:13-22).

After Darius I, Xerxes ruled Persia. He reigned from 486 to 464 B.C., during which period the majority of the Jewish population remained in what was once Babylon. Esther, a Jew, was selected to be his wife and God providentially used her to preserve the nation of Israel from a conspiracy to exterminate the Jews.

Ezra, Religious Reformer

In 458 B.C., fifty-eight years after the temple was rebuilt, Ezra the scribe led another group of returning exiles from Babylon to Jerusalem. Artaxerxes I (or Artaxerxes Longimanus[3]) was now on the Persian throne, having assumed power in 464. Artaxerxes was agreeable to Ezra's request to beautify the house of the Lord, permitting any who were *"minded of their own freewill to go up to Jerusalem"* with Ezra (Ez. 7:1-13). He gave Ezra official permission to establish local government in Judah according to the laws of God and to teach the law to those that knew it not (7:25).

Approximately 1700 people returned with Ezra, whose burden was clearly to labor for the spiritual and internal, as opposed to mere physical and external, reformation of the people. Upon his arrival, Ezra began the work of restoring the spiritual life of the nation by proclaiming a fast and seeking

---

[3] Nehemiah was cupbearer to this same Artaxerxes, king of Persia.

God's guidance (8:21). He then recommissioned the priests for service and burnt offerings were made to the God of Israel.

The hopeful work of spiritual renewal, however, was short-lived. A new crisis was revealed. It came to Ezra's attention that a number of the original 42,000 exiles who had returned some 80 years earlier had repeated the old sin of mixing themselves among the heathen nations around them. They had intermarried with the surrounding nations and adopted their idolatrous and pagan practices (9:1-2).

Ezra was horrified. He knew that the repetition of the very sins for which the nation had been sent into captivity threatened to undo all that had been accomplished. He tore his garment and plucked the hair from his head and beard. This display of penitence and mourning drew a crowd of devout Jews who were likewise burdened. Ezra's subsequent prayer is one of the most moving expressions of contrite confession anywhere in the Bible (9:1-15).

After prayer, a great congregation of Israelites assembled to Ezra who instructed them to repent at a radical level by dismissing the strange wives they had taken and to apply to God for mercy. The people complied and any further judgment from God was diverted.

Nehemiah the Wallbuilder

In 445 B.C., thirteen years after Ezra's migration back to Jerusalem, a Jewish man named Nehemiah was serving in the

Persian palace at Shushan[4] as cupbearer to king Artaxerxes Longimanus. Nehemiah knew of Ezra's expedition to beautify the house of the Lord (for the same Artaxerxes that now reigned had commissioned Ezra) and was anxious to know the progress of the work.

A visit to Shushan from Hanani and other men of Judah lately come from Jerusalem brought the answer: *"The remnant that are left of the captivity there in the province are in great affliction and reproach: the wall of Jerusalem also is broken down, and the gates thereof are burned with fire"* (Neh. 1:1-3). The polar opposite of all Nehemiah's hopes, this report so burdened him that he spent the next three months[5] weeping, fasting, and praying. His prayer to the God of heaven in 1:5-11 is an impassioned petition for guidance and blessing on the basis of God's covenant faithfulness.

At some point during that 100 day interval, Nehemiah began to entertain the prospect of personal involvement. Perhaps God would use him to remedy the deplorable circumstances of the people and city he loved so well. Motivated by a concern for God's glory and the prosperity of His kingdom, Nehemiah prayed that God would open the door of providence

---

[4] The Greeks called this capital of the Perisan empire "Susa". Near the turn of the 20th century, archaeologists uncovered there the palace of Xerxes where Esther lived.

[5] Compare 1:1 and 2:1. The month Chisleu is comparable to *mid-November-mid-December* of our calendar. The month Nisan corresponds to our *mid-March-mid-April*.

so he might gain leave of his palace duties in order to journey to Jerusalem (1:11).

This was no small request. Although Artaxerxes had granted Ezra the scribe permission to return to his homeland, it was highly unlikely that he would release Nehemiah. Unlike Ezra, a religious teacher, Nehemiah was nothing more than a high-class slave (1:11b). As cupbearer to the king, he occupied a fiduciary position that required unusual integrity. The element of trustworthiness necessary to the role of cupbearer meant that finding a replacement for him would be no small challenge. The prospect that Nehemiah would be granted a "leave of absence" in lieu of both his responsible position and the fact that he was a "civilian" rather than a "cleric" like Ezra was so unlikely as to be virtually impossible.

But nothing is too hard for the God who holds the hearts of all men in His sovereign hands. One day, Artaxerxes made inquiry about Nehemiah's apparent sadness. After a silent "arrow prayer" sent heavenward, Nehemiah revealed his burden. Remarkably, Artaxerxes not only agreed to release him, but appointed him governor of Judea. He also provided a military escort to Jerusalem, and government funds to aid in the repair of the city (Neh. 2:1-8).

Upon his arrival in Jerusalem, Nehemiah spent three days formulating his plan. Then he shared his vision with the people (2:11-20). Though neighboring political figures named Sanballat, Tobiah, and Geshem ridiculed the venture, the people "had a mind to work". In just a matter of days, one-half of the city walls had been rebuilt (4:1-6).

When rhetoric had proven unsuccessful, the enemies of the Jews resorted to threats and intimidation. They *"conspired all of them together to come and to fight against Jerusalem, and to hinder it"* (4:8). But Nehemiah countered the threat by humble prayer and wise planning (4:9).

The relentless external pressure and the mammoth amount of work yet to be done, however, was wearing on the builders: *"And Judah said, The strength of the bearers of burdens is decayed, and there is much rubbish; so that we are not able to build the wall. And our adversaries said, They shall not know, neither see, till we come in the midst among them, and slay them, and cause the work to cease"* (4:10-11). Nehemiah moved quickly to remedy the spreading infection of discouragement.

How did he meet this crisis? First, Nehemiah reminded the people of the "big picture": *"Be not afraid of them: remember the Lord, which is great and terrible, and fight for your brethren, your sons, and your daughters, your wives, and your houses"* (4:14). Second, he reorganized the work on the wall so that families and people of communal interest could build together (4:19ff). This wise counter-tactic proved the undoing of the planned attack.

Nehemiah also had to deal with other crises such as internal strife (Neh. 5) and personal plots against his life (Neh. 6). He met each challenge with wisdom, courage, and dependence on God, and *"the wall was finished…in fifty-two days"* (6:15). Nothing but the providential blessing of God could account for such a monumental achievement as the reconstruction of 2 ½ miles of wall in less than 2 months (6:16).

With the physical challenge of reconstructing the walls of Jerusalem complete, Nehemiah proceeded to tackle the social challenge of repopulating the city.

Convincing the people to move into and reinhabit the city was indeed a social challenge, for the returned exiles had lost their sense of identity. But how would he revive their sense of identity? He would do so by reminding them of their common spiritual interests as the covenant people of God.

Like a wise engineer, Nehemiah found a genealogical register of the exiles who had returned to Jerusalem and summoned them to the city (Neh. 7). Then, he turned the program over to Ezra the scribe. Ezra called for the book of the law of Moses and began to read God's word to the people, while the priests mingled with the crowd interpreting, explaining, and applying the truths they heard (Neh. 8:1-8). The rediscovery of God's word exercised a profound effect upon the people.

The next day, the crowd observed the feast of booths, a reminder of their rich heritage and the pilgrim character of their faith (8:13-18). Three weeks later, they met again for a worship service (9:1ff). This service began with contrition and confession of sin, and ended with a renewed commitment to keep God's covenant and not to forsake the house of the Lord (9:38 – 10:39).

This season of spiritual renewal resulted in the decision to bring 10% of the population then in Israel to repopulate the city of Jerusalem (11:1). Almost 3000 people volunteered to move into the city (11:2-19). Once Jerusalem was reinhabited, Nehemiah organized an elaborate ceremony to dedicate the wall. It was a happy time of thanksgiving and praise, and "the joy of Jerusalem was heard even afar off" (12:27-43).

The book of Nehemiah reads like a personal journal. It details the historical circumstances of Jerusalem's restoration. Indeed, it is a testimony to its central character – Nehemiah. It depicts him as a man of prayer, integrity, courage, wisdom, and perseverance. But, the book of Nehemiah is more than a testimony to human ingenuity, character, and achievement. Far and away, this book is a testimony to the covenant faithfulness of God. He is the hero of this story. It was His providence that softened the king's heart, directed Nehemiah's decisions, won the ears and hearts of the people to Nehemiah's vision, sustained the builders in the face of relentless opposition, and restored a sense of identity and solidarity to the people.

The restoration of Jerusalem was, in other words, no mere human production. God alone is able to accomplish such an impossible feat, and He alone deserves the glory.

Restoration of the Theocracy

Chapter 16

THE POST-EXILIC PROPHETS
Haggai, Zechariah, Malachi

Three prophets ministered to Israel after the Babylonian captivity: Haggai, Zechariah, and Malachi. Haggai and Zechariah prophesied during the silent interim between the laying of the temple foundation and the reconstruction of the temple (or, if you please, between the events recorded in Ezra 4 and those recorded in Ezra 5-6). Malachi was contemporaneous with the Persian king Artaxerxes I. His prophetic career followed on the heels of Nehemiah's reforms.[1]

Historical Background

The year was 520 B.C. Sixteen years had passed since Cyrus liberated the Jews. The foundation for the rebuilt temple had been laid in Jerusalem, but Cambyses, influenced by the enemies of the Jews, issued an interdict to halt the reconstruction efforts. For at least a decade, no further progress toward the restoration of Divine worship and community life in Jerusalem had been made.

It was into this lackluster scene that God sent and commissioned two prophets to challenge the apathetic nation to resume the work of reconstruction. Their names were Haggai and Zechariah.

---

[1] See "Timeline of Post-Exilic Period" at beginning of Part 3.

Because of the success they enjoyed, the people petitioned the new Persian king Darius I (who had assumed the throne in 522 B.C.) for permission to resume the rebuilding program (cf. Ezra 5:1ff; 6:14). They reminded him of Cyrus' original edict. After investigating that lead, Darius permitted the resumption of the work and in a mere four years, the new temple was completed.

The Prophet Haggai

Little is known about the prophet Haggai. Besides his very brief, two-chapter prophecy (consisting of only 38 verses), he is mentioned twice in Ezra (5:1; 6:14).

He suddenly appears on the scene in 520 B.C. and delivers four messages in a time-frame of four months. Each message is precisely dated (cf. 1:1; 2:1; 2:10; 2:20), and the period corresponds to the months August to December on the Gregorian calendar. After delivering his final message, Haggai disappears from the scene.

Like his ministry, Haggai's messages are brief and "to the point". The first discourse appears in 1:1-11. It might be appropriately titled by the twice repeated phrase "Consider Your Ways" (vs. 5, 7). A brief historical account of the effect the message had on his hearers follows in 1:12-15. The second address is recorded in 2:1-9. It is a message of encouragement to the builders with a strong Messianic overtone. This discourse might be titled "Be Strong in the Lord" (v. 4).

The third address appears in 2:10-19. Here, the prophet teaches the people the important principle that God blesses His people in obedience. The final discourse appears in 2:20-23 and is a message concerning the Messianic hope of the nation.

Haggai Challenges Spiritual Apathy (1:1-15)

The book of Haggai (as well as Zechariah) reveals the anemic spiritual condition of Israel in the aftermath of their return to Jerusalem. It is important to note, however, that Israel was not at this time an immoral or ungodly society. The circumstances attending Haggai's ministry were unlike conditions within the nation before the exile, when God sent prophets to warn them of impending judgment. Haggai's audience is the faithful remnant that has returned from Babylon to the land of their fathers.

But all is not quite right. The euphoria experienced and enthusiasm exhibited at their liberation from Babylon has now given way to a spirit of indifference and inactivity. In a period of only sixteen years, a certain spiritual coldness has paralyzed the nation.

What has contributed to this spirit of apathy and inactivity? Obviously, the hostile opposition of their neighbors tended to their discouragement. As time passed, their initial attitude of caution degenerated into a settled spirit of complacency. Another possible reason for the lethargy of the day was their own lack of experience. Many of them had lived in Babylon since birth, during which time they had adjusted to worship without the temple. These people had never even seen God's house of worship. In fact, since the return of Zerubbabel's delegation, the Jews had been worshipping without the benefit of a temple (cf. Ezra 3:2ff). Perhaps they thought that was good enough.

Whatever the reason, the Jews near Jerusalem had settled in to a lifestyle characterized by the priority of personal enterprise. Divine worship in the house of God was not central, but peripheral, to them. This secular orientation toward life made them cavalier toward spiritual things.

Haggai bursts onto the scene to challenge their self-centered lifestyle: "*Is it time for you to dwell in your ceiled houses, and this house lie waste?*" (1:4). The people were neglecting spiritual responsibilities and pursuing their own material prosperity. Haggai, however, challenges them with the facts: "*Consider your ways. Ye have sown much, but bring in little; ye eat, but ye have not enough; ye drink, but ye are not filled with drink; ye clothe you, but there is none warm; and he that earneth wages earneth wages to put it into a bag with holes*" (1:5-6). Though they worked diligently for personal prosperity, they were not, in fact, prosperous. He exhorts them to evaluate their priorities in the light of the hardships with which they met. God was not blessing them for all their industry, for they had not made His house the priority of their lives (1:9-11).

Haggai's confrontational message had a powerful effect upon the people: "*The Lord stirred up...the spirit of all the remnant of the people and they came and did work in the house of the Lord of hosts, their God"* (1:14). The revival that resulted must have brought tremendous encouragement to the heart of Haggai.

Is this not a picture of the modern situation? How salutary is this reminder! When God's people invert the priorities of life, making earthly comfort preeminent to the kingdom of God, they will enjoy neither earthly comfort nor the benefits of God's kingdom.

Haggai Encourages Faith (2:1-9)

After challenging the religious apathy of the people, Haggai next encourages their faith. He bids the workers to *"be strong... and work, for I am with you, saith the Lord"* (v. 4). The thrice repeated injunction "be strong" is a military term, a fact that serves to remind us that serving God involves conflict and requires a soldier's courage. But the fight of faith is a "good fight" — i.e. a battle worth waging.

How does Haggai encourage these builders? He exhorts them to faith by reminding them of a previous promise and by revealing to them a future prospect.

First, he reminds them of God's covenantal presence: *"According to the word that I covenanted with you when ye came out of Egypt, so my spirit remaineth among you: fear ye not"* (2:5). Second, he reveals the future prospect of a superior glory: *"The glory of this latter house shall be greater than the former...and in this place will I give peace, saith the Lord of hosts"* (2:9).

This prospect of the future glory of God's house is a reference to the coming Messiah. Indeed, the actual rebuilt temple was not more glorious than the Solomon's original temple. It was both structurally and aesthetically inferior to the "former house" (2:3). But God promised to "fill this house with glory" (2:7), a glory that would be superior to the former glory (2:9). This superior glory would be realized when "the desire of all nations shall come" (2:7). In the "temple" of Messiah's body (cf. Jno. 2:21; Jno. 1:14), the glory of God would be displayed in its fullness.

This passage teaches that the coming of the Messiah and fulfillment of God's covenant purpose through Him is the ultimate encouragement to our faith. It is the presence of God that makes His people strong, especially His presence in the person of His Son. What better incentive exists to "be strong and work" in the service of the Lord than the great fact of Christ's glorious person and successful redemptive work on the cross?

Haggai Teaches Obedience (2:10-19)

In the third address, Haggai exhorts the people to holiness. He does so by asking the priests for a ruling on how an object may be made either clean or unclean: *"If one bear holy flesh in the skirt of his garment, and with his skirt do touch bread...shall it be holy?"* (2:12). In other words, can holiness be communicated by contact? The priests correctly answered "no". Then he asked, *"If one that is unclean by a dead body touch any of these, shall it be unclean?"* (2:13). In other words, is sin communicable? The priests correctly answered "yes".

God now applies this principle to the nation (2:14). Because of her spiritual apathy, everything that Israel touched was contaminated. The people did not prosper in any endeavor because their priorities were out of place (cf. Hag. 1). Since their repentance, however, the situation will be reversed: "*...from this day and upward...will I bless you*" (2:15a, 18a, 19b).

The practical lesson is unmistakable: Sinfulness in certain areas of life will eventually affect every area of life, bringing with it misery, frustration, and pain. Blessing, on the contrary, results from the conscious decision to serve and obey the Lord.

Haggai Anticipates the Messiah (2:20-23)

Haggai concludes his prophecies with a message to Zerubbabel, the leader of the remnant. Again, it is a message of encouragement with a strong Messianic component. God tells Zerubbabel that though the political scene would be altered (vs. 21-22), yet he would be kept safe and secure, like a king preserves his own signet ring (v. 23).

Interestingly, Zerubbabel is listed in the genealogy of Jesus (Mt. 1:12-13). Through this man's lineage would come the Messiah who would rule over the kingdom of God forever. Regardless of the immediate dangers and difficulties of rebuilding the city of Jerusalem and the temple for Divine worship, God's purpose to establish His kingdom would be realized in the coming Messianic King. Zerubbabel could take great comfort in that fact.

Zechariah

Zechariah, the son of Iddo, was Haggai's prophetic colleague. He began his career only two months after Haggai spoke his first prophecy and ministered during the same static interval of the reconstruction of the temple. His book serves as a supplement to Haggai's prophecy.

Like Haggai, Zechariah was born in Babylon and returned to Jerusalem with Zerubbabel's migration in 536 B.C. Beside his literary prophecy, Zechariah is mentioned in Ezra 5:1; 6:14; and Nehemiah 12:16. His name means "Jehovah remembers" and his prophecy—with its portrait of Israel's glorious future and promise that the universal dominion of the Messiah would, in fact, be realized—echoes that theme.

Style of the Book

Though Haggai and Zechariah are co-laborers in the quest to animate the nation to resume reconstruction of the temple, the contrast between their respective styles is revealing. Haggai takes a practical approach, challenging the people to evaluate their priorities in lieu of the small success they had experienced.

Zechariah's prophecy, on the contrary, is more theoretical. He aims to excite the people by explaining their situation in terms of God's promise to revive the nation. Zechariah aims to help his readers to interpret their current crisis in the larger context of God's kingdom objective. He seeks to motivate them to action by the vision of Divine activity. He wants them to see the unfolding of the big picture and to interpret their present challenges in that context.

It is not surprising, therefore, that *Zechariah* has been called the Old Testament equivalent of the book of *Revelation*. It is arguably the most eschatological or apocalyptic of the Old Testament prophecies.   Like *Revelation*, this book aims to encourage the people to present faithfulness by a view of future glory.

Perhaps more than any other book, *Zechariah* reveals how all the promises of the universal dominance of God's kingdom, the primary theme of the Old Testament, converge in the person of the coming Messiah. By blending a proliferation of Messianic prophecies with an elaborate theology of Spiritual Renewal, Zechariah encourages his readers to action by reminding them of the truth that *the ultimate revival will be realized with the coming of the Messiah.*

Structure of the Book

After an introductory "call to repentance" (1:1-6), the prophecy of Zechariah falls into two primary divisions. Chapters 1-8 consist of prophetic visions with a more immediate, historical application. Chapters 9-14 contain verbal prophecies with a more remote, or eschatological significance. A superficial outline of *Zechariah* might look like this:

I. Eight Night Visions (chs. 1-8)
   A. Vision #1 - Horses & Riders
   B. Vision #2 – Four Horns & Four Carpenters
   C. Vision #3 – Surveyor
   D. Vision #4 – Joshua's Acquittal
   E. Vision #5 – Golden Lampstand
   F. Vision #6 - Flying Roll
   G. Vision #7 – Woman in Ephah
   H. Vision #8 – Four Chariots
II. Kingdom Prophecies (chs. 9-14)
   A. Israel's Deliverance through the Messianic King (9-10)
   B. The Shepherd-King's Humiliation (11-12)
   C. The Cleansing Fountain (13)
   D. The Messianic Kingdom (14)

Themes of the Book

The two structural divisions of the book are doctrinally significant. Zechariah's "night visions" in chapters 1-8 develop a doctrine of revival. His verbal prophecies in chapters 9-14 focus on the character and coming of the Messiah.

A Theology of Revival (Zech. 1-8): Zechariah 1 through 6 contain the prophet's eight "night visions". Chapters 7-8 offer a portrait of the triumphs of revival life. Chapter eight is actually a summary of the various elements involved in revival with the key text being verse nineteen: *"The fasts...shall be...cheerful feasts,"* teaching that what had previously been an occasion for mourning would now be an occasion for celebration. The whole tenor of chapter eight is one of jubilation and exuberance. It is in these night visions that God reveals His purpose to revive the nation.

The first night vision, the vision of the horses and riders (1:7-17) addresses *God's motive for revival*: *"...I am jealous for Jerusalem and for Zion with a great jealousy"* (v. 14). The jealousy of God is a phrase that always expresses His desire for the glory of His name. Vision #2, the vision of the four horns and the four carpenters (1:18-21), discloses *the results of revival*. The four horns are symbolic of the powers who had scattered the people of God. The four carpenters "fray," that is, terrify and oust, the horns, teaching that revival results in deliverance from one's enemies. A similar thought is developed in vision #7 (5:5-11), the vision of the woman in the ephah (barrel) who was banished to Shinar (Babylon). Vision #3, the vision of the surveyor (2:1-13), together with vision #4, the vision of Joshua the high priest (3:1-10), together with vision #5, the vision of the golden lampstand (4:1-14) and vision #8, the vision of the four chariots (6:1-8) all speak of *the nature of revival*. Let's be more specific.

The vision of the surveyor (Zech. 2) discloses the nature of revival in terms of *the presence of God in the midst of His people*.

"Sing and rejoice...for, lo, I come, and I will dwell in the midst of thee...and many nations shall be joined to the Lord in that day...and I will dwell in the midst of thee...be silent, O all flesh, before the Lord: for He is raised up out of His holy habitation" (2:10-13).

The manifest presence of God is the very essence of revival; hence, the early church frequently witnessed strangers who would come into their assembly and fall to the ground in worship, "*confessing that God was in them of a truth*" (I Cor. 14:25). When "*the Lord awakes as one out of sleep, and like a mighty man that shouteth by reason of wine*," smites "his enemies" and reestablishes His church (Ps. 78:65-66); when He "*rends the heavens and comes down*" (Is. 64:1-3); when He "*arises with healing in His wings*" (Mal. 4:2; Ps. 44:23-26) and "visits" His people (Ps. 80:14-19) with outpourings of His Spirit; then, and not until then, is she revitalized.

The vision of Joshua the high priest (Zech. 3) teaches that revival *involves corporate forgiveness*, as God removes the iniquity of the land (v. 9) and plucks His people from the fire of judgment (v. 2). The vision of the chariots (Zech. 6) corresponds to this thought of forgiveness, symbolizing *the pacifying of God's wrath* (v. 8).

Thirdly, the nature of revival is disclosed in the vision of the lampstand (Zech. 4). Revival is *a sovereign work of the Holy Spirit*, i.e. "not by might, nor by power, but by my Spirit". Man cannot manufacture or work-up this fire; it must be sent down by God. When God revives his people, they respond by giving Him the glory, saying "grace, grace unto it" (vs. 6-7).

The only vision left is the sixth, the vision of the flying scroll (Zech. 5:1-4). This vision completes Zechariah's theology of revival by addressing the subject of *antecedents to revival*. The flying roll is "a curse" (v. 3), that is a divine judgment, which enters into the house of society's lawless (v. 4), and it teaches us that *divine judgment is frequently the precursor of spiritual renewal*. It's a sad indictment against mankind that judgment is frequently necessary to reawaken a sense of moral and spiritual obligation. That such is the case is an undisputed fact, both in scripture and history. This thought, that revival comes on the heels of cultural upheaval through divine judgment, is a thought pronounced in scriptures such as Psalm 79:4-9, Psalm 80, Psalm 85:4-7, and Habakkuk 3:2. God may utilize circumstances such as war, famine, disease, pestilence, or even natural disaster to awaken people to divine matters and introduce a spiritual revival.

The Messianic King (Zech. 9-14): *Zechariah* chapters 9 through 14 contain the prophet's verbal prophecies of the coming Messiah. In this section, Zechariah seeks to energize the people to action by restoring focus on the big picture. By reminding them of the coming Messianic kingdom in language so specific as to indicate that the long anticipated hope was an imminent reality, Zechariah demonstrates the primarily pastoral purpose of Biblical prophecy, a principle of Bible interpretation that finds its fullest expression in the book of *Revelation*.

Chapters 9-10 describe Israel's deliverance through her coming Messianic King. This message must have encouraged the anemic faith of a nation that had been so long oppressed and opposed by others. How they longed for deliverance from their enemies! Such deliverance would be realized when Messiah makes his advent (9:1-8): *"Rejoice greatly, O daughter of Zion; shout, O daughter of Jerusalem: behold, thy King cometh unto thee: he is just, and having salvation..."* (v. 9).

But how would he come? Would he arrive in the pomp and circumstance of a conqueror's victory parade? Would he ride on a stately steed? Contrary to all expectations, Messiah would come *"lowly, and riding upon an ass, and upon a colt the foal of an ass"* (v. 9b). Furthermore, He would *"speak peace unto the heathen and his dominion shall be from sea even to sea, and from the river even to the ends of the earth"* (v. 10). These paradoxical prophecies blending Messiah's meek and humble character and the global extent of His dominion would prove to be a stumblingblock to the Jews. Who had ever heard of a humble King, and what could Zechariah possibly mean by the prediction that Messiah would speak "peace" to the Gentiles?

Zechariah 9:11-12 anticipates the means by which Messiah would deliver the people: *"By the blood of thy covenant I have sent forth thy prisoners out of the pit wherein is no water..."* Ultimate deliverance for God's covenant people from their miserable state in sin would come by the blood of the everlasting covenant. Though they are still classified as "prisoners" after Messiah delivers them, they are now His prisoners – "prisoners of hope" (v. 12).

Zechariah's message is that the deliverance so desperately needed by God's people would be purchased only by means of their King's humiliation. This prophecy was literally fulfilled when Jesus made his triumphal entry into Jerusalem to be crucified (cf. Mt. 21:4-7).

Chapters 11-12 further reveal the character of the coming Messiah in terms of his humiliation and suffering. Zechariah 11 predicts three specific facts associated with the coming Shepherd-King: (1) His rejection by Israel and God's subsequent judgment upon the nation (vs. 4-11; cf. Jno. 1:11; Mt. 23:37-39); 92); (2) His betrayal by Judas Iscariot for thirty pieces of silver (vs. 12-14); (3) the eschatological rise and fall of the Antichrist (vs. 15-17; cf. Jno. 5:43).

Zechariah 12 predicts the "pouring of the spirit of grace and supplications" upon God's people and the consequent conviction of sin that comes with the realization of responsibility for crucifying the Messiah (v. 10). Though this chapter may indeed refer to the prospect of a yet future gospel conversion (see Mt. 23:39; Acts 1:6-7; Rom. 11:13-24), it certainly applies to events recorded in Acts 2 on the Day of Pentecost (e. g. Acts 2:1-13, 18, 36-41).

Chapter 13 focuses on the effects of Messiah's suffering and death. Zechariah reveals that the ultimate humiliation and indignity suffered by the coming King would be death by crucifixion (v. 6), but that death would result in the satisfaction of God's wrath (v. 7), the cleansing of guilt and sin (v. 1), and the restoration of true worship (vs. 8-9). Verses six and seven describe both the physical and the spiritual sufferings of Christ, respectively: *"What are these wounds in thy hands? ...Those with which I was wounded in the house of my friends"* (v. 6); *"Awake O sword against my shepherd, and against the man that is my fellow, saith the Lord..."* (v. 7).

Finally, chapter 14 describes the blessings of life in the Messianic kingdom. Like so many prophecies in Scripture, this passage is an example of *prophetic foreshortening*—a passage that does not distinguish between the first and the second advents of Christ,

301

but commingles the two.[2] Verse 4 anticipates the second coming and verse 9 describes a universal theocracy, the goal of redemptive history. The spiritual principles of the dominance of God's kingdom and the hallowing of all things, even the most common vessels, for the worship of Jehovah, however, anticipate the blessings of the Gospel day ushered in by Messiah's first advent and the establishment of His gospel kingdom.

Indeed, God's purpose to establish a theocratic kingdom through the Messiah was realized when the Lord Jesus Christ came to cleanse the sins of all of His people (v. 8). That kingdom is now a present reality (cf. Lk. 16:16; 17:20-21; 18:16), albeit a microcosm of the future prospect when it is globally and universally manifest that Christ is the only Potentate, King of kings and Lord of lords (Lk. 21:31; 1 Tim. 6:15; 1 Cor. 15:22-28). This "already" and "not yet" model of God's "kingdom" program is exclusive to those of us who live between the two comings of the Messianic King. Though Zechariah looked forward to the first advent of Christ and understood that it would bring victory over sin, we look forward to the second advent in the understanding that it will bring final victory over all evil. That day will prove to be the greatest revival of all.

Malachi

The final post-exilic prophet was Malachi. His book concludes the Old Testament canon. It also serves as a transitional book between the Testaments in the sense that it

---

[2] Isaiah 61:1-3 and Job 19:25ff are other examples.

"sets the stage" for the spiritual conditions prevailing among the Jews when Christ came.

Malachi penned his prophecies in *circa* 400-425 B.C. The reconstruction of the temple that concerned the prophecies of Haggai and Zechariah and the rebuilding of the walls of Jerusalem under Nehemiah's direction have been completed. A century has elapsed since the Jews had returned from Babylonian captivity, sufficient time for a movement away from God, and the various spiritual, practical, and moral departures cited by the prophet describe a people who were, once again, suffering a spiritual and moral free-fall. Such a scene of declining spirituality forms the first of four dominant themes comprising the book of Malachi.

Spiritual Declension, Yet Again

Though the nation had enjoyed a period of revival characterized by the restoration of Divine worship and recommitment to holiness, it had since backslidden, yet once again, into the attitudes of religious apathy and ethical autonomy. Malachi records a number of Divine allegations against the nation, each of which the people refuse to acknowledge. The repeated formula *"You are guilty of 'such and such' sin/Yet you say, Wherein have we committed this sin"* demonstrates Malachi's use of a literary style known as dialectic rhetoric, an intriguing feature of prophetic literature.

First, He charges Israel with *the failure to acknowledge His kindness to them* (1:1-5). The glorious promises of Israel's future that Zechariah had made had not yet been realized; furthermore, the nation was still under Persian control. Many of the people were beginning to ask if God truly loved Israel. But such a question revealed an ungrateful attitude toward past mercies, and the Lord took offense at it.

Second, God accuses them of *dishonoring His name by offering Him diseased and malformed animals for sacrifice* (1:6-8). Such measly offerings reflected an attitude of apathy toward Divine things.

Third, He indicts them on the charge of *begrudging obedience* (1:13). They were not serving the Lord "with gladness" and entering His presence "with thanksgiving", but going through the motions in a tired and purely mechanical way.

Then, God accuses the priests of *breaking the Levitical covenant by their selective adherence to the law* (2:1-9). Spiritual leaders bear a greater responsibility for integrity, for the effects of failures in leadership are felt in the lives of those who follow (vs. 7-8). No doubt the rift between religious leaders and the common people that existed when Jesus lived had its roots in Malachi's day.

Fifth, God alleges that their *moral laxity was hindering the acceptability of worship* (2:10-16). The people had relaxed the standards of the covenant of marriage. Many were marrying non-Jewish women (vs. 10-12), and divorce was becoming a pervasive problem among the Jews (vs. 11-16). The marriage covenant had been redefined in secular, not sacred, terms.

Next, the Lord charges the nation with *theological departure* (2:17). They denied that there were any consequences in disobedience. The general consensus was that judgment does not follow sin. "You can live as you please and God will still accept you" was the message they dared to promote.

Chapter 3 records two final allegations. God accuses the people of *stealing from him by withholding the tithe* (3:8-12) and of *fighting against him by murmuring and complaining words* (3:13-15). They could not make sense of the fact that the proud were happy while they struggled beneath so many burdens; hence, they concluded, "It is vain to serve God."

All in all, the charges leveled against Israel are intended to induce them to repent. But when the Lord bids them to "return unto Me", they refuse to admit that they have departed: *"But ye say, Wherein shall we return?"* (3:7).

Messiah's Purification of Divine Worship

It is against these apparent departures that God promises to send the Messiah to *"purify the sons of Levi...that they may offer unto the Lord an offering in righteousness"* (3:3). Though they eagerly anticipated the coming Messiah (3:1), God reveals that His coming will not be pleasant to those who have deviated from the prescribed pattern of Divine worship (3:2, 5).

Of course, the Lord Jesus Christ spoke his most scathing denunciations against the religious leaders among the Jews (cf. Mt. 15:8-9; Mt. 23). Repeatedly, He described the "clerics" of his day as hypocrites, more married to human tradition than to the worship of God.

Promises to the Godly Remnant

In spite of this Divine diatribe against a nation that had fallen back into the same, past patterns of religious indifference and moral lethargy, Malachi describes another group of people who remained faithful to the Lord. This faithful "remnant" is identified by their "fear of the Lord" (2:5; 3:5; 3:16; 4:2). In contrast to the casual and cavalier attitude that characterized the sinful majority, the godly minority "feared God's name" and reverently obeyed him.

This "remnant" is called God's *segulla*, i.e. "treasured possession", in 3:17. Though God's covenant loyalty toward the entire nation was still a reality, yet only the remnant would escape judgment on the nation. To the unfaithful majority, Messiah's coming would be like the refiner's fire, burning the dross and tin in judgment (Mal. 3:2). But to faithful minority, it would be the dawn of a new day, bringing healing to their souls like sunshine revives the earth (Mal. 4:2). They would be "spared" from the judgment that would fall upon the nation in A. D. 70 (3:17). Such a distinction between the true and false worshippers (cf. Jno. 4:24) would be apparent when Messiah comes (Mal. 3:18).

Messiah's Forerunner: An Elijah-like Prophet

The prophecy of Malachi concludes with a prediction of the forerunner of the coming Messiah: *"Behold, I will send you Elijah the prophet before the coming of the great and dreadful day of the Lord: and he shall turn the heart of the fathers to the children, and the heart of the children to their fathers, lest I come and smite the earth with a curse"* (Mal. 4:5-6). These words from the final canonical prophet affirm God's purpose to send yet one further prophet whose ministry would be identical in character to the first man who occupied the office of prophet in the Old Testament.

John the Baptist, the forerunner of Christ, ministered in the spirit and power of Elijah (Lk. 1:17). Like his illustrious predecessor, John was fearless and unflinching in the face of opposition. His message was, largely, ethically-oriented. He preached repentance at a grass roots level, urging a return to basic and fundamental relationships in order to prepare people to receive the more spiritual message of the Lord Jesus Christ.

With this specific announcement of the Messiah's harbinger, the message of the Old Testament is concluded. All has been building in rising action to the coming of the Messiah, the eschatological hope of the Abrahamic covenant. All that remains is for that hope to be realized. Four hundred years would pass, however, before the advent of the One who would be born King. During that intertestamental period, the religious decline would proceed apace, albeit mitigated by the presence of a godly remnant who, like Anna the prophetess, "waited for the kingdom of God."

The Post-Exilic Prophets

TOPICAL INDEX
This index is not exhaustive.

TOPICAL INDEX

BIBLIOGRAPHY

Archer, Gleason L. *A Survey of Old Testament Introduction*, Moody Press, 1994.

Boice, James Montgomery. *The Minor Prophets*, Kregel Publications, 1986.

Complete Works of Flavius Josephus, Translated by William Whiston, Kregel Publications, 1981.

Edersheim, Alfred. *Bible History: Old Testament*, William B. Eerdmans Publishing Company, January 1984 Reprint.

Freeman, Hobart E. *An Introduction to the Old Testament Prophets*, Moody Press, 1968.

MacArthur, John Jr. *The Love of God*, Word Publishing, 1996.

McGee, J. Vernon. *Thru the Bible Commentary Series*, Thomas Nelson Publishers, 1991.

Pratt, Richard L. Jr. *He Gave Us Stories: The Bible Student's Guide to Interpreting Old Testament Narratives*, Wolgemuth & Hyatt Publishers, 1990.

Sproul, R. C. *The Holiness of God*, Tyndale House Publishers, 1988.

VanGemeren, Willem A. *Interpreting the Prophetic Word*, Zondervan, 1990.

www.ingramcontent.com/pod-product-compliance
Lightning Source LLC
Chambersburg PA
CBHW031942080426
42735CB00007B/229

9 781929 635344